SERMONS FOR REVIVAL
BY
E. A. JOHNSTON

SERMONS FOR REVIVAL

© by E. A. Johnston
October, 2013

ISBN: 978-1-56632-170-9

Foreword by:
Rev. Dr. Colin N. Peckham
Principal Emeritus—Faith Bible College
Edinburgh, Scotland

Publishing, Formatting & Editing Facilitated by:
The Old Paths Publications, Inc
142 Gold Flume Way
Cleveland, GA 30528

Regarding the cover photo: The author is in the pulpit of St. Mary de Crypt, Gloucester, England, from which George Whitefield preached his first sermon and sent 15 people mad.

DEDICATION

This book of sermons is dedicated to my darling daughter Carly who, through difficult days, has been a constant ray of sunshine in my life.

Dad
Evangelist and Author, E A. Johnston
October, 2013

TABLE OF CONTENTS

DEDICATION 3
TABLE OF CONTENTS 5
FOREWORD 9
INTRODUCTION 11
CHAPTER 1: AMERICA: REVIVAL OR RUIN 13
    Bible Text: Amos 3 13
    Preached on: Wednesday, July 25, 2012 13
CHAPTER 2: A TOUR OF HELL 23
    Bible Text: Luke 16:23 23
    Preached on: Wednesday, July 25, 2012 23
CHAPTER 3: A SILENT CHURCH AMIDST A SINFUL NATION 35
    Bible Text: Jeremiah 5:21-31 35
    Preached on: Tuesday, March 5, 2013 35
CHAPTER 4: GOD'S LOVE LETTER 41
    Bible Text: John 3:16 41
    Preached on: Tuesday, May 14, 2013 41
CHAPTER 5: AN AWAKENING SERMON 47
    Bible Text: Psalm 7:11-12 47
    Preached On: Saturday, April 13, 2013 47
CHAPTER 6: THE CAPPUCCINO CHURCH 59
    Bible Text: Ezekiel 11:12 59
    Preached On: Wednesday, July 3, 2013 59
CHAPTER 7: THE IMPLOSION OF AMERICA 67
    Bible Text: Jeremiah 1:13-14 67
    Preached on: Tuesday, April 16, 2013 67
    Principle #1 67

Principle # 2 69
Principle #3 70
CHAPTER 8: CHRIST'S RECEPTION OF SINNERS 73
Bible Text: Gospel of Matthew.. 73
Preached on: Saturday, January 12, 2013 73
CHAPTER 9: THE KING OF GLORY OF REVIVAL........................ 81
Bible Text: Psalm 24... 81
Preached On: Tuesday, September 10, 2013.............................. 81
CHAPTER 10: TEN MISTAKES OF MODERN EVANGELISM....... 89
Preached On: Tuesday, July 30, 2013 89
Mistake #1... 91
Mistake #2... 92
Mistake #3... 92
Mistake #4... 93
Mistake #5... 94
Mistake #6... 95
Mistake #7... 96
Mistake #8... 97
Mistake #9... 98
Mistake #10... 99
CHAPTER 11: THE POWER OF A HOLY LIFE 103
Bible Text: 2 Kings 4:8-9.. 103
Preached on: Tuesday, July 3, 2012 103
CHAPTER 12: WALKING WITH GOD 111
Bible Text: Genesis 5:24... 111
Preached on: Sunday, August 5, 2012 111
CHAPTER 13: THE OUTPOURED WRATH OF A LONG-PROVOKED GOD 123
Bible Text: Zephaniah 1:14-18 123

TABLE OF CONTENTS

Preached On: Tuesday, July 23, 2013 123

CHAPTER 14: THE HEART THAT CARES FOR THE SOULS OF MEN **129**
    Bible Text: Romans 1:16 129
    Preached On: Saturday, January 5, 2013 129

CHAPTER 15: THE SOLEMN ASSEMBLY **137**
    Bible Text: Joel 1:10-15 137
    Preached on: Wednesday, February 27, 2013 137

CHAPTER 16: WEARING THE ARMOR OF GOD **143**
    Bible Text: Ephesians 6:10-18 143
    Preached on: Wednesday, January 2, 2013 143

CHAPTER 17: WHERE A TREE FALLS IT SHALL LIE **151**
    Bible Text: Ecclesiastes 11:3 151
    Preached on: Sunday, August 19, 2012 151

CHAPTER 18: UNCTION IN PREACHING **163**
    Bible Text: Luke 3:16 163
    Preached on: Thursday, December 27, 2012 163

CHAPTER 19: HELL-SHAKING PRAYER **169**
    Bible Text: James 5:16 169
    Preached on: Wednesday, May 15, 2013 169

CHAPTER 20: ISN'T JESUS WONDERFUL! **175**
    Bible Text: Revelation 2:1-5 175
    Preached On: Sunday, July 29, 2012 175

CHAPTER 21: THE ROOT OF SIN **183**
    Bible Text: Luke 3:7-9 183
    Preached On: Tuesday, August 6, 2013 183

CHAPTER 22: AMERICAN CHURCH BUFFET **189**
    Bible Text: Hosea 4:17 189
    Preached On: Friday, August 16, 2013 189

CHAPTER 23: THE LEGEND OF THE KING'S SWORD 195
   Bible Text: Jeremiah 6:16 195
   Preached On: Thursday, July 18, 2013 195

CHAPTER 24: LIFEBOAT OF GRACE IN A SINKING WORLD 201
   Bible Text: 2 Peter 3:3-9 201
   Preached On: Thursday, August 22, 2013 201

CHAPTER 25: TEXTUAL DECISIONISTS 207
   Bible Text: Romans 8:9 207
   Preached On: Tuesday, September 10, 2013................................... 207

CHAPTER 26: THAT BLOODY CROSS 213
   Bible Text: Romans 5:9 213
   Preached On: Monday, September 16, 2013 213

CHAPTER 27: WHAT PAUL PREACHED 219
   Bible Text: Romans 1:16 219
   Preached On: Thursday, September 19, 2013 219

CHAPTER 28: LOST GENERATION WITH ONE FOOT IN HELL 225
   Bible Text: Book of Judges 225
   Preached On: Tuesday, October 1, 2013 225

CHAPTER 29: ONE FOOT IN THE AISLE AND THE OTHER IN HELL 231
   Bible Text: Matthew 7:13-27 231
   Preached On: Saturday, October 12, 2013 231

CHAPTER 30: REVIVAL: AN ABUNDANCE OF RAIN 239
   Bible Text: 1 Kings 18:30-40 239
   Preached On: Sunday, October 13, 2013 239

INDEX OF WORDS AND PHRASES 245

ABOUT THE AUTHOR 253

FOREWORD

The famous World Missionary Convention held in Edinburgh, Scotland, in 1910, came to the conclusion that the state of the church "was such as to prove itself utterly unfit for the work of God put before it." Andrew Murray then wrote a book called *The State of the Church* in which he took these assessments and further analyzed the church as being self-centered, with little consecration, vision, spiritual dynamic or prayer. It is a vivid and scathing assessment.

One hundred years later, Dr. E. A. Johnston has done the same, and has been even more explicit. He has looked at the Western church in its crises with half-hearted congregations sound asleep. The standards fall; there is a lack of fervent, burdened praying; the witness is feeble; the worship is often shallow and anthropocentric (centered on 'me'); holiness is on the back-burner and is an embarrassing subject; preaching is often mechanical and professional; the poorly attended prayer meetings consist so often of merely listing our needs before God; conversions are infrequent, for sinners are only sought halfheartedly; the church is cold and is in a state of spiritual declension.

Christian people today are often more materialistic and self-sufficient. Even those who are seeking God are in danger of being numbed by the passivity of the prevailing Christian attitudes. There is little burdened preaching. Christianity has become cerebral. The Bible may be taught, but the heart is not touched.

Spurgeon in his *Sermons on Revival* said,

> It seems to me to be perfectly dreadful that there should be this constant dying, this constant ruin, this constant spread of error, and no progress in the church!

Even in his day, he felt the chilly blast from a cold, cold church. How much more we today!

The Psalmist said, *"Horror hath taken hold upon me because of the wicked that forsake thy law"* (119:53). But there is not much horror today—we are conditioned to the godlessness around us and have ceased to feel the horror.

Burdened, broken, bold praying is the nerve center of revival. There is a price to be paid, a price of curbed freedom, of resolute concentration, of agonizing supplication. Intercession costs. There is a burden, a passion, an agony, and yes—glory! The breaking through of God into a meeting, the evidence of His felt presence is everything!

And to get that, costs everything. True intercession is sacrifice. Because of the high demands of taking up this burden, many cannot pay the price and consequently do not gain the rewards and benefits of brokenness and soul-travail in God's presence. Their ministry becomes ordinary; good and biblical, but ordinary! The price is too high. Yet God says, *"I the LORD build the ruined places, and plant that that was desolate ... I will yet for this be enquired of by the house of Israel, to do it for them"* (Ezekiel 36:36-37). Jesus said, *"Watch and pray"* (Mark 13:33). When last did we pray with broken hearts? When last did we feel that pain-filled fellowship of the pierced hand?

Oh, how we need the refreshing breath of the Spirit where glowing coals are fanned into a white-hot flame! Revival is a many splendorous thing, but at its heart is the revelation of the holy presence of God. It is the localized presence of deity, the consciousness of the Eternal, where God takes the field and stands in the midst as the mighty Conqueror, and where the glory of the Lord returns to the church.

May the stirring challenge of this book speak to us all, and may it cause the church to acknowledge the heights from which it has fallen and appreciate the greatness and holiness of God. May it cause us to repent and turn from our superficiality to seek God whole-heartedly, fervently, and constantly until He reigns righteousness upon us, and we watch as He extends His kingdom in the demonstration of the Spirit's power and unction. This book is a serious call to holy living, to repentance, to total commitment, and to prayer in the Holy Ghost. May God use it for His glory.

Rev. Dr. Colin N. Peckham
Principal Emeritus—Faith Bible College
Edinburgh, Scotland

INTRODUCTION

In a day of moral decline in society and spiritual declension in the church, there is a great need for spiritual awakening and revival. God has seemed pleased to send revival to His church and national awakening to the land in former times, through the preaching of the great doctrines of grace. This was the case in America in 1740 under the searching preaching of Jonathan Edwards and the mighty preaching of George Whitefield and other "revival men" such as Gilbert Tennent and Jonathan Parsons and a host of other firebrands who called sin black and hell hot and preached the necessity of repentance and the need of God to perform a work of regeneration upon the heart of sinful man.

There is a great difference between preaching "about" revival and preaching "for" revival.

It is the hope and prayer of this poor preacher that God will be pleased to bless the enclosed messages and send a mighty outpouring of His Spirit in this sin-soaked land today!

All glory to His holy Name!

E. A. Johnston, Ph.D, D.B.S
Evangelist and Author

CHAPTER 1: AMERICA: REVIVAL OR RUIN

Bible Text: Amos 3
Preached on: Wednesday, July 25, 2012

When I was a little boy in the 1950s, things were different in America back then. I remember this country when Hollywood had censors, politicians had a conscience, and America had a moral compass. Hemlines were lower and morals were higher and sin was called sin and not social disorders. Of course, we didn't have the technology that we have today. Back then if you said Microsoft they thought you were referring to your mattress. And we didn't have Wi-Fi. We had hi-fi. It was a time when only women wore earrings and only sailors had tattoos. I remember America when it still had a strong work ethic and business abounded in honesty and integrity and a man's word and handshake was as good as gold. And I remember in America when a parent did not have to worry about what their children saw on TV and marriage was between a man and a woman. There was such a thing as shame in society back then.

I remember America when the church still had authority and there was still a fear of God in the land. I remember a nation that stood on biblical principles and looked to God for guidance and to the church for direction. It was okay to pray in public school back then and the Ten Commandments were publicly displayed. And if any atheist cried out against it, there were more than enough Christians to shout that person down because God had the majority in the nation back then. And I remember an America that was looked up to by other nations and we were a country that held on to the principles of our founding fathers and Old Glory was never stomped on and set on fire because we respected too much what it stood for. Back then there was such a thing as a weekly prayer meeting in the church and people actually came to pray. And they weren't embarrassed to cry when they prayed and they prayed loud and long and did so until they grabbed hold of God and the fire fell and consumed the sacrifice. The church back then didn't operate on money and manpower, but by God and Holy Ghost power. Back then the church influenced society instead of society influencing the church. And I remember preachers who preached about the blood and the cross and they warned that hell was hot and a future judgment awaited all mankind. Those kinds of preachers weren't afraid of men, but they sure feared the Almighty.

I keep using the word remember because all I have is my memory of these former things. Today America is facing ruin and only a heaven-sent revival will save this nation from complete destruction.

You see, Christianity was always meant to be counter-cultural. In the New Testament, when the church met the world, there was a clash because the church went in one direction and pagan society went in the other. Now they travel side by side and there is just a rub between them.

We wanted to reach the world so we brought the world into the church. Where has it gotten us? It has only corrupted the house of God. When the people of God begin to drift away from the heart of God, then God will send remedial judgments to call His people back to Him.

My message today is entitled, "America: Revival or Ruin." It is about the remedial judgments of God and we want to begin in the book of Amos, chapters 3 and 4.

Amos was a fiery prophet of God whose main message was judgment. God's timetable was up and the people of God would not return to Him, so He sent a series of judgments upon them; remedial judgments, each one being stronger and harsher than the previous one. God was seeking to get their attention, but they refused to listen. Is God seeking to get our attention today? Is America under the chastisement of the Almighty? Have we not turned our backs on God in this country today?

You know, 9/11 was a wakeup call, but almost everyone went back to sleep. God is still, in His mercy, seeking to get our attention. But the timetable is quickly running out. This is the most critical time in the history of this nation, because if things don't drastically change and there is a turning of this nation back to God, then there will be no nation to turn. It will be gone.

Look at ancient Rome and their military might that ruled the world with an iron fist. Can you fear an Italian army today? No. It is laughable. America is now laughable in the eyes of the world.

Well, look in your Bibles at Amos chapter 3, verse 3. What does it say? *"Can two walk together, except they are agreed?"* Can you walk with God and still hang on to your wretched sins? Can you name the name of Christ and live like the devil? If you want to walk with God you must turn from your sins and pursue a life of holiness. God is holy. God's Word declares: *"Follow ... holiness, without which no man shall see the Lord"* (Hebrews 12:14).

The problem with Israel here in Amos was that they had quit walking with God. They preferred their sins over God. They turned their back side to God. And yet they still believed they were alright in God's eyes; that God had somehow adjusted Himself to their wicked ways; that He tolerated their sins because of His great love for them. God was angry with the Jews and God is angry with the church member who claims to be Christian yet who still hangs on to his sins.

"Can two walk together, except they be agreed?" Can they?

Picture in your mind the story of Elijah and his contest with the prophets of Baal on Mount Carmel. He was up against 450 prophets of Baal; remember that? Elijah built an altar and challenged the prophets of Baal to call on their gods to consume the sacrifice and their gods didn't show up. Finally Elijah began to mock them and said that perhaps their god was on vacation. But listen to what Elijah said to the assembled crowd that day: *"And Elijah came unto all the people, and said, How long halt ye between two opinions? if the LORD be God, follow him: but if Baal, then follow him. And the people answered him not a word"* (1 Kings 18:21).

In other words, if you want to walk with God, you can't have one foot with God and with the other play footsie with the world. Notice he said *"If the LORD be God."* Is Jesus your Lord or is He just your insurance policy against hell?

In Amos chapter 3, verse 6 the text reads: *"shall there be evil [calamity] in a city, and the LORD hath not done it?"*

Never in my lifetime have there been so many frequent natural disasters in this country, one right after another. Why do you think that is? Is it global warming or mother nature? Or is it God allowing Satan to wreak havoc on our society and on our land? In the book of Job, Satan brought a great wind to collapse the house of Job and remove his family and his wealth. God gave Satan permission to do it. Satan is not on the same level as God. There is not an equal war between good and evil. Satan is only a created being; a judged created being whose time is short and he knows it. The last days will be so terrible you will not want to be alive if God does not send revival.

Let us now look at how God sends remedial judgments to a people who have turned their backs on Him. Look at Amos chapter 4 beginning in verse 6: *"And I also have given you cleanness of teeth in all your cities, and want of bread in all your places: yet have ye not returned unto me, saith the LORD."*

Judgment number one was that God sent a famine in the land. In His mercy He sent them a famine. But how did they respond? *"Yet have ye not returned unto me, saith the LORD."*

Well, look at judgment number two in verse 7. It is more severe: *"And also I have withholden the rain from you, when there were yet three months to the harvest: and I caused it to rain upon one city, and caused it not to rain upon another city: one piece was rained upon, and the piece whereupon it rained not withered."*

See, you can go a week without food, but man cannot live long without water. God sent a drought to His disobedient people. Now do they turn back to Him and repent and seek His face? No. *"... yet have ye not returned unto me."*

You see, back then the local Jewish weather men told them it was just mother nature acting up again, or women nature. They would just have to grin and bear it. But they didn't return to God. So He brings an even more severe judgment. Look at judgment number three in verse 9: *"I have smitten you with blasting and mildew: when your gardens and your vineyards and your fig trees and your olive trees increased, the palmerworm devoured them: yet have ye not returned unto me, saith the LORD."*

God sent a financial collapse. Our economy is growing worse and worse and a global depression is on the horizon. Have we turned back to God? God is seeking to get our attention. Are we paying attention or are we asleep? The remedial judgments of God when unheeded become the increasing judgments of God.

Look at how severe judgment number four is. Look at verse 10: *"I have sent among you the pestilence after the manner of Egypt: your young men have I slain with the sword, and have taken away your horses; and I have made the stink of your camps to come up unto your nostrils: yet have ye not returned unto me, saith the LORD."*

He has removed young men of the city by death. You know, take the young men out of a community and the community has little future. God sent death to them through pestilence and war. What is it going to take in America? What kind of terrible national calamity will have to fall upon this nation before it turns back to God? Will it ever turn back to God? When the Christian leaders refuse to acknowledge that God is judging America and judging the churches in America, then we have the blind leading the blind.

Pastors of former generations were wiser and preached revival sermons to turn the hearts of the people back to God. Listen to a sermon preached by a leading pastor in Boston in 1755 when an earthquake shook that city. Listen to the title of his sermon:

"Earthquakes the works of God and tokens of his just displeasure being a discourse on that subject wherein is given a particular description of this awful event of Providence made public at this time on occasion of the late dreadful earthquake which happened on the 18th of November 1755."

The text of the sermon was Psalm 18:7, *"Then the earth shook and trembled; the foundations also of the hills moved and were shaken, because he was wroth."*

The leading pastors in New England all preached similar sermons at that time. They called the congregations to fast and pray and repent of their sins and fall on their faces before the God of terrible majesty. Even the President of the United States had a fear of God back then and called the entire nation to a time of humiliation before an offended Creator. Consider this notice in a newspaper from 1798: "A discourse delivered in the First Presbyterian Church of Philadelphia on Wednesday, May 9, 1798, recommended by the President of the United States to be observed as a day of fasting, humiliation and prayer throughout the United States of America."

How much more urgent is the great need for America today? We can't look to the White House to help us. We can't even look to the church house to help us. Who will take a stand for God in this land today? Who? It is time for the people of God to turn from their wicked ways and fast and pray and seek His holy face in repentance and humiliation or there will not be a nation left to pray in. When will the churches in this land stop playing church and get right with God and call a time of solemn assembly where the people of God cry out to God in nights of desperation and prayer? Why complain about the direction of this nation when you are not willing to do anything about it? God says: *"Return unto me, and I will return unto you"* (Malachi 3:7).

How bad do we want Him? Listen to this warning from the book of Romans:

The night is far spent, the day is at hand: let us therefore cast off the works of darkness, and let us put on the armour of light. Let us walk honestly, as in the day; not in rioting and drunkenness, not in chambering and wantonness, not in strife and envying. But put ye on the Lord Jesus Christ, and make not provision for the flesh, to fulfil the lusts thereof. (Romans 13:12-14)

Let me tell you what can happen to a church. Things can get between you and God. Leonard Ravenhill used to tell a story about a friend of his who was on fire for God. Every time Ravenhill got around this man he was more thirsty for Christ and things of eternal worth. Do you know people like that, people that make you thirsty for God? Well, this man was like that. Every time he got around him he wanted to talk about Jesus and winning souls. Then one day he began collecting stamps. As his collection grew, so did his enthusiasm for stamp collecting. Leonard Ravenhill said, "This man called me up one day and said, 'Come on over and I will show you my new stamp collection of British colonials that cost me $50,000.'" Ravenhill said that pretty soon this man no longer wanted to talk about Jesus or the things of God. He just wanted to talk about stamps. A harmless little thing like a stamp drew that man away from God.

What is it with you? What is the thing, no matter how seemingly harmless, that has stolen your affection from Jesus? Why is your Bible a closed book? Why is your prayer life so stale and so infrequent? Why is your walk so up and down?

You see, a church has influence for God in a community as long as the church members have influence with God. A church is only a reflection of its members. The members of a church will either draw people to God like a magnet or turn people away from Him by their inconsistent and worldly lives.

Let me share a story with you. A traveling preacher was passing through a certain city and he wanted to go by and visit a historic church that had a long reputation for doing good for the Lord. But when he got into town he stopped at a local restaurant to grab some lunch and ask directions to that famous church. The owner of the restaurant was well familiar with that church and when the traveling preacher went on and on about all the great things that church had done, the owner of the restaurant looked at him strangely and commented, "Yes, it used to be that way some time ago. If you want directions to that church, go up the road a piece and turn right at the next stop sign. Then go up a hill and at the top of the hill there will be a sign telling you the way to that church." "What does the sign say?" asked the traveling preacher? The man paused and with a sad look said, "The sign says, 'Caution, children at play.'"

I am sorry to say I have known churches like that, too many, that once did great things for God, that God did great things through them, and now there are signs out front that say, "Caution, children at play."

The hour is late, friends. It is time to get serious with God. Get serious with God and God will get serious with you. If your free time is spent on anything other than prayer and Bible study and things of eternal worth, I feel sorry for you. There is a bema seat for believers. And there we will receive gold, silver, and precious stones or wood, hay, and straw. When the works of your life pass through the fire, what will remain? Will it be gold, silver, and precious stones? Will your life for Christ shine like a brilliant jewel reflecting His glory? Or will you stand there knee deep in the ashes of a wasted life and bend over and press those ashes into His nail-pierced hand? Do you want to be found playing with the marbles of the world when Jesus appears at the rapture? If we really believe we are living in the last days, our lives don't reflect it. If we really believed that Christ is returning soon, we would not be so consumed with this world. Some of you within the sound of my voice may be living your last years. How do you want to spend them? Chasing a little white ball around a golf course? I used to do that until God showed me what golf stood for—Golden Opportunities Lost Forever.

What occupies your time? Are we redeeming the time because the days are evil? You may think I am morbid, but I read the obituaries every day. I take time to read each one and contemplate on their life and how they lived it. You can learn a lot about a person from his obituary. I often read, "He was an avid golfer. He loved to ride motorcycles. He had a passion for bowling and he was a deacon at such and such Baptist church."

Seldom do I read an obituary about a man that says he had a passion for God and was consumed with things of eternal worth. He lived to bring the lost in. He loved Jesus with his whole heart. No, it is usually he loved his antique cars, or his bass boat, and so on. I read an obituary recently about a church member whose friend wrote the article and said the deceased loved martinis.

Like I said, you can learn a lot about a person by what consumes their time here on earth. My late mentor, Dr. Steven F. Olford, used to quote, "Only one life, 'twill soon be past. Only what's done for Christ will last."

What will they write about in your obituary? That you were a success in life, but a failure for God? As blood-bought, born-again believers, shouldn't we be consumed with things of eternal worth? Should our model be eat, drink, and be merry, and live for today for tomorrow we die? Or should our motto be as believers, "Only one life, 'twill soon be past. Only what's done for Christ will last"?

And as I lie dying, how good it shall be, if the lamp of my life has been burned out for thee.

But, I repeat, only a heaven-sent revival will save America from ruin. These are, indeed, the end times. Do you believe that? And the end is drawing closer and closer every day. We are living in the day and the spirit of antichrist right now. Our society grows darker and darker with each new day. You'd better forget about your theory of relax and be raptured. I believe in the rapture of the church, but I believe the American church is going to go through fire and persecution before

Christ comes again. Persecution is on the way to America and it is right around the corner. The chaff will be separated from the wheat.

But there is hope of revival for America. The Word of God gives us a pathway to revival. It is found in 2 Chronicles, chapter 7 and verse 14: *"If my people, which are called by my name, shall humble themselves, and pray, and seek my face, and turn from their wicked ways; then will I hear from heaven, and will forgive their sin, and will heal their land."*

Let me ask you a question. Does our land need healing? Let me ask you the next question. Are you willing to pay the price for revival and really do what this verse says and get serious with God and humble yourselves before Him, pray and seek His face in these dark days? And are you willing to do the last part of this verse which God requires from us? And that is to turn from your wicked ways? Are you willing to repent of your sins and come clean with God not only for your sake and the sake of your family, but for the sake of our nation? For the nation is merely the reflection of its people. America used to be a God-fearing nation because the Christians used to fear God and live holy lives toward Him. We are to be salt, the Bible says. You see, salt is a preservative. We are to be a preservative from evil for this nation to do good for the glory of God.

Listen, friends. God promises us in His Word, *"Return unto me, and I will return unto you"* (Malachi 3:7). Are we willing to do it with a sincere heart? The passage in 2 Chronicles mentions duties on our part that we must do to gain the ear of the Almighty. I believe the average church member is willing to do the first two aspects of this text, humble themselves and pray. But very few are willing to comply with the most solemn aspect of this text, and that is repent and turn from their wicked ways.

Listen to me. God will not move one inch until we comply with His demand of repentance on our part. If we humbly seek His face in prayer and supplication and turn from our wicked ways, He then promises to do two big things for us, hear and heal. This is an if/then proposition in Scripture. If the people of God will do such and such, then God will do such and such. God says that if my people do these things, then I will hear their prayers and heal their land.

You see, there was revival in the days of Hezekiah because he complied with the precepts of 2 Chronicles 7:14. King Hezekiah gathered his religious leaders together and told them: *"Hear me, ye Levites, sanctify now yourselves, and sanctify the house of the LORD God of your fathers, and carry forth the filthiness out of the holy place"* (2 Chronicles 29:5).

Hezekiah was instructing them to do two things. Number one, clean the temple of its idols and, number two, clean the altar of their hearts in repentance. We see this in 2 Chronicles chapter 29 and verses 15 through 16. Listen to what the people of God did in response to the king's request of getting right with God. The text reads:

> *And they gathered their brethren, and sanctified themselves, and came, according to the commandment of the king, by the words of the LORD, to cleanse the house of the LORD. And the priests went into the inner part of the house of the LORD, to cleanse it, and brought out all the uncleanness that they found in the temple of the LORD into the court of the house of the LORD. And the Levites took it, to carry it out abroad into the brook Kidron.*

This is what the people of God did. They searched the temple to find unclean idols and then brought them out, took them to the brook Kidron, and burned them there. They sanctified themselves and God brought a mighty revival under King Hezekiah because he did that which was right in the sight of the Lord.

It is up to the church in America today to do the same: to search our sanctuaries to see what idols we have set up which displease and grieve God, and take those worldly idols back out of our churches and get rid of them. Then we are to search our hearts under the bright spotlight of the Holy Spirit to see if there is anything grievous to God in our lives and turn from it in repentance. Then, and only then, will our prayers have power with God to the degree that He will indeed hear and heal: hear our prayers and heal our land.

You know, we don't hear much preaching today on the cross in the life of the believer. But if we want God to hear us and to take us seriously, we must crucify anything in our lives that is displeasing to Christ Jesus. When we get serious with God, He will get serious with us and answer our prayers and bring a Holy Ghost revival to America that will shake the gates of hell from coast to coast.

This is a call to fall on our faces and seek Him in sincerity of heart. Will we do it? Will we do it? America: revival or ruin. Will we heed the warnings? God help us if we don't.

CHAPTER 2: A TOUR OF HELL

Bible Text: Luke 16:23
Preached on: Wednesday, July 25, 2012

When I was a little boy I visited a museum in Chicago and in that museum was an exhibit which fascinated me. It was called "The Coal Mine" and it was like an amusement park ride. You got into an elevator and it gave you the sensation of going deep into the ground to a coal mine. The elevator became darker and colder and the walls of the elevator were a conveyor belt which looked like rock walls. As the walls of the elevator moved you believed you were descending deep into the bowels of the earth. All your sensations told you that you were going deep into a coal mine beneath the ground.

Today I'm going to be your tour guide and escort you into the nether regions underground. For I'm going to take you on a tour of hell. We don't hear much about hell these days and many do not believe in a literal hell. But Jesus did and that's good enough for me. Amen?

I bring this message for two reasons. Number one, to bring glory to the Father. Number two, to warn those outside of Christ to flee from an eternal punishment called hell and to seek refuge in your only hope, Jesus Christ.

Our text today is from Luke, chapter 16 and verse 23: *"And in hell he lift up his eyes, being in torments."* You see, friends, hell is a place of torments; a place of everlasting burnings where the worm dieth not. I must issue a disclaimer here before we proceed on this tour of hell. This message is not for the faint of heart but it is for the stony heart. People must be warned of hell.

What happens to persons when they die? Is it just a blank void of nothingness? Is there some kind of life after death? Some people believe in reincarnation where a person gets several chances in life to get it right. But my Bible says we only have one life to live and after that we face the Judge of all the earth.

This is what it says in Hebrews: *"And as it is appointed unto men once to die, but after this the judgment"* (9:27). When a believer dies, he or she goes to heaven to be with Jesus. My Bible tells me that to be absent from the body is to be present with the Lord. When an unbeliever dies, they awake in a terrible place called hell.

There is a book I read about hell that was written by a cardiologist at the UT School of Medicine in Tennessee. His name is Dr. Maurice Rawlings. He was an avowed atheist until he witnessed some near-death experiences of his patients; patients who had been clinically dead on the operating table. They had come back to life and what these patients experienced during that time of death startled Dr. Rawlings. Some of his patients went to hell and back; hence the title of his book, *To Hell and Back.*

What he witnessed in these patients disturbed him because their faces would be twisted in a grimace of terror. At times they would shriek in horror and cry out in agony and their eyes would dilate as they described horrific scenes of tortured souls and a burning hell. This so shocked Dr. Rawlings that he began to wonder if there really was a heaven and hell after all. So he began to study the Bible and what it said about hell and the afterlife. Through his study he got saved and became a Christian and he wrote several books on this topic of hell and its torments.

We don't hear much preaching today on the subject of hell. You know, old time preachers used to preach on hell often as a means to awaken the lost to see their real condition and perilous position outside of Christ. But we preach nice little messages today that don't disturb anybody. Well, Jesus preached about hell and warns us not to go there. See, there's an invisible world all around us.

There's a story about Charles Spurgeon, the famous British preacher. Spurgeon was in a hotel room in France where he lay dying. His close friend then, aide Joseph Harrold, related the following story. He said that as he gazed out the window toward the hills beyond, under a cloudless sky, he was astonished at what he saw. To his dying day Joseph Harrold claimed he saw, out on the hillside that day, a company of angels hovering above the hills looking as though they were waiting for someone. They did not have long to wait; Spurgeon died shortly thereafter.

I believe that. I believe that when we die as believers, angels take us up to heaven. Does not Jesus Himself say so? In our passage of Scripture today from Luke's gospel, the Lord Jesus is describing the beggar, Lazarus, who dies, and Jesus said, *"And it came to pass, that the beggar died, and was carried by the angels into Abraham's bosom"* (16:22). I believe that. I also believe that when an unsaved person dies, demons drag that person down to hell.

Come with me now as we descend into the nether regions and see what the Bible has to say about the existence of a literal hell. This is what the Bible says: hell is a place of punishment for sin, hell is inhabited by demons, hell is an abode for the wicked dead, and hell is a place of eternal suffering.

Let's look at the first of these: hell is a place of punishment for sin. The fact that God punishes sin is found throughout God's Word. My Bible states that God is angry with the wicked every day. Look at the biblical record. In Genesis we find the following evidence that God punishes sin:

> *And GOD saw that the wickedness of man was great in the earth, and that every imagination of the thoughts of his heart was only evil continually. And it repented the LORD that he had made man on the earth, and it grieved him at his heart. And the LORD said, I will destroy man whom I have created from the face of the earth.* (6:5-7)

In the biblical record found again in Genesis we see that God will punish sin. God told Abraham that He would destroy the wicked inhabitants of Sodom and Gomorrah. The Bible record says, *"Because the cry of Sodom and Gomorrah is great, and because their sin is very grievous"* (18:20). And the Word of God proves that a holy God will punish sin, for the text reads, *"Then the LORD rained upon Sodom and upon Gomorrah brimstone and fire from the LORD out of heaven; And he overthrew those cities, and all the plain, and all the inhabitants of the cities, and that which grew upon the ground"* (19:24-25).

See, the trouble with our society today is that people sleep well at night because they don't believe God will punish sin. Even many church members today don't believe in a God that will punish sin. They do not believe in that kind of God; their God wouldn't act that way and send people to hell. But listen, friends, the God of the Bible will, because the God of the Bible punishes sin. But some church members don't let their profession of faith interfere with their daily living because they just don't believe God will punish sin. Even when you witness to people today and you talk about Jesus dying on the cross, they're not interested because they don't believe God will punish sin. And no one will be interested in what Christ did on the cross until they believe that God will punish sin.

We have forgotten what the message of the gospel is. In your day and mine, in our generation, we are fed a diluted gospel message of the cross that speaks only about an offered Christ, but there is no use to offer a remedy to people who don't need a remedy. There is no use to preach the second message of the cross, the forgiveness of sins through Christ's blood. Listen, friend, this generation doesn't think it needs its sins forgiven; they just don't think there's any need. But we still go on and only offer the second message of the cross; Christ and His forgiveness of sins. However, this generation of hell bound sinners needs to hear the *first* message of that bloody cross and that message is, God will punish sin. Every time they nailed those nails into the flesh of the Son of God, every stroke of the hammer said, God will punish sin, God will punish sin, God will punish sin.

But in our day of weak evangelism we beg people to come to Jesus, but they don't feel like they need Him. A man won't go to the doctor unless he discovers he's deathly ill. When a man is sick to the point of death and the doctor has a remedy that will cure him, that man will give that doctor every cent he has to get well and live. But he doesn't need a cure if he doesn't think he's sick.

Listen to me, dear ones. If you do not hear anything else I say today, remember this; God *will* punish sin. That's the first message of the cross and after somebody believes that you can come in with the second message of the cross; that substitute who hangs there in my stead. Christ is God's sacrifice and my substitute.

So the first thing you need to accept on this tour of hell is the fact that hell is a place of punishment for sin. People go to hell because God sends them there to punish them for sin. People do not send themselves to hell; that's a ridiculous statement. Listen, Jesus hung on a bloody cross for sinful man. God was reconciling the world through the death of His Son. Jesus said that men are cast into hell: *"Wherefore if thy hand or thy foot offend thee, cut them off, and cast them from thee: it is better for thee to enter into life halt or maimed, rather than having two hands or two feet to be cast into everlasting fire"* (Matthew 18:8).

Hell itself exists because of sin. Hell is a place of punishment for sin. Sin is not sent to hell but sinners are sent to hell to be punished for their sins and rebellion against a holy God who hates sin so much He cannot look upon it. That's why God looked away from His precious Son on the cross and Jesus cried out, *"My God, my God, why hast thou forsaken me?"* (Matthew 27:46).

Jesus took our sins and took the wrath of God upon Himself. For those who believe in Him shall not see death but have everlasting life. Listen, *"He that believeth not the Son shall not see life; but the wrath of God abideth on him"* (John 3:36). The wrath of God. God will pour out His wrath on those Christless individuals in hell for all eternity.

Well, let's continue our tour of hell and notice this, that hell is inhabited by demons. When I was a teenager my family moved into a haunted house. There was an evil presence in that house. Right after we moved in, my parents and I were sitting in the living room and upstairs above us we heard very strong footsteps walking down the hall. We looked at each other alarmed. My father tried to laugh it off but it happened again and again. We came to accept the fact that our house was haunted.

A TOUR OF HELL

One night as we were sitting downstairs in the living room, we heard those heavy footsteps walking up and down the hall upstairs and I ran upstairs to see if there was an intruder up there. But there was no one there, at least no one I could see with my eyes. It was an eerie feeling.

But even worse than that, occasionally in that house something horrible, something frightening, would occur suddenly and without warning. There was a door beneath the stairwell upon which, without warning, a loud pounding would begin on that closed door so loud it would startle you and stop you in your tracks. After that loud pounding one day I slowly crept over to that door and opened it and I felt cold air come out on me even though it was a warm summer day. Demons inhabited that house. There was an unseen evil presence there. I sure was glad when we finally moved away.

Hell is inhabited by demons. In hell you will be surrounded by demon entities and you will not be able to get away from them but they will brush up against you, tear you, and attack you and there will be no one to help you. Not only will you not be able to move away from them, rather you will be at their mercy. That hell is inhabited by demons is seen from the words of Christ: *"Then shall he say also unto them on the left hand, Depart from me, ye cursed, into everlasting fire, prepared for the devil and his angels"* (Matthew 25:41).

Several of the patients of Dr. Rawlings, the cardiologist, spoke of seeing demons in their near-death experiences. They described them as dark shrouded entities, slimy and disfigured, grotesque in appearance and smell. These demon entities were the first ones you saw in hell. In Dr. Rawlings book, *Beyond Death's Door,* he writes about it in a chapter called "Descending to Hell." He writes the description of what his patients saw there. He describes the experience of a patient apparently dying with a heart attack and coming back to life. She attended church every Sunday and considered herself an average Christian. These are her words:

> I remember getting short of breath and then I must've blacked out. Then I saw that I was getting out of my body. The next thing I remember was entering this gloomy room where I saw in one of the windows this huge giant with a grotesque face that was watching me. Running around the windowsill were little imps or elves that seemed to be with this giant. The giant beckoned me to come with him. I didn't want to go but I had to. Outside was darkness but I could hear people moaning all around me; I could feel things moving about my feet. As we moved on through this tunnel or cave things were getting worse. I remember I was crying.

Then for some reason the giant turned me loose and sent me back. I felt I was being spared.

Not only is hell inhabited by demons, but as we go deeper into this tour of hell we see it is also an abode for the wicked dead. Psalm 9, verse 17 tells us, *"The wicked shall be turned into hell, and all the nations that forget God."* Hell is crowded right now with wicked individuals. Think of all of mankind that have died since the beginning of civilization. The wicked in each generation have been cast into hell—all the idolaters and adulterers, drunkards and atheists, thieves and murderers. The most vile of humankind are in hell right now. Hitler is there, serial killers are there, rapists are there, perverts are there. All of the wicked who were on the earth in the days of Noah are there. The inhabitants of Sodom and Gomorrah are there. The evil Roman emperors are there. Hell is crawling with the refuse of mankind. God haters and every sociopath from every generation of man are there. People that you would be afraid to be left in a room alone with will rub up against you in hell. Their sweat will get on you and there won't be a thing you can do about it. Hell is a very crowded place.

It's been estimated that eighty-three people a minute die apart from Christ. Do the math and that comes to almost 5,000 an hour. Every day 120,000 people fall into hell. That's over 800,000 a week. Every month that adds up to three million people falling into the terrors of hell. Through the course of a year, forty million new people populate the regions of hell. Let ten years go by and another 400 million souls are shut in there to scream in agony. Now, think back in your mind of all the generations since the time of Adam and add all the hordes of people who have died apart from Christ and occupy hell right this moment. I repeat, hell is a very crowded place.

Jesus spoke of the narrow way and the broad way. Jesus said, *"Enter ye in at the strait gate: for wide is the gate, and broad is the way, that leadeth to destruction, and many there be which go in thereat: Because strait is the gate, and narrow is the way, which leadeth unto life, and few there be that find it"* (Matthew 7:13-14). Jesus calls it a strait gate because of the difficulty of the passage. If you are truly regenerated you make the attempt to go through the strait passage; others attempt but they are quickly discouraged and get off on that easier broader road which leads to hell.

That's where the world is. There's a vast crowd on that road today. This is the road of sin, unrighteousness, and disobedience. The majority travel this wider road and they have in every generation. Few are they who travel along the narrow way of true salvation which is self-denial, mortification, and gospel obedience. Few passengers take this course; they love their sin and stay on the broad way and are led like animals into a snare and a net. Sudden death takes them away and without warning. Just turn on the TV and see how sudden death takes people away in America today through tragedy, through sudden accidents.

Listen what the Bible says in Ecclesiastes, chapter 9, verse 12: *"For man also knoweth not his time: as the fishes that are taken in an evil net, and as the birds that are caught in the snare; so are the sons of men snared in an evil time, when it falleth suddenly upon them."*

You have no guarantee of tomorrow. Your plans for the future may not be realized. You may be like the rich man of whom Jesus spoke.

> *The ground of a certain rich man brought forth plentifully: And he thought within himself, saying, What shall I do, because I have no room where to bestow my fruits? And he said, This will I do: I will pull down my barns, and build greater; and there will I bestow all my fruits and my goods. And I will say to my soul, Soul, thou hast much goods laid up for many years; take thine ease, eat, drink, and be merry. But God said unto him, Thou fool, this night thy soul shall be required of thee.* (Luke 12:16-20)

Sudden death happens every day in this country—a car crash, a murder, an accident, a heart attack. Listen, God can remove you in an instant without notice and you can suddenly enter eternity. If you are truly born again, if you die you will be carried by angels into His presence, but if you are unsaved you will die in your sins and be thrown into hell. You have no guarantee of tomorrow. You are in grave danger if you have been living in known sin and living in rebellion to the God who made you. You are like the person spoken of in Ecclesiastes, *"He that diggeth a pit shall fall into it; and whoso breaketh an hedge, a serpent shall bite him"* (10:8).

The Bible declares that God is a righteous judge who acts justly and by no means clears the guilty. The great danger of suddenly dying and dropping into hell should awaken everybody out of their spiritual slumber, for it is far better to repent immediately and beg for God's mercy now than die apart from Christ and awaken to torments of the prison of hell.

Our next stop on this tour of hell is that hell is a place of eternal suffering. Physical suffering in this world eventually ends if we are Christians and we are suffering a terrible slow death. When we die there's an end to that suffering. Often we hear of a loved one who has passed away and we hear, "Well, at least they're no longer suffering. They are now with the Lord." But for the unsaved this is not so. Their suffering continues into the next world; a world of eternal misery and physical torments to which there is no relief and no end.

The following images may give you a glimpse into hell. Think of your worst fear. Think of your absolute worst fear. Some people are afraid of the dark. Well, hell is called outer darkness; there's no light there, only deep darkness. You will not be able to see your hand in front of your face, but you will be able to hear the cries of the damned all around you, you will be able to smell their putrefying burning flesh, you will be able to feel pain, and you will experience a thirst that is never quenched.

Listen, hell is a lonely place. You will have no friend there to talk to; you'll not be able to get out your cell phone and send texts to one another. There are no cell phone signals in hell. You are cut off from your companions. You will long for someone to be kind to you, someone to talk to you. There'll be loneliness all around you. Hell is a place of immense agony and separation.

Jesus describes hell as a place of weeping and gnashing of teeth. Listen, we can speak to great loss and grief and gnashing of teeth signifying great anger and regret. In hell, you will regret the day that you spurned the love of Christ, that you turned away from the invitations of the gospel, that you did not lay hold of Christ in a saving way while you had a chance. You will hate the evangelist or the preacher who fed you a false gospel and told you that you were saved when you were still lost. His name will be a curse word to you for all eternity. You will hate yourself for not seeking Christ while He was to be found. You will hate your sins because while on earth you took pleasure in them, but in hell there is no pleasure in sin, only torment.

Listen, friends, if you die in your sins you *will* wake up in hell. Imagine your shock, your confusion, your tongue so dry it feels like it'll fall right out of your mouth, your heart breaking because of your foolishness and sin. But you were overtaken in hell by demons that tear at you and rend you and come again upon you and they do not stop. Your cries are drowned out by the awful shrieks around you. Look, if you went to every hospital in your city tonight and took every patient off of their pain medication, and did not give them anything for pain, not even an aspirin, their cries of agony would keep your town awake tonight.

Another terrible thing about hell is the physical pain. To be burned to death is the worst way to die. It is said to be the most painful. That is why when you see a building on fire people often leap to their deaths rather than stay inside and be burned in the flames. During the tragedy of 9/11 when the Twin Towers were on fire, many leaped to their deaths from a hundred stories high, rather than be burned up in the flames.

But hell is everlasting burnings. The Bible declares from the book of Isaiah, *"Who among us shall dwell with the devouring fire? who among us shall dwell with everlasting burnings?"* (33:14). Hell is said to be a lake of fire. Revelation speaks to this, *"And whosoever was not found written in the book of life was cast into the lake of fire"* (20:15). Jesus tells us that hell is prepared for the devil and his angels. *"Depart from me, ye cursed, into everlasting fire, prepared for the devil and his angels"* (Matthew 25:41).

The torments in hell are forever, friends. Listen, *"And the smoke of their torment ascendeth up for ever and ever"* (Revelation 14:11). Listen, friends, hell is continual; it is an unquenchable fire. Matthew tells us, *"He will burn up the chaff with unquenchable fire"* (3:12). Jesus tells us hell is a place *"where their worm dieth not, and the fire is not quenched"* (Mark 9:44, 46, 48).

Once you are in hell there is no appeasing God's wrath upon you and that terrible furnace of fire which our Lord spoke of in Matthew, *"And shall cast them into the furnace of fire: there shall be wailing and gnashing of teeth"* (13:50). Listen, that furnace is terrible.

I used to work in a grocery store when I was a teenager. One of my jobs was to take the boxes that the produce came in and bring them to the back of the store and throw them into a cast iron furnace. When I would open the door to that furnace, the flame in there was so hot it was a white flame. And the heat was so intense it would singe my face just to be near it.

Malachi tells us that God's anger *"shall burn as an oven; and all the proud, yea, and all that do wickedly, shall be stubble: and the day that cometh shall burn them up, saith the LORD of hosts"* (4:1). Hell is prepared for you if you are outside of Christ.

Listen, friends, in the state of Florida there is a phenomenon called sinkholes. The ground is sand and it gives way and it caves in. Entire houses have sunken without warning into these deep sinkholes. If you are outside of Christ, you are sitting on a sinkhole, for beneath you is hell and its torments and only the grace of God can keep you out of hell at this moment. God could end your life this minute if He chose to, and open the ground beneath you and drag you down to hell.

We are warned by God of the danger that lies in our not surrendering to the claims of Christ and to the gospel. *"He, that being often reproved hardeneth his neck, shall suddenly be destroyed, and that without remedy"* (Proverbs 29:1). If you have ignored the invitations of the gospel and have rejected the Christ of the gospel, you are on slippery ground.

Listen to what God says: *"To me belongeth vengeance, and recompence; their foot shall slide in due time: for the day of their calamity is at hand, and the things that shall come upon them make haste"* (Deuteronomy 32:35).

Listen again to what God says in His Word: *"Surely thou didst set them in slippery places: thou castedst them down into destruction. How are they brought into desolation, as in a moment! they are utterly consumed with terrors"* (Psalm 73:18-19).

Listen, friends, to die suddenly and wake up in hell is to be utterly consumed with terrors. Death is even called the King of Terror. I beg you, examine yourself right now. The apostle Paul warns us in 2 Corinthians, chapter 13 and verse 5. He says: *"Examine yourselves, whether ye be in the faith; prove your own selves. Know ye not your own selves, how that Jesus Christ is in you, except ye be reprobates?"*

I ask you now if Jesus Christ is in you. Are you truly born again? Are you washed in the blood and born of the Spirit? Do you know that your sins are forgiven? Have you been under conviction of sin? Have you ever experienced contrition with sound humiliation of the soul where sin is seen to you to be very odious and yourself vile in your own eyes because of your sin? Are you seeking Christ and His righteousness? Is your heart prepared to seek Him? Can you renounce your own righteousness and cast yourself upon Christ alone and His righteousness; coming to Him in complete and utter surrender where you lay down your arms of rebellion, putting your neck under His yoke, and following a crucified Savior? He must be the risen Lord of your life; you cannot have Jesus apart from His lordship. The Bible does not say believe on Jesus and be saved. It says rather, believe on the Lord Jesus Christ and be saved. You are a rebel. You must throw down your shotgun of rebellion and come to Christ in total surrender; in repentance and faith. I earnestly implore you on behalf of Christ to reconcile yourself to God if you are apart from Him. Listen to Paul's words in 2 Corinthians: *"Now then we are ambassadors for Christ, as though God did beseech you by us: we pray you in Christ's stead, be ye reconciled to God"* (5:20).

Listen, friends, I speak to you seriously today because of the words of God in Ezekiel, chapter 3, verses 18 and 19. Listen to these solemn words:

> *When I say unto the wicked, Thou shalt surely die; and thou givest him not warning, nor speakest to warn the wicked from his wicked*

way, to save his life; the same wicked man shall die in his iniquity; but his blood will I require at thine hand. Yet if thou warn the wicked, and he turn not from his wickedness, nor from his wicked way, he shall die in his iniquity; but thou hast delivered thy soul.

Listen, I do not want your blood on my hands, therefore I have faithfully declared to you the full counsel of God. Repent from your sins, turn to Christ, ask Him for the faith that brings you to Christ. I have given you this tour of hell today through the Scriptures with the express hope and prayer that you do not tour it in person yourself. Listen, friends, hell is a one stop prison. Once you get in there you cannot get out. There is no doorway out; there is no exit sign outside of hell. It is a bottomless pit which you cannot climb out of. Do not go there, friend. Seek Christ and seek Him now.

Listen to the pleas of the gospel,

> *Seek ye the LORD while he may be found, call ye upon him while he is near: Let the wicked forsake his way, and the unrighteous man his thoughts: and let him return unto the LORD, and he will have mercy upon him; and to our God, for he will abundantly pardon.* (Isaiah 55:6-7)
>
> *If any man thirst, let him come unto me, and drink. He that believeth on me, as the scripture hath said, out of his belly shall flow rivers of living water.* (John 7:37-38)
>
> *And the Spirit and the bride say, Come. And let him that heareth say, Come. And let him that is athirst come. And whosoever will, let him take the water of life freely.* (Revelation 22:17)

My friends, listen, the gospel is for the hungry, the weary, and the thirsty. Are you hungry for salvation? Are you weary of your sins? Are you thirsty for Christ? Then come. There is a promise to those who come to Christ in a sincere way and with a sincere heart; they will not be turned away. *"All that the Father giveth me shall come to me; and him that cometh to me I will in no wise cast out"* (John 6:37).

This tour of hell is now over and I pray that you will never, ever have to go there in person. Listen, friend, repent and seek Christ now. He is your only hope.

CHAPTER 3: A SILENT CHURCH AMIDST A SINFUL NATION

Bible Text: Jeremiah 5:21-31
Preached on: Tuesday, March 5, 2013

I have a video of Martin Lloyd Jones as he is touring England and visiting the sights where George Whitefield labored. While standing at the site of the Bell Inn where Whitefield was born, Lloyd Jones describes the moral climate of London in the days of Whitefield. He said that morality was at an all-time low; spirituality in the churches was almost nonexistent; and that in London every fifth house was a gin-house; and that it seemed the city itself was in a drunken debauchery and spiritual stupor. And Lloyd Jones glares into the camera and comments, "And where was the church in all of this?"

Today in America, our situation is far more grim than in the days of Whitefield and Wesley, our national sins more multiplied. Evil increases at a rapid rate and our society slides into a sinkhole of perversion and debauchery. Our civic leaders call evil good and good evil. God has been legislated out of our once great country. The spirit of antichrist grows in the land and I ask the same question, "Where is the church in all of this? Where is the church? She is shamefully silent amidst a sinful nation."

And that's the title of my message today, "A Silent Church Amidst a Sinful Nation." It reminds me of the days of Nazi Germany where a German pastor made the following comments about the increasing evil in his day and his failure to cry out against it. He said, "First they came for the communists and I didn't speak out because I wasn't a communist. Then they came for the socialists and I didn't speak out because I wasn't a socialist. Then they came for the trade unionists and I didn't speak out because I wasn't a trade unionist. Then they came for the Jews and I didn't speak out because I wasn't a Jew. Then they came for the Catholics and I didn't speak out because I wasn't a Catholic. Then they came for me and there was no one left to speak for me."

Dear friends, this is a graphic picture of the church in America today. Evil abounds and the church is silent. God is systematically removed from society and the church is silent. Perversion permeates the fabric of our society and the church is silent. The government mocks God and His authority and the church is silent. The church sleeps a sleep of death and slumbers on corporate cushions of self-indulgence and soon they will come for her. Persecution is on the way to the church in America. We have missed our opportunity to cry out; we have remained silent for too long and the hour is now too late. We have been busy building our own islands and fortifying them by growing our church campuses and building a corporate environment where we can be entertained. The nation has passed the boundaries of decency and crossed the line of blasphemy against a holy God and an offended Creator. Yet the church is silent and her silence is deafening.

I can sum up the American church by this description of a recent visit to a Baptist church. The church service led off with a Hollywood video. The content was banal and offensive, yet the church laughed. The music minister laughed, the pastor laughed, the congregation laughed because they were embarrassed. I sat there looking down at the floor and my insides groaned within me. I wept inside at the state of the church in America today that has wedded Hollywood and the world with sacred things of God. The pastor preached a doctrinally sound sermon but there was no power of the attending Holy Spirit because the Holy Spirit had been grieved away before the pastor entered the pulpit. What occurred in that church service was a religious ceremony without spiritual transformation; worship without the presence of God. We have become, as a people of God, impotent, apathetic, and indifferent. We'd rather be entertained than challenged spiritually. We have turned into a cappuccino church; all froth and no substance.

Listen to the wise words of Samuel Chadwick, a pastor of former days, "When a church is run on the same lines as a circus, there may be crowds but there is no Shekinah." Oh, friends, where is the Shekinah glory in our churches today? How the glory has departed from among us and we have not even noticed. We are like Samson who left the tent and shook himself but knew not that the Spirit of God was no longer upon him.

Listen to the comments of another pastor, a godly man, W. Graham Scroggie, as he pleaded with pastors in his day.

> Make a show. The people love a show and you will gain the end of your ambition at once. The crowd is always ready for a sensation and alas there are always those who are disposed to stimulate religion, to fill the churches by the method of sensationalism.

Listen, friends, to yet another man, another pastor, who was much wiser than us in his day. Listen to Alan Redpath, former pastor of the Moody Church in Chicago. Listen to his words.

Today, the Christian church is helpless. Behind the scenes and away from the public arena, we are facing powers of darkness too strong for us because somewhere in our personal lives we have forfeited our right to the Spirit's anointing, His authority, and His power. In His absence, all we can do is to substitute planning and organization, schemes and techniques.

Alan Redpath's stinging observation can be modified for our day by adding to our substitution of God, forms of entertainment in the sanctuary of God.

Dear pastor brother, Hollywood has no place in the sanctuary of God. How can you introduce strange fire into your assembly and still have the fire of God? You cannot. These idols should be removed from the house of God. When I visit churches and see the deplorable spiritual condition of the church in America today, I weep and groan and beg God to forgive us for our spiritual slumber and dishonoring of Him. We have tried to shrink God down to our size and taken salvation out of the hands of God and placed it in the hands of man. Society crumbles all around us and there is little hope for the future of America, as we, as a nation, have filled up the cup of our iniquity before an offended God. It reminds me of the people of God in the days of Jeremiah, as described in Jeremiah, chapter 5, verses 21-31. Allow me to read this striking passage to us today.

> *Hear now this, O foolish people, and without understanding; which have eyes, and see not; which have ears, and hear not: Fear ye not me? saith the LORD: will ye not tremble at my presence, which have placed the sand for the bound of the sea by a perpetual decree, that it cannot pass it: and though the waves thereof toss themselves, yet can they not prevail; though they roar, yet can they not pass over it? But this people hath a revolting and a rebellious heart; they are revolted and gone. Neither say they in their heart, Let us now fear the LORD our God, that giveth rain, both the former and the latter, in his season: he reserveth unto us the appointed weeks of the harvest. Your iniquities have turned away these things, and your sins have withholden good things from you. For among my people are found wicked men: they lay wait, as he that setteth snares; they set a trap, they catch men. As a cage is full of birds, so are their houses full of deceit: therefore they are become great, and waxen rich. They are waxen fat, they shine: yea, they overpass the deeds of the wicked: they judge not the cause, the cause of the fatherless, yet they prosper; and the right of the needy do they not judge. Shall I not visit for these things?*

> *saith the LORD: shall not my soul be avenged on such a nation as this? A wonderful and horrible thing is committed in the land; The prophets prophesy falsely, and the priests bear rule by their means; and my people love to have it so: and what will ye do in the end thereof?*

What a sad, tragic picture that is of a people of God who have backslidden far away from the heart of God. Well, what did God do with such a strange people? This is what He did in the form of a severe judgment upon them as seen in Jeremiah 5:15-17.

> *Lo, I will bring a nation upon you from far, O house of Israel, saith the LORD: it is a mighty nation, it is an ancient nation, a nation whose language thou knowest not, neither understandest what they say. Their quiver is as an open sepulchre, they are all mighty men. And they shall eat up thine harvest, and thy bread, which thy sons and thy daughters should eat: they shall eat up thy flocks and thine herds: they shall eat up thy vines and thy fig trees: they shall impoverish thy fenced cities, wherein thou trustedst, with the sword.*

God will bring a swift judgment upon America if the nation does not turn back to Him. It will be such a sudden and widespread calamity that it will be numbing in its intensity of destruction of human life. It will be such a national calamity that the government will be powerless to help anyone because they will be rendered powerless themselves. God's answer to a wonderful and horrible thing committed in the land is judgment upon a sinful and disobedient people. And I ask, "Where is the church in all of this? Why is she silent while she still has the time to do something about it? Why, brother pastor, would you rather show Hollywood movies in your church and entertain your people rather than lead them in a time of brokenness before God in humility, in repentance, and in prayer? Why?" Because the people love to have it so. So you give them what they want instead of what they need.

God says, "No." We have misused the time given to us in this nation of ours. We have misspent it on ourselves and our own selfish desires. Now it is time to pay the piper and we as a nation are unprepared for what is about to befall us from the hand of an offended God. "Then came they for the Jews and I didn't speak out because I wasn't a Jew. Then they came for the Catholics and I didn't speak out because I wasn't a Catholic. Then they came for me and there was no one left to speak for me."

A SILENT CHURCH AMIDST A SINFUL NATION

O Great God, forgive us for our national sins. Forgive America for grievously offending thee. Forgive us of our multiplied sins. Forgive our blind leaders who lead falsely. Forgive us for our allowing our nation to be permeated and saturated with perversion. Forgive us, O Lord, for our adultery and fornications, for our idol worship. But forgive us most of all, O Lord, for forsaking thee. We as a nation, a people, have forsaken thee. Forgive us for corrupting the house of God with abominable things. Forgive us for mixing true worship with strange fire. Forgive us for our vast personal and corporate sins. We beseech thee, O Great God, look down and hear our cry; we seek thy face and favor. Once again, visit us with a national revival, I beg you, rather than a national calamity that will come in judgment. In thy wrath, remember mercy. In thy wrath, remember mercy. Come again, O Lord, and fill our sanctuaries with your presence and preeminence. We pray in the strong name of our Lord Jesus Christ. Amen.

CHAPTER 4: GOD'S LOVE LETTER

Bible Text: John 3:16
Preached on: Tuesday, May 14, 2013

There was an Englishman who traveled frequently to India for business purposes. His main business took place in the city of Calcutta. It was there while shopping in an Indian bazaar that he purchased a necklace for his little girl. He would often bring his eight-year-old daughter trinkets back from his travels. On this trip to India he bought his daughter a pretty little jade necklace at an inexpensive market bazaar. After she wore it a few days the metal clasp broke and this Englishman took it to a London jeweler to be repaired. A few days later the man returned to the jeweler to pick up the necklace for his little girl. The jeweler emerged from a back room with the necklace and with an excited look on his face. The jeweler asked, "May I ask you, sir, how much you paid for this jade necklace?" The man replied, "I believe I paid twenty pounds for it, nothing more." The jeweler smiled and said, "Look into this magnifying glass. See the letters carved on each piece of jade? It is French lettering. When you lay these seventy-eight pieces of jade side-by-side they form a love letter written from Napoleon to Juliette. This jade necklace is worth well over half a million pounds."

Listen, friends, the Bible is comprised of 66 books and they form a love letter. It is God's love letter to us, for the Bible is a story about God's love toward sinful man in reconciling the world back to Him through the death and resurrection of His dear Son, Jesus Christ. And the love of Christ was demonstrated for us by the pouring out of His blood on an ignoble cross so we could escape the wrath of God through a sin substitute who died on our behalf. *"For God so loved the world, that he gave his only begotten Son, that whosoever believeth in him should not perish, but have everlasting life"* (John 3:16).

And Jesus is seated on a heavenly throne right now, right now where He reigns in glory. He sits at the right of the Father and He earned that right by way of a bloody cross. I repeat, the Bible is God's love letter to sinful man. It speaks of the broken heart of God over sin. It is a book of letters which tells of the love of God and it is a book which declares the good news concerning the gift of God, the Lord Jesus Christ. And the gospel itself is truly a love letter from Jesus to sinful man. It is a love letter signed with His very own blood.

Listen, the blood of Christ His Son cleanses us from all sin. The gospel of Christ, the death of Christ, the blood of Christ, all speak of such a love letter poured out from the very heart of God. Never was there such a love letter as this. Ephesians 2:4 declares, *"For his great love wherewith he loved us."* How great is this love?

There is a story which always moves me when I hear it. It's about a farmer's dog which had been very useful to him but was getting old. His master decided one day to get rid of him by drowning him. Taking the dog with him to a large river near his farm, he got into a boat and rowed out to the deepest part of the river. Around the dog's neck he tied a cord attached to a heavy stone. Then he threw both of them into the water. The poor dog sank but the cord broke, and rising to the surface with a whine, the dog frantically tried to get into the boat again. Unmoved, his master pushed him off a number of times with an oar but every time the dog faithfully swam back. Finally, in desperation, the farmer stood up in the boat intending to strike the dog such a blow with the oar that it would send the dog to the bottom of the river. As the farmer swung the oar at the dog's head, he lost his balance and fell into the water himself. Well, the farmer could not swim and would have drowned, but when the dog saw his master struggling in the water, in spite of the cruel treatment he had just received from him, the dog swam up to him, caught hold of his clothes and paddling with all its might, the faithful friend brought his master safely to the shore. Did the farmer end up killing that dog? Of course not. He was so overwhelmed by the loyalty and love of his dog that he cared for it for the rest of its days.

When you, friends, are confronted with the message of the gospel of the Son of God, it should so overwhelm you with God's love towards you that you should be brought savingly to Christ. How could you read that love letter and not have your own heart broken over your sins? But what happened when Jesus came into this world doing good, healing the sick, giving sight to the blind, raising the dead, and giving rest to the weary? Wicked men said, "Away with Him. Crucify Him!" They took the Lamb of God and nailed Him to a tree.

Look at that blessed Man on that bloody cross. Even when they railed at Him while He hung on that cross, His love flowed out in a prayer to the Father, *"Father, forgive them; for they know not what they do"* (Luke 23:34). The cross was the place where men sought to get rid of Him but through His death that same cross becomes the place where His saving power flows out to all who come in repentance and own Him as their Savior and Lord.

"In this was manifested the love of God toward us, because that God sent his only begotten Son into the world, that we might live through him. Herein is love,

not that we loved God, but that he loved us, and sent his Son to be the propitiation for our sins" (1 John 4:9-10).

Some time ago I read the story about how our Bibles came to have red lettering for the words of Christ. There was a man named Louis Klopsch who was good friends with D. L. Moody and also the editor of *The Christian Herald* magazine. When reading Jesus' words one day, *"This cup is the new testament in my blood, which is shed for you"* (Luke 22:20), he thought of printing all of Jesus' words in red, the color of His blood, to remind people of that sacrifice. So that is how we came to have our red-letter Bibles.

Listen to this; the gospel is a love letter written in red. When Jesus was scourged every stripe is a letter. When they hammered those nails into His hands, every nail is a capital letter. Every bleeding wound in His flesh is a sentence. The blood-stained cross is an exclamation point. The gospel of Jesus Christ is truly a love letter written in red, with His precious blood. Even your sins are crimson red. Is that not what God declares in this love letter of his? *"Come now, and let us reason together, saith the LORD: though your sins be as scarlet, they shall be as white as snow; though they be red like crimson, they shall be as wool"* (Isaiah 1:18).

Red like crimson, your own bloody sins nailed Christ to that tree. And you need a substitute for sin. If you can't stand on your merit against the severity and strictness of God's holy law, you will be condemned for breaking that law. And the punishment is a burning hell, where once you're shut up in there you cannot get out.

I know I've broken God's law because I'm a sinner, and I need a substitute for sin in the person of Jesus Christ, and so do you. I repeat, the gospel of Jesus Christ is a love letter from God written and signed with His very blood. How can you not surrender to God after hearing about such love? You are a rebellious soul with a filthy heart. Your sins nailed Him to that tree. Be thankful for the blood of Christ, that fount of blood which washes sin away. Can you not love Him, He who first loved you? Or will you love your sins more? Will you spurn the love of Christ? Will you reject Him? How can you not part with your sins after knowing that God parted with His Son, allowing Him to be sent to a cross to die for you? How can you not part with your sins after knowing that Christ was willing to endure all that suffering and shame for you, that Christ was content to be forsaken that you might not be forsaken, that Christ would be content to be condemned and sentenced that you might be acquitted. How can you not be swallowed up in this divine love?

How can you spend your thoughts and live your life in rebellion against this Christ who gave His all for you?

Look on Jesus who died that you might live. Who, because of His tender love for you, became a sacrifice for sin so that you would not suffer and burn in hell for eternity. Will you not come to Jesus Christ and love Him?

It is recorded that the martyr, Ignatius, so continually meditated on the great things Christ suffered for him, that he so entirely loved Christ that when he was persecuted, and it was demanded of him to reject Christ or to be torn and devoured of wild beasts, he answered that he could not forget Him because of His suffering for him. He declared, "O, His sufferings are not transient words or removable objects but they are indelible characters so engraven in my heart that all the torments of earth can never raze them out." The love of Christ so overwhelmed the early Christians that they'd rather die than deny Him.

Do you love Jesus like that? Or do you love your sins more than Jesus? There must be a satisfaction to divine justice and this was accomplished through the death of the Son of God. If those damned souls in hell could reach you with their cries, they would warn you not to come there. They died in their sins. They died apart from Christ. Those suffering in hell right now would love to hear a gospel invitation. But it is too late for them. But you have an opportunity to hear of this love letter from God which declares, *"For God so loved the world, that he gave his only begotten Son, that whosoever believeth in him should not perish, but have everlasting life"* (John 3:16).

Listen to this call of love from this love letter:

> *Ho, every one that thirsteth, come ye to the waters, and he that hath no money; come ye, buy, and eat; yea, come, buy wine and milk without money and without price.* (Isaiah 55:1)

> *And the Spirit and the bride say, Come. And let him that heareth say, Come. And let him that is athirst come. And whosoever will, let him take the water of life freely.* (Revelation 22:17)

Listen to Jesus, as He calls you to partake of this love letter:

> *If any man thirst, let him come unto me, and drink. He that believeth on me, as the scripture hath said, out of his belly shall flow rivers of living water.* (John 7:37-38).

GOD'S LOVE LETTER

This love letter from God calls the hungry, the weary, and the thirsty to come to Him. Will you come to Him? This love letter declares that Christ came to save lost sinners.

"But God commendeth his love toward us, in that, while we were yet sinners, Christ died for us" (Romans 5:8).

This love letter from God both woos and warns. *"Blessed are all they that put their trust in him"* (Psalm 2:12). But listen to its warning if you spurn the love of God and reject His dear Son, Jesus Christ, *"How shall we escape, if we neglect so great salvation?"* (Hebrews 2:3).

Today, I have read you portions of a love letter from God dipped in the ink of the blood of His Son. But you must repent of your sins and place your faith in Jesus Christ to receive this great love. Let me ask you a question, "Would you gladly receive this love letter from God in the person of His Son Jesus Christ by placing your faith in Him? Or will you carelessly tear up this love letter and trample the offered sacrifice for sin?"

Look to Christ, friend. Look to Christ. *"And as Moses lifted up the serpent in the wilderness, even so must the Son of man be lifted up: That whosoever believeth in him should not perish, but have eternal life"* (John 3:14-15). I beg you to turn from your sins and go to God now and ask Him for the grace of repentance and faith and accept the offered Christ today. Repent of your sins and place your faith in Jesus Christ and receive this great love, friend. Look and live.

CHAPTER 5: AN AWAKENING SERMON

Bible Text: Psalm 7:11-12
Preached On: Saturday, April 13, 2013

We live in a day of a compromised gospel, a powerless pulpit, and a worldly church. I can sum up the American church today as described by a recent visit of an Oriental pastor who came to America to see for himself what the churches were like. He said, "First karaoke, then a lecture." That sums it up, friends. We have very little preaching in our pulpits today. It is mainly teaching; teaching informs, preaching transforms.

The message you're about to hear is not a politically correct gospel; rather it is a full presentation of the gospel of the Son of God preached in the full counsel of God. Listen to it very carefully.

As the day begins and the sun rises, it paints a picture of hope for a new today and a better tomorrow. Yet, this is not always the case. Listen to the words that describe a solemn scene as the sun rose over the plains:

> *The sun was risen upon the earth when Lot entered into Zoar. Then the LORD rained upon Sodom and upon Gomorrah brimstone and fire from the LORD out of heaven; And he overthrew those cities, and all the plain, and all the inhabitants of the cities, and that which grew upon the ground.* (Genesis 19:23-25)

Surely the Sodomites did not know in advance what utter destruction was about to fall upon them. They, in their warm and comfortable homes, lying together and burning in their lusts for each other, would soon face, at the break of day, rather than a pleasant sunrise to warm them, rather than the sound of birds singing to them, fire dropping out of heaven and burning the very flesh off their bones. So great was the sudden judgment from God, so overtaking and consuming in its finality of destruction, that we're given the scene of this from the eyes of Abraham as he stands on the mountain and views the smoking cities below: *"And Abraham gat up early in the morning to the place where he stood before the LORD: And he looked toward Sodom and Gomorrah, and toward all the land of the plain, and beheld, and, lo, the smoke of the country went up as the smoke of a furnace"* (Genesis 19:27-28).

When I was a boy, years ago in high school, I worked as a sack boy in a local grocery store. One of the duties of my employment was to take the cardboard boxes that the produce came in and break them down with a box cutter to where they were flat, and then take them to a cast iron furnace and burn them. I remember to this day the sensation I felt as I would carefully open that heavy furnace door, the heat was so intense that my face would be singed from it. I would have to stand back and throw those boxes into an oven full of white hot flames. The heat and intensity of it was powerfully frightening. I can only imagine the intensity of the engulfing flames that fell upon the inhabitants of Sodom that morning, how relentless the fire and brimstone was to where the smoke of the country went up as the smoke of a furnace. A furnace fueled with burning bodies, burning livestock, burning homes and buildings and commerce and livelihoods. How great was the cry of those being burned alive at the break of day.

Yet it was not as great as the cry which God had heard beforehand; before He sent the fire that would consume them. Listen to the words from verses 20 and 21 from Genesis 18: *"And the LORD said, Because the cry of Sodom and Gomorrah is great, and because their sin is very grievous; I will go down now, and see whether they have done altogether according to the cry of it, which is come unto me; and if not, I will know."*

What cry is God speaking of? Would it not be the cry of rape? Did not the men of Sodom want to take the angels from the house of Lot with violence and rape them? These Sodomites had become so hardened in their sins that they thought nothing of raping any boy or man they could lay their hands upon. Surely, the cry of the victims went up to the ears of the Lord, so the cry of their sins reached the ears of heaven and moved God to go down to have a look for Himself. And what He saw made Him so filled with wrath that He sent a consuming fire upon all the inhabitants of that country, and the cry of their torments went up as the smoke of a furnace.

Oh, what a horrible noise Sodom on fire must have made that particular morning; a morning normally filled with the breeze in the treetops and the gentle sounds of birds singing, filled with cries and shrieks of pain and anguish from all who resided there as flames engulfed their homes and their city was burned to the ground. Surely, had they known such a horrible and painful fate awaited them at sunrise they would have done everything in their power to reform themselves and repent before God and avoid such a final catastrophe. But they had no warning, and they perished in an onslaught of falling flames, and their cry went up along with the smoke of their burning city.

AN AWAKENING SERMON

The day before in Sodom was quite a normal day, quite ordinary. All the men of the city were engaged in their lustful enterprise. They were enjoying themselves to the full. They were filling the cup of their iniquity and had no regrets for what they were doing so wickedly before the eyes of a holy God.

In the days of Noah, when he was building the ark, the inhabitants of his country would observe him and his family as he labored building the ark and preaching righteousness to them. But they mocked and laughed at such a spectacle of an old man building such a monstrosity as an ark, when it was obvious to anyone with any sense that there was no need for it.

And God looked down and beheld the wickedness of man and it grieved Him. In Genesis 6 we read,

> *And GOD saw that the wickedness of man was great in the earth, and that every imagination of the thoughts of his heart was only evil continually. And it repented the LORD that he had made man on the earth, and it grieved him at his heart. And the LORD said, I will destroy man whom I have created from the face of the earth; both man, and beast, and the creeping thing, and the fowls of the air; for it repenteth me that I have made them.* (verses 5-7)

Here is a land full of people whose hearts are corrupt and their lives are an overflow of that corruption. They grieve God by their sinfulness. Even their evil thoughts grieve God. So God calls a man named Noah; a man that the Scripture says of, *"Noah was a just man and perfect in his generations, and Noah walked with God"* (Genesis 6:9). Here was a man, in the midst of an evil nation, who stood out from his countrymen in that he walked with God Almighty while the other inhabitants of the land grieved the heart of God through their wickedness and sin. And their destruction came upon them suddenly and without warning, and they all were drowned except eight persons in the family of Noah. Christ spoke of this in the gospels saying that they were eating and drinking and being given in marriage up until the very day that the flood came and destroyed them. The apostle Peter speaks of those destroyed by judgment as examples to us today: *"And spared not the old world, but saved Noah the eighth person, a preacher of righteousness, bringing in the flood upon the world of the ungodly; And turning the cities of Sodom and Gomorrha into ashes condemned them with an overthrow, making them an ensample unto those that after should live ungodly"* (2 Peter 2:5-6).

Surely, had the people of Noah's day known in advance what tragedy would befall them, what rains and floods would surround and engulf them, the extent of the raging waters that would drown them, and their cattle, and all the beasts of the field; that their homes would float, and then sink, and that they would be helpless to alleviate their entire circumstance. Imagine the sorrow and regret that filled their hearts as they were drowning, as they did not heed the warnings of Noah and book passage on the ark of safety. Rather they laughed, mocked, and they drowned.

Surely, had they known all of this, they would not have become so foolish. They would have become grave and serious and reformed themselves and repented before God to avoid such a horrible end as drowning.

Today in the land, people go about the normal activities of their day, and they eat and drink, they laugh and enjoy themselves, they pursue their goals and their careers, they build, they gather, they work, they labor, and they do wickedly against the holy God, for any sin is grievous to a holy God. And man is simple, man is corrupt, man is alienated from God, and the world is oblivious to Him. Your average person today cares little about eternity. They seldom think of a final judgment and a burning hell. Why, there are so few preachers of righteousness today who even speak or warn of such things. Mostly, in pulpits, you will hear about God's great love and heaven, but you will seldom hear about God's wrath for sin and sinners in a burning hell prepared for them. No, there are few preachers of righteousness today warning men to flee from the wrath to come. Rather, they speak, *"Peace, peace; when there is no peace"* (Jeremiah 6:14).

Although we have a Bible to warn us of these things and bring us to repentance before God, many today are unconcerned about spiritual things. They could care less about matters of eternity. Why, just about everyone you would ask would tell you that they are alright in the eyes of God; that He is just fine with them and they won't go to a place called hell. The God of today wouldn't send people to such a terrible place. He is just a God of love. And many preach that nonsense. But the fact remains that God will judge every man at the great judgment and every knee will bow to the Lord Jesus Christ and acknowledge Him. Those who die in their sins enter a Christless eternity. They are forever separated from God.

A person has to be awakened to his sinful condition before he can even realize these solemn things. Only the Holy Spirit of God can awaken you to your danger. Only God can awaken you to the fact that you are on the wrong side of Him, that you are lost before a just and holy God, and that you stand in a place of great danger. You see, you need to be warned of your danger. If you were driving your car and the bridge ahead of you down the road was so unstable, that as soon as your vehicle got on it, the bridge would give way and plunge you to your death in

AN AWAKENING SERMON

the waters below, you would want to know about it. You'd want to be warned in advance.

The true gospel warns you to flee to Christ because of the great danger. You are standing on your own merit, but you compare yourself to the men of Sodom, and the wicked of those days, and others in our day, and you say to yourself that you are not as bad as they. You think your sins aren't as great as others. But the Bible says, *"All we like sheep have gone astray; we have turned every one to his own way"* (Isaiah 53:6).

You see, friend, sin is going *our* way, when we know it isn't *God's* way. And God views all sin as rebellion against Him. You are a rebel against a holy God. You need to be warned. The apostle Paul states in 2 Corinthians 5:11, *"Knowing therefore the terror of the Lord, we persuade men."* You must be awakened to the fact that you're on the wrong side of an offended God, and you stand in great danger and peril.

Listen, friend, in Psalm 7:11-12 the Bible declares, *"God is angry with the wicked every day. If he turn not, he will whet his sword; he hath bent his bow, and made it ready."* You foolishly believe yourself to be standing in a place of safety. But God stands against you. At any moment a sudden accident or calamity can remove you from this earth and send you into an eternity unprepared to meet the God of that eternity. Have you ever seen yourself as lost? How can you consider yourself saved if you have never been lost? Has there ever been a time in your life when you knew you were on your way to hell and that you deserved to go there? How then can you feel a need for a Savior and a remedy for sin if you have never considered yourself in need of that remedy?

I fear many today have entered the church and walked an aisle and made a decision for Christ and believed themselves to be saved, but they have never seen themselves as lost; that Jesus came to seek and save that which was lost. To be off here effects our destiny. You have to be lost before you can be saved or you will be consigned to an eternal place of torment, a place of fire and flames, heat and agony, and anguish and regret. There will be no escape from the regions of hell. It is a final prison engulfed in flames and torments. As the tree falls so it shall lie; as a man dies in his sins, so shall he surely go to hell.

I remember the day well when God showed me that I was lost. I was a church member in good standing, but standing on the wrong side of God. I was reading a sermon by Solomon Stoddard and suddenly God revealed to me that I was on my way to hell, and not only that, that I deserved to go there. I couldn't believe it. I questioned God and wrestled in prayer until I was convinced that I *was* lost. It was terrifying. I was shaking off my self-righteousness. All my props were kicked out from beneath me and I stood guilty before a holy God. I then became a seeker, a seeker of Him, and became the recipient of His saving grace. How about you?

Listen to these words from the Word of God which describe a lost sinner's condition. This is how the Bible describes man apart from God, Ephesians 2:1 states, *"And you hath he quickened, who were dead in trespasses and sins."* You need to realize that you are dead in sin, and if you die in your sins, you will be consigned to an eternal hell and be locked in that prison for all eternity, separated from God.

Perhaps this next verse in Ephesians can show you that if you were dead in sin, you were on the wrong side of God and an object of His wrath, *"Among whom also we all had our conversation in times past in the lusts of our flesh, fulfilling the desires of the flesh and of the mind; and were by nature the children of wrath, even as others"* (2:3). Did you hear those words *"were by nature"*? You were born with a sin nature. Because of the sin of Adam, the entire human race enters the world spiritually dead and with a depraved nature that is inclined to sin. Did you hear also the words *"children of wrath"*? That is a vivid description of a lost person on their way to hell under the condemnation of a holy God who hates sin and must punish it.

You must be awakened, friend, to the fact that you are an object of God's wrath and you can die in a moment and slip into hell and never get out of there, for there are no exit doors in the regions of hell. Once you are in there you can never get out, and you fall into hell without a moment's notice. You have no guarantee of tomorrow. To think you do is foolish, for you could die tonight unexpectedly and tragically.

I was in Edinburgh, Scotland, at a hotel. I had just stepped into the shower. It was a death trap. The floor of the shower had just been waxed. As soon as I stepped in there, it was like stepping on slippery ice. My feet slipped from beneath me and I did a somersault through the air and landed on a hard concrete bathroom floor. My arm broke the fall, but I hit my head and I broke my wrist as my head hit the floor. I could have easily been removed from this earth suddenly and without warning. My foot slid unexpectedly.

Listen to the Word of God as it describes your perilous position outside of Christ, *"To me belongeth vengeance, and recompence; their foot shall slide in due time: for the day of their calamity is at hand, and the things that shall come upon them make haste"* (Deuteronomy 32:35). How many times have you sat carelessly in church thinking you were just fine, and in reality you were lost, and at any

AN AWAKENING SERMON

moment an unexpected accident or heart attack could make you slip and fall into hell. Hell opens before you, waiting to receive you. The demons reach up to grab you and drag you down to hell and its horrors. You do not realize your perilous position apart from a true saving knowledge of Christ. You may be a good church member who just believed on the fact of the death of Christ, and you believed that believing in that fact was good enough to save you, but in reality, you cannot be saved by believing just on the death of Christ; you must believe on the Christ who died.

Perhaps you have reformed yourself to look your best in the company of others, but when you are alone you know how unchanged you really are, and there's never been a true work of regeneration upon your heart. You have never been born again, never been washed in the blood and born of the Spirit. You have no assurance that you are truly saved. Is your Bible a closed book? Why do you not regularly witness to the lost? Why do you still hang on to your sins and sit on the throne of your life? Where is your joy, the joy of your salvation? Why do you lie? Why do you not obey Christ's commands? Jesus said, *"If ye love me, keep my commandments"* (John 14:15). Why do you not conform to Christ and grow in holiness and obedience to Him? Is it because you have never exercised true repentance towards God?

You see, friend, when we come savingly to Christ something happens. Self is dethroned and another is enthroned there. Self is dethroned and Christ is enthroned in our lives, for He is a risen Lord; He sits on a throne at the right hand of the Father and He got there by way of a bloody cross. How can you claim to know Christ and take His name as a follower of His and call yourself a Christian if you are still in your sins, if you have never been washed in the blood and born from above? If you only knew of your great danger. You do not realize how close you are to being past your day of grace and dropping down into hell unexpectedly. You can slip into death at any moment in this dangerous world. You can be run over while jogging, killed in a car accident, or your heart could just stop beating. You have no guarantee of tomorrow. Life is uncertain and unpredictable. The very ground you're walking on is a slippery place and your foot is ready to give way from underneath you. *"Surely thou didst set them in slippery places: thou castedst them down into destruction. How are they brought into desolation, as in a moment!"* (Psalm 73:18-19).

You may be young and feel you have all your life ahead of you, or you may be in perfect health and pleasant circumstance and feel like you'll live to a ripe old age. But that is presumption on your part for you have no guarantee of tomorrow. Today might be your very last day upon this earth and then you die and go unto another world quite unexpectedly. *"For man also knoweth not his time: as the fishes that are taken in an evil net, and as the birds that are caught in the snare; so are the sons of men snared in an evil time, when it falleth suddenly upon them"* (Ecclesiastes 9:12).

You could be the victim of a terrorist attack, you could be in a plane crash, you could be gunned down in a movie theater or killed while you stand in line. You live in an evil day where death surrounds you at every turn. Where would you be if you died tonight? Would you drop into hell quite suddenly? Are you certain that you are joined to Christ in a saving way? Are you in a vital union with a living Lord? Do you have the Holy Spirit within you? Is your name written in the Lamb's Book of Life?

Perhaps you have been the victim of poor evangelism and some evangelist told you that you were saved, but the Spirit of God has never given you that assurance. Perhaps you walked an aisle and became a church member but your life was never transformed by the person of Christ. When Jesus was here in His earthly ministry, when He entered a village, the persons that He encountered were changed. Other lives were transformed and forever changed. Is your life different since you have become a Christian or have you merely reformed some of your gross sins?

John Wesley said that conversion was a change which God works upon the heart. I repeat, have you been changed? Are you different since you accepted Christ? Please, do not stand upon a false foundation or rest upon a false hope. Do not rest your hopes on a feeling or a verse of Scripture. Have you met the living Lord? Have you seen a revealed Christ? Is Christ real to you as your Savior?

There are no second chances in hell. There are no gospel invitations in hell. Rather, hell is a sentence carried out on those who die in their sins without a saving knowledge of Jesus Christ. Christ will say to those unregenerate church members on that day, *"I never knew you: depart from me"* (Matthew 7:23).

Do you know that you are a sinner? Having a recollection of sin is not the same thing as being convicted of sin by the Holy Spirit. Only the Holy Spirit can convict you of sin. Have you ever fallen under the conviction of sin? God's law is unyielding: *"Thou shalt not kill. Thou shalt not commit adultery. Thou shalt not steal. Thou shalt not bear false witness"* (Exodus 20:13-16). Every man will be held up to God's perfect law and no man will be able to stand against that law. All will fail that test, for man is a sinner, and unless he has a sin substitute he will fail the test of standing alongside the utter strictness of the law of God.

AN AWAKENING SERMON

God reveals the purpose of the law in Romans 3: *"That every mouth may be stopped, and all the world may become guilty before God. Therefore by the deeds of the law shall no flesh be justified in his sight: for by the law is the knowledge of sin"* (verses 19-20). Then it goes on to say, *"For all have sinned, and come short of the glory of God"* (verse 23).

Listen, the shortest definition of sin found is in the Bible: *"All we like sheep have gone astray; we have turned every one to his own way"* (Isaiah 53:6).

Hear me, how will you stand against the strict law of God and not be cast down to hell? Do you see your need of a sin substitute? Do you thirst for Jesus? Like I said, you must be awakened to your lost condition. Dear friend, have you ever been lost? How can you claim to be saved if you've never been lost? You have a conscience, you know right and wrong, that is given to every man—a law written on the heart. When the law of God, from His written Word, is applied to your conscience, then the Holy Spirit has the power to grind you under the conviction of sin and show you that you are guilty before a holy God and that He is just to send you to the hell that you deserve. You then know you are a sinner on your way to hell and you deserve it.

You then become a seeker of God, you desire the grace of repentance. Oh, how you wish you could turn from your wretched sins, you want a new start. You don't want to live that way any longer; you desire a true ability to turn from your sins, to agree with God about what He says about them, to be able to loathe them as He loathes them, to turn from them in a true work of repentance towards God and faith and Jesus Christ.

This is saving faith; this is grace. God is the author of salvation. He can give it or withhold it and still be a just God. Jesus said, *"But ye believe not, because ye are not of my sheep"* (John 10:26). Jesus said, *"And ye will not come to me, that ye might have life"* (John 5:40). Jesus also declared, *"No man can come to me, except the Father which hath sent me draw him: and I will raise him up at the last day"* (John 6:44).

Saving faith is a grace given. You cannot earn it. You certainly don't deserve it, but you can become a seeker of God. Seek Him earnestly through grace, repentance, and faith. Oh, friend, if you are under the conviction of sin, I can promise you that if you will come to Christ, if you will come to Him savingly. Jesus declared, *"If any man thirst, let him come unto me, and drink. He that believeth on me, as the scripture hath said, out of his belly shall flow rivers of living water"* (John 7:37-38).

Listen, friend, to this promise to you from Scripture: *"Ho, every one that thirsteth, come ye to the waters, and he that hath no money; come ye, buy, and eat; yea, come, buy wine and milk without money and without price"* (Isaiah 55:1).

Are you thirsty for Christ? Then come and be filled. Listen to His promise: *"And the Spirit and the bride say, Come. And let him that heareth say, Come. And let him that is athirst come. And whosoever will, let him take the water of life freely"* (Revelation 22:17).

The pearl of great price is for the thirsty, the hungry, the weary. Come.

When we come to Christ and surrender our lives to Him, when we throw down our shotgun of rebellion and lay the arms of our rebellion at His sovereign feet, when we take up our cross and follow Him, we die to the world and now live for eternity. For we are bought with a price and that price was His blood. We are no longer our own; we have a new Master. Listen to the words of the apostle Paul, *"And that he died for all, that they which live should not henceforth live unto themselves, but unto him which died for them, and rose again"* (2 Corinthians 5:15).

When you come to Christ savingly, He plants a new disposition in you, a disposition for holiness. You will want to live for Him and be pleasing to the Father. You will have the evidence of your salvation.

George Whitefield, the great British evangelist, came to America in 1740 during the Great Awakening and under his preaching many thousands were melted down under conviction of sin and were converted. He was once asked by a Boston pastor, "Mr. Whitefield, how many converts have you had since you've been to America?" To which the great Whitefield replied, "I don't know, sir, but I will be back this way in a year or two and I shall look for the evidence of their salvation."

Let me ask you, dear friend, is there an evidence of your salvation? Does the Spirit of God bear witness with your spirit that you are a son of God? Do you long for holiness? Do you enjoy reading your Bible? Do you spend time in prayer on a regular basis? Do you witness for Christ and share your faith on a regular basis? Surely, you cannot be truly born again and not witness for Christ regularly. Do you weep over the lost and perishing? Do you hunger and long for revival? Do you thirst after Christ and yearn for more of Him each day? Can others see the evidence of your salvation? Can your family members testify that you have a new disposition towards them? Are you truly saved?

Examine yourselves whether ye be in the faith. Prove your own selves. No, you're not your own now that Jesus Christ is in you except ye be reprobates. Is

Jesus Christ in you? Come to Him now and trust Him to save you. Seek God and ask Him to give you the grace of repentance and faith.

When I stand up against the strictness and severity of God's holy law, I know I will fail the test. I'm a sinner. God's law requires perfection. I have failed that test. I need a substitute for sin in the person of Jesus Christ. So do you, friend. You cannot stand on your own righteousness. Your righteousness is like a filthy rag in God's eyes. You need to rest in the merits of Christ as a substitute for sin. If you die apart from Christ you will die in your sins and stand guilty before a just and holy God, and you will have no excuse.

Surely, had the men of Sodom been forewarned of their coming destruction, they would have reformed themselves and sought repentance towards God. The people in Nineveh, under the preaching of Jonah, repented from the king down to the beast. They were clothed in sackcloth as they turned to God and repented to avoid their own destruction. Had the people in the days of Noah only had a second chance, they never would have mocked Noah and the ark, but they would have run to the ark of safety to avoid being destroyed in the flood.

Jesus is the ark of safety; He is the only way to salvation. Flee to Him now. You have been given a better opportunity than the people of Sodom and Gomorrah, for you have been warned. You have been warned in this message. You have heard a full presentation of the gospel. I have spoken about ruin, repentance, redemption and regeneration. Christ paid the price on a bloody cross for your wretched sins. The very nails in His hands were driven there by *your* sins. Because of sin you stand guilty before a holy and just God who *must* punish sin to be true to *His* nature.

He is a God who is angry with the wicked every day. But in His great love He sent His only beloved Son into the world to die for sinful man. And that, *"He that believeth on the Son hath everlasting life: and he that believeth not the Son shall not see life; but the wrath of God abideth on him"* (John 3:36).

I don't preach a politically correct gospel. I'm not here to impress you. I will be faithful to God and to the Word of God. I preach the full counsel of God and today you have heard it and you have a duty of immediate repentance. God demands repentance. Jesus told His disciples, *"Except ye repent, ye shall all likewise perish"* (Luke 13:3, 5). That means you, friend. Don't be fooled by the watered down gospel of this generation that removes the need of repentance and does not proclaim the reality of a future judgment and a burning and literal hell. A clear gospel that does not warn you that God is angered with the wicked every day is no gospel.

Friend, you have been warned; you have no excuse now. I beg you to flee from the wrath to come and fly to Christ. Fly to Him now, repent now, and become a seeker of Christ before it's too late. All that matters is eternity. Where will you spend eternity? Ask yourself. Will it be in heaven or in hell? Flee to Christ now.

CHAPTER 6: THE CAPPUCCINO CHURCH

Bible Text: Ezekiel 11:12
Preached On: Wednesday, July 3, 2013

We are living in a critical time in which spirituality in the church is near an all-time low and immorality in society is near an all-time high. The pulpits of the land have lost their influence upon society because they have let the world into the church and cheapened the gospel message in an attempt to grow their church campus. Many church members profess to know Christ, but their lives do not display the evidence of true conversion.

When George Whitefield, the great British evangelist, came to America in 1740 during the Great Awakening, he was asked by a Boston minister, "Mr. Whitefield, how many converts have you had since you've been among us?" To which the great Whitefield replied, "I don't know, sir, but I shall return to these parts in a year or two and look for the evidence of their salvation." Few church members today demonstrate credible evidence of their salvation.

Listen, friends, when the church fails to carry out the mandate of the Great Commission and proactively storm the gates of hell, then a vacuum is created. The vacuum begins within the church until the church compromises the gospel message, places man and his needs as the center and focus of the church, and everything rotates around the happiness of man.

My message tonight is on the apostate church in America. It is entitled "The Cappuccino Church" because it's all froth and no substance. I am not insinuating that the entire institutional church in America is apostate; please don't misunderstand me. There are many sound Christian churches throughout our land with solid shepherds leading them, but I have seen a drastic change in a majority of churches that have cheapened the gospel message with the express purpose of growing their church. They've made it a lot easier to become a Christian than what Jesus stated. Jesus said the way is narrow and the passage difficult. He said, *"Except ye repent, ye shall all likewise perish"* (Luke 13:3, 5). I have been around for a long time and have witnessed the tragic spiritual declension of the church in America. It breaks my heart to bring this message tonight, but I must unburden my heart of what the Lord has given me regarding the church in America today.

When I was a little boy in the 1950s and you went to church, you knew you were safe there. You knew that in all probability you would hear the true gospel, and be surrounded by real Christians, and receive spiritual good. Today in America, the church looks the same on the outside, but instead of being a place of blessing, it is now a church that harms you spiritually. It harms the soul with its diluted gospel and man-centered theology. Sinners are fed a false gospel and given a false security. So many pulpits preach death instead of life and damn their hearers instead of blessing them. I'm even afraid to take my teenage daughter to church these days because it seems to be more hurtful to her rather than helpful. You think you're doing good putting your child in a youth group at church but often it's more corrupting in influence than spiritually helpful. That's how bad things have gotten in the church in America in our day.

When I go around and visit churches, I can barely make it through the service without being offended or embarrassed by the minister in the pulpit. The pulpit today in America has not only lost its authority, it's lost its dignity through many of the immature men who occupy it. The church in America has become a Cappuccino Church, all froth and no substance. Instead of being a place of spiritual good, it often has a damning influence.

Many churches in America today are indistinguishable from the local country club. They offer all the comforts of a country club including yoga classes and Zumba dancing and coffee bars whose focus is on making man happy and gratifying his flesh. The gospel of the apostate church speaks of a comfortable Christianity which has no restrictions, and it speaks of a Jesus who has no requirements. But the Jesus of the Bible did not speak of a comfortable Christianity, rather he said, *"Foxes have holes, and birds of the air have nests; but the Son of man hath not where to lay his head"* (Luke 9:58).

The members of the apostate church are quite happy and content there. They are entertained weekly like they belong to a special social club, and they meet on a regular basis. They even pay their monthly dues to this country club church by tithing, and this helps to ease their conscience. But the sad fact is that this apostate church is a church that damns. The Cappuccino Church is a worldly church with a worldly program for its worldly members. It is of the world and of the devil. The Cappuccino Church has a pastor who is more like Jay Leno than a true shepherd. This comedian pastor tells jokes to make his people laugh. The jokes may even be off-color to embarrass them to laugh. He tells funny stories to arouse emotions, and his ministry is based on his professionalism and personality rather than the power of God through a surrendered life under the discipline of the Holy Spirit.

Can you imagine Jonathan Edwards telling jokes to the congregation in Enfield, Connecticut, to warm up his crowd with laughter before he preached

THE CAPPUCCINO CHURCH

"Sinners in the Hands of an Angry God"? But we have jokesters in the pulpits today who make you laugh rather than prophets who cry with authority, *"Thus saith the LORD."* Sadly, few want to have an encounter with God in the church today. They just want to be entertained. The church was never intended to be a place of laughter and entertainment, but a house of prayer and worship. The church in America today has become a party church with fun and laughter rather than a weeping church, broken over the sins of the land, and burdened for the lost and perishing around them. The church has become self-focused, self-sufficient, and self-absorbed.

God is a million miles away from the Cappuccino Church in America today. The Cappuccino Church is a feel-good church. Like the coffee drink, it makes you feel good. I remember being in church as a boy and there was a sense of God's presence there, and a certain solemnity that attended it, and you worshipped God because of His presence. But today in churches, they have a party and laugh and sing because of His absence. The church in America back then was a place where true believers gathered to pray and lay hold of God and weep over the lost. You heard a message about the blood and the cross and the need for repentance because you were a sinner who needed to be reconciled back to an offended God. You heard about a terrible place called hell and you were warned not to go there. But today, in the churches in the land, you'll hear a funny story and feel-good messages to make you feel better about yourself before it's time for you to leave and enjoy your lunch.

Listen, friends, the apostate church fails to warn the sinner to flee from the wrath to come and it's run on man-power and methodologies rather than God and Holy Ghost power. The Cappuccino Church presents a God that has no claims or rights upon a person's life. It omits the need of repentance, the plan of redemption, the blood of Christ, and the bloody cross on which He died. Rather, it preaches a feel-good message which doesn't upset anybody or confront them with their sins. The underground church in China suffers persecution as they follow a crucified Savior. The aboveground church in China is the Three Self Church and it's a tool for the communist government.

The apostate church in America will be the vehicle used by Antichrist when he appears. You will be able to distinguish a true Christian then. They'll be the ones being persecuted for their faith and testimony in Christ Jesus. Martin Luther cried out against the corrupt church in his day and he was persecuted for it. The apostate church will persecute true believers as the Antichrist appears.

Well, that's my introduction for my message tonight on "The Cappuccino Church." My text is found in the book of Ezekiel, in chapter 11 and verse 12. This text accurately describes the church in the West today. Listen to how God describes His rebellious people: *"And ye shall know that I am the LORD: for ye have not walked in my statutes, neither executed my judgments, but have done after the manners of the heathen that are round about you"* (Ezekiel 11:12).

Notice several outstanding remarks from this passage from the Word of God: First, God says something to His people which is quite extraordinary. He declares, *"And ye shall know that I am the LORD."* You see, many that claimed to know Him did not know Him. They had a perverted view of God and their god was not the God of the Bible. Today in our land, I fear many church members have a perverted view of God and they have fashioned a god of their own making and they worship that idol rather than know the true and living God of the Bible.

God was telling His rebellious people that through coming judgments, they will know the true God and *"know that I am the LORD."* This will be true when judgment falls upon America from the hand of God. Times will become so desperate and people so despondent, they will turn to the government for help and the government will be bankrupt and entirely helpless themselves. This situation will be so drastic and so bad that people will realize that God is the author of their calamity and God will be able to say, *"And ye shall know that I am the LORD."*

Notice the next indictment God has against His straying people. He says, *"For ye have not walked in my statutes."* Today's apostate church has members who live in sin and have no remorse for it. They feel that because they are "once saved, always saved," they can sin all they want to without any repercussions since they won their ticket to heaven through a false, easy believism.

God reprimands His people for their disobedience to His commands. Today's church that damns, preaches an easy-belief gospel that allows you to take Christ as Savior and remain in your sins, whereas the Bible declares that Jesus came to save His people from their sins. Jesus never preached a sinning religion, but a self-crucifying one. He said, *"If any man will come after me, let him deny himself, and take up his cross, and follow me. For whosoever will save his life shall lose it: and whosoever will lose his life for my sake shall find it"* (Matthew 16:24-25). But the church that damns declares you can have Jesus and the world, too. You can have Jesus and hold on to your rotten sins and it's okay with Him. But, God says, "No." God says, *"Be ye holy; for I am holy"* (1 Peter 1:16). And in Hebrews 12:14 it declares that without holiness no one will see the Lord.

Notice the next urgent matter that God brings before His rebellious people. He says to them, *"neither executed my judgments."* The people of God were careless stewards of the things of God. Rather than declare to the heathen the purposes of God, they kept all their knowledge to themselves selfishly. Today's church that damns has no real gospel witness to the world. There's no message of God's true gospel which speaks of ruin, redemption, repentance, and regeneration. You will not hear of the blood, nor the cross, nor sin, nor hell, nor of a future judgment for all mankind. Rather, it's a selfish gospel which creates selfish followers who think only of themselves and their own amusements. Their number one aim in life is to gratify their flesh. They know nothing of the cross in the life of the believer nor have they ever surrendered to the lordship of Christ with all His claims and demands upon their lives. The church that damns speaks nothing about the strict and severe law of God which every man will be judged against and that all will fail that test. All men are sinners and need a sin substitute in the person of Jesus Christ.

The rebellious Jews did not execute God's judgments and defend a holy God and fear Him. Rather, they put their own needs and desires first in their lives to the neglect of the things of God. The Jews put themselves first and God second in their lives and God said, "No."

Finally, notice the last thing in this verse from Ezekiel; notice the last indictment from God to His straying people. He tells them, *"but have done after the manners of the heathen that are round about you."* In other words, they worshipped God like the heathen. They brought false fire into the house of God. They let the world in and pushed God out. I fear many churches in America today have walked God to the back of the church and pushed Him out the back door and then they've gone and opened their front door and invited the world in. The Cappuccino Church looks just like the world; there's no telling them apart.

I have a hard time finding anybody today preaching on the blood and the cross and calling sin "black" and hell "hot" and warning sinners to flee from the wrath to come. No, they just want to make you laugh and want to entertain you. They don't want to upset anybody by mentioning sin or the need for repentance. They're afraid to offend man so they offend God. God help us.

When Jesus preached, He always upset His hearers. They wanted to take Him to the top of a hill after He preached and throw Him off it. After one preaching session, the people picked up stones to stone Him, but He escaped them by walking through their midst. And one time, after Jesus preached a hard message, the crowd left Him and many said, "Who can understand it?" And Jesus turned to His men and asked, "Will you leave me too?"

When Christ preached, He divided the crowd into sheep and goats but many of the pygmies that stand in our pulpits today want to be accepted by their hearers because of their pride, so they speak, *"Peace, peace; when there is no peace" (Jeremiah 6:14, 8:11).* The true gospel declares we are enemies of God because of sin and we need to be reconciled to Him through the blood of Jesus Christ. We need to repent of our rotten sins and fall on our faces and turn back to God in true contrition and brokenness over our sins. We need to humble ourselves before an offended Creator and beg Him for mercy.

Listen, friends, judgment is not coming to America because of the White House. Judgment is not coming to America because of the courthouse. Judgment is coming to America because of the church house. God is sending judgments upon America because the professed church of God does not walk in His statutes, nor execute His judgments, but has done after the manners of the heathen that are round about them.

The only hope for America and Canada is revival. But there is good news. God is calling out His remnant to stand strong for Him. God called out a remnant in the days of Ezekiel. Listen to verses 19 and 20 from chapter 11. Listen to God's mercy: *"And I will give them one heart, and I will put a new spirit within you; and I will take the stony heart out of their flesh, and will give them an heart of flesh: That they may walk in my statutes, and keep mine ordinances, and do them: and they shall be my people, and I will be their God."*

I believe that God is calling His remnant today in the land to go to their knees and humble themselves before His face. I believe it will be God's remnant who emerge in the coming days of the appearing of Antichrist. The remnant will be the sufferers for Christ. The remnant will be the ones in prison for Him. The remnant will be the ones martyred for Him and His glory. This is a call to the people of God to go to our knees and ask the Holy Spirit to show us anything in our lives that is grievous to Him.

Listen, friends, I got rid of television in my home. I was hooked on too many news programs and cooking programs and golf programs. I got rid of the damning influence of television in my home. People call me odd but I don't care. I spend that time I used to watch TV, now, in my Bible and in prayer. Christ is calling His own to separate themselves from the world. Are we willing to do it?

THE CAPPUCCINO CHURCH

The Cappuccino Church is a feel-good church with a feel-good message and it allows you to profess Christ and remain in your sins. Jesus said if you die in your sins, you will go to hell. The Cappuccino Church is damning its members to hell rather than warning them not to go there.

In the coming days of these end times, the apostate church will grow in influence and popularity, and it will spread over the land like the great plague that it is. For it is an indictment against the people of God who have not walked in His statutes, nor executed His judgments, but have done after the matters of the heathen that were round about them. God have mercy on us.

CHAPTER 7: THE IMPLOSION OF AMERICA

Bible Text: Jeremiah 1:13-14
Preached on: Tuesday, April 16, 2013

In 1960, the Soviet Premier, Nikita Krushchev, visited the United Nations. He outraged the country by banging his shoe on the table. But I recall his comments in an interview from that time. He was asked by a journalist how he viewed the threat of America as a military power. Krushchev replied that he was not concerned so much about America the great superpower, because eventually America would implode on the inside and self-destruct. I look back on his words because in a sense, they were prophetic. America is imploding today. No national threat overtakes us; it doesn't have to. We are our biggest enemy. The book of Proverbs says, *"Where there is no vision, the people perish"* (29:18). How true this is, especially for our generation.

There are three principles I would like to share with you today that describe a nation's downfall and ultimate destruction. These principles are described by the word "absence." For in actuality, there are three great absences that bring a nation down and make it fall. These three are as follows: 1. When there is an absence of spiritual leadership in the church, the people of God backslide and depart from God. 2. When there is an absence of godly leadership in a nation, the nation falls into gross immorality. 3. When there is an absence of prophets in the land, God is clearing the land for great judgment. All three of these great absences contribute to a nation's ruin and ultimate destruction.

My message today, friends, is entitled "The Implosion of America," for this is what is taking place in this once great land of ours. A land that God once favored is now a land that God has forsaken. A land which God once favored with mighty movements of His presence in revival and spiritual awakenings is now a land desolate by the withdrawn presence of God. There is no fear of God in the land today and God has vacated the premises, leaving us to our own fleshly devices.

Principle #1

Let us examine Principle #1: When there is an absence of spiritual leadership in the church, the people of God backslide and depart from God. Turn in your Bibles to Exodus 32:1. *"And when the people saw that Moses delayed to come down out of the mount, the people gathered themselves together unto Aaron, and said unto him, Up, make us gods, which shall go before us; for as for this Moses, the man that brought us up out of the land of Egypt, we wot not what is become of him."*

Notice two striking statements from this passage. First, notice the comment that it was Moses that brought them up out of Egypt, rather than God who delivered them from Egypt. Already the people of God refused to acknowledge the great deliverances and blessings that God had bestowed upon them. Instead they say, *"This Moses, the man that brought us up out of the land of Egypt,"* and they deride him.

Next, notice the comment, *"We wot not what is become of him."* Moses is absent. There is no spiritual leadership in the camp of Israel. Aaron is an appointed leader by God, yet is a poor spiritual guide as he heeds to the people's sinful demands and makes an idol of gold to worship. So the principle here stated is this, when there is an absence of spiritual leadership in the church, the people of God backslide and depart from God.

Look at their great departure found in verses 3-6:

> *And all the people brake off the golden earrings which were in their ears, and brought them unto Aaron. And he received them at their hand, and fashioned it with a graving tool, after he had made it a molten calf: and they said, These be thy gods, O Israel, which brought thee up out of the land of Egypt. And when Aaron saw it, he built an altar before it; and Aaron made proclamation, and said, To morrow is a feast to the LORD. And they rose up early on the morrow, and offered burnt offerings, and brought peace offerings; and the people sat down to eat and to drink, and rose up to play.*

Here is a sad and tragic picture of the people of God, who have so departed from the heart of God that they turn from God to idols and worship them. Their hearts are so hardened through this departure from God that they quickly descend into debauchery. And the sad thing is, that they find it perfectly natural to have an orgy at this feast. It's alright in their eyes, and they think it's all pleasing in the sight of God.

Listen how God views this horrid thing. Listen to verses 7-10:

> *And the LORD said unto Moses, Go, get thee down; for thy people, which thou broughtest out of the land of Egypt, have corrupted themselves: They have turned aside quickly out of the way which I commanded them: they have made them a molten calf, and have*

worshipped it, and have sacrificed thereunto, and said, These be thy gods, O Israel, which have brought thee up out of the land of Egypt. And the LORD said unto Moses, I have seen this people, and, behold, it is a stiffnecked people: Now therefore let me alone, that my wrath may wax hot against them, and that I may consume them: and I will make of thee a great nation.

In the churches of America and Great Britain, there is an absence, a dearth of spiritual leadership, so the countries deteriorate and depart from the living God. The church in America and Great Britain is in spiritual decay and decline. Deadness is all around. The church is powerless to impact a sinful society because of her own sinfulness in departing from God and the Word of God. Rather than repent and do that first work, the church entertains herself and rises up to play. This impacts the nation as a whole, as unbelievers view the church as hypocritical and judgmental. Rather than being salt, which preserves a nation from sin, the people of God add to the sinful departure of a nation from God through their own departure from God. Yet, in their eyes, they see nothing wrong in their idolatries.

The church in America and Great Britain has done two terrible things. They have thrown open the front doors of their church and let the world in. Secondly, they have opened up the back door of the church and escorted God out saying, "We don't need you anymore. We are fine without you." And the people that fill our churches cry out for more entertainment, rather than cry out in anguish over the things that break the heart of God. They serve and worship themselves rather than serve the true and living God of the Bible. The priests are ruled by their means and the people love to have it so.

I remember in America in the 1950s when the Methodist church wielded such authority that they kept a TV commercial off the air because they felt it was crude. The church back in those days influenced society, rather than today where society influences the church. The very absence of the voices of authority in places of spiritual leadership who cry out against the sins of the land show how America is imploding and soon will be a desolation.

Principle # 2

Let's examine the second principle of great absence. When there is an absence of godly leadership in a nation, the nation falls into gross immorality. Look at America and Great Britain today. Friends, how the gold has dimmed. Two nations, once mighty in mission outreach and the printing and distribution of Christian literature, now produce multiplied sins against a holy and offended God. The governments of both these nations stand in bold defiance to God and His Word.

They mock God's authority. They mock the people of God and the church of God and they institute laws which profane the very direct commands of God. And what is the result of all of this? Pick up a newspaper or turn on the national news and see the gross immorality that permeates and saturates the very foundation of America and Great Britain.

Two nations that once did great things for God and God did great things through them, lie spiritually impotent and have become a laughingstock in the eyes of the world. Look at the absence of godly rulers in both these nations and how God has brought judgment upon them in the form of gross immorality and increasing judgments from the hand of God.

Now, look at the principle found in Scripture describing the rule and reign of wicked King Manasssah. It is found in 2 Kings 21:9: *"Manasseh seduced them to do more evil than did the nations whom the LORD destroyed before the children of Israel."*

And look at God's response to such a wicked king and to such a disobedient people. Look at verse 12: *"Therefore thus saith the LORD God of Israel, Behold, I am bringing such evil upon Jerusalem and Judah, that whosoever heareth of it, both his ears shall tingle."*

A nation will surely deteriorate and eventually implode under ungodly rulers. Look at ancient Rome and the Caesars; how corrupt that society became until it, too, eventually imploded. Rome, that once ruled the world with an iron fist, even today is a joke as a superpower. And Great Britain, which once ruled the seas with her mighty Royal Navy, can hardly rule herself. America, which once all other nations looked up to in admiration, is now looked at with ridicule and derision. Third World countries used to tremble at America's feet but now hold up an angry and defiant fist and shake it in her face, and she is impotent to do anything about it because of her leadership. Yes, Nikita Krushchev was right in his summation of America over fifty years ago. The last five decades of America have been a time of national departure from God, and a time of growing decadence in America.

Principle #3

Let us examine this third and last principle of yet another great absence, and I fear it is the most alarming of all three. When there is an absence of prophets in the land, God is clearing the land for a great judgment. I vividly remember the comments of Dr. Adrian Rogers to me at the funeral of Stephen Olford. I was standing in front of Adrian Rogers, and he had his arms folded across his chest and he looked very disturbed as he asked me a question. He said, "Do you know what concerns me?" I answered him, "No, Dr. Rogers, what concerns you?" He replied, "I see God calling up men like J. Sidlow Baxter and Stephen Olford and I look around and I don't see any come-uppers and that concerns me." I told him it concerned me, too.

I look around today in America and Great Britain and I see a void, an absence of prophets in the land. I see God calling up men like Leonard Ravenhill, Vance Havner, and David Wilkerson, and I see no replacements for them. Men who were not afraid to call a nation to repentance with the words, *"Thus saith the LORD."*

To me, dear friends, this is the most alarming aspect of the three absences which I have mentioned, for it means that God is clearing the land for a final judgment. That alone should drive us to our knees in desperation, to sit in sackcloth and ashes in our sanctuaries and cry out to God for forgiveness for the great sins in our land. We should all be on our knees right now, in repentance and humility before an offended God, begging God to have mercy upon us. Instead, we are so spiritually blinded and so far away from the heart of God in a backslidden condition, that we simply rise up to play. We sacrifice to our idols while an impending judgment faces the land.

Listen to the vivid imagery found in Jeremiah about a seething pot, ready to spill out its contents upon the land in judgment. Listen to Jeremiah 1:13-14: *"And the word of the LORD came unto me the second time, saying, What seest thou? And I said, I see a seething pot; and the face thereof is toward the north. Then the LORD said unto me, Out of the north an evil shall break forth upon all the inhabitants of the land."*

Listen, friends, in America and Great Britain today there has not been a time more critical than this hour, when God's hand of judgment is ready to spill out across our lands because of our gross national sins and a departure from a holy God. During the first part of the last century, both Great Britain and America were still considered Christian nations and doing good for the Lord. But now, their combined, sad departure from God, and spiritual decay in the people of God, is a stark contrast to what they both once stood for and did for a holy God.

"I see a seething pot; and the face thereof is toward the north," the prophet answered. But where, O where, are the prophets today, to warn our once great nations of our sad departure from a holy God and lead us into great national repentance back to God, to avoid a sudden and final judgment from the hand of God? *"Then the LORD said unto me, Out of the north an evil shall break forth upon all the inhabitants of the land."* Unless we, as nations, heed the signs all around us and repent of our sins and turn back to God with our whole heart, the

ears of our nations will tingle at the coming judgment upon us. The coming judgment will be so widespread in its severity that it will ring out in history as a tragic reminder of what befalls a nation when it departs from the living God. The unraveling of society is tied directly to the implosion of our country.

Will we turn back to God before it's too late? I pray that we will!

CHAPTER 8: CHRIST'S RECEPTION OF SINNERS

Bible Text: Gospel of Matthew
Preached on: Saturday, January 12, 2013

Matthew Henry, the great Bible commentator, had this to say about Christ's reception of sinners. He said, "Christ was born in an inn. An inn receives all commerce and so does Christ. He hangs out the banner of love for His sign and whoever comes to Him He will in no wise cast out. Only unlike other inns, He welcomes those who come without money and without price." My message today is entitled "Christ's Reception of Sinners."

Our text is found in the gospel of Matthew, chapter 11 and verse 28, *"Come unto me, all ye that labour and are heavy laden, and I will give you rest."* It is an invitation from Christ to the sinner to come and He will welcome you. Christ wants to pardon and receive sinners. Jesus is willing for sinners to come to Him for He states, *"Him that cometh to me I will in no wise cast out"* (John 6:37). The thief on the cross can come and the biggest sinner in your community can come. All are invited to come to Christ, for the Son is willing in His reception of sinners and He casts none out that come in.

Jesus came down here so that we can go up to heaven. Jesus said, *"For I came down from heaven, not to do mine own will, but the will of him that sent me"* (John 6:38). Christ was on an errand, a mission, to save souls and He has a warm reception for sinners. Oh friends, look at Jesus as He went about in His earthly ministry. He went from town to town, village to village, wearing Himself out to preach the glad tidings of the gospel. He was so tired from His incessant labors that He had to rest at the well in Samaria. He was so worn out from going from coast to coast that He slept soundly in a boat through a violent storm. Jesus was tireless in His efforts to invite poor sinners to come to Him.

At the last day of the Feast of Tabernacles, Jesus stood and cried out, *"If any man thirst, let him come unto me, and drink"* (John 7:37). Well, what is that but an invitation to come to Him whose arms are open wide, ready to receive every single sinner that is thirsty for Him? No one is turned away, *"Ho, every one that thirsteth, come ye to the waters"* (Isaiah 55:1). Listen to His pleas to come to Him, *"And the Spirit and the bride say, Come. And let him that heareth say, Come. And let him that is athirst come. And whosoever will, let him take the water of life freely"* (Revelation 22:17). Christ not only invites, He stands ready to receive all that come to Him.

Listen to the mercy of the Lord and His readiness to receive poor sinners: *"Let the wicked forsake his way, and the unrighteous man his thoughts: and let him return unto the LORD, and he will have mercy upon him; and to our God, for he will abundantly pardon"* (Isaiah 55:7).

Did you hear those last words? He will abundantly pardon? Oh friend, He is merciful and ready to pardon you if you would only come to Him, but you won't come. He is not willing that any should perish. *"For I have no pleasure in the death of him that dieth, saith the Lord GOD: wherefore turn yourselves, and live ye"* (Ezekiel 18:32).

He is willing, but you are unwilling to come to Him. Look at the freeness of God's love for you, *"For God so loved the world, that he gave his only begotten son."* His only Son, He gave His Son for you, *"that whosoever believeth in him should not perish, but have everlasting life"* (John 3:16). But you refuse to believe in Him. That is, you may mentally acknowledge Him but you refuse to turn your life over to Him in a full surrender of yourself to Him. You refuse to die so that you can live. You refuse to die to yourself, your needs, your lusts, so even though the love of the Father is free, and the love of Christ is clearly demonstrated in His death on the cross, and the invitations of the gospel are calls of welcome to come to Christ freely, without money or without price, and eat, still you do not come. You are unwilling.

Let us look at Christ's reception of sinners from God's own sworn promise as found in Ezekiel 33:11, *"Turn ye, turn ye from your evil ways; for why will ye die, O house of Israel?"* Oh, the goodness of God in His mercy extended towards you; He pleads with you to turn from your sins and repent towards Him; to have faith in Christ Jesus, but you will not. You love your sins.

See how Jesus came to win souls to Himself, how He came to woo you to Him, how He came into the world to save you, *"This is a faithful saying, and worthy of all acceptation, that Christ Jesus came into the world to save sinners"* (1 Timothy 1:15). Oh friend, He came on a divine mission to save you, but you do not want to be saved. You are unwilling to be saved. Jesus weeps tears over your not repenting and coming unto Him.

Look at Him as He stands on the hillside looking down at the city of Jerusalem, and how He bemoans the hard-heartedness of sinful man in his refusal to come to Christ, *"And when he was come near, he beheld the city, and wept over it, Saying, If thou hadst known, even thou, at least in this thy day, the things which belong unto thy peace! but now are they hid from thine eyes"* (Luke 19:41-42). He weeps. He weeps over your ignorance of Him as your Redeemer. He weeps over your lack of peace because of your refusal to acknowledge Him as Lord of your life and come to Him in glad submission and throw down your shotgun of rebellion and surrender to the King of Kings. He is ready to receive you, dear friend. Won't you come to Him? Won't you come? You won't because you are unwilling; you are blind to your own condition.

George Whitefield, the great British evangelist, once described the sinner in this way; he likened him to a poor blind beggar who walks along a dangerous road with his cane and little dog beside him. The poor blind beggar comes to a precipice where he totters and he loses his cane and his little dog deserts him. And there the poor blind beggar stands ready to fall to his death and die in his sins. You are blind, blind to your sins, blind to the free grace of God, blind to the mercy of God. Not only blind, but deaf; deaf to the calls of God to come to Him through His Son, Jesus Christ. Why, oh why, won't you come? Why do you not respond to the Word of God and the pleas of God? This is why, *"But the natural man receiveth not the things of the Spirit of God: for they are foolishness unto him: neither can he know them, because they are spiritually discerned"* (1 Corinthians 2:14).

But listen to Jesus as He tells of His errand here on earth, *"And Jesus answering said unto them, They that are whole need not a physician; but they that are sick. I came not to call the righteous, but sinners to repentance"* (Luke 5:31-32).

You have no need of Him because you do not realize that you are sick; you do not realize your desperate condition without God in the world. You are blinded to your perilous position outside of Christ and how you can die at any moment and perish into a Christless eternity. But Jesus came to call sinners to repentance; He came to seek and save.

Christ's reception of sinners is a broad welcome to come to Him and He will receive you. Listen to Christ's moans and groans and broken heart over the hard heart of man who refuses to hear His voice, *"O Jerusalem, Jerusalem, thou that killest the prophets, and stonest them which are sent unto thee, how often would I have gathered thy children together, even as a hen gathereth her chickens under her wings, and ye would not!"* (Matthew 23:37). Look at the tenderness of Christ's own heart, the heart of God Himself in His bemoaning the hard heart of sinful man and his refusal to come to Him; how He likens Himself to a mother hen gathering her chicks about her with care and love. The warnings of the prophets, the death of Christ, the invitations of the gospel, *"And ye would not."* You will not come to Him. Why won't you come? Christ stands ready to receive you if you will only come to Him now. Christ's reception of sinners is seen plainly throughout the Scriptures; His readiness to receive you if you would only receive Him. But you would not.

The abundant mercy of God should make you run to Him. Look at the story of the prodigal son and how he finally came to his senses and said, *"I will arise and go to my father"* (Luke 15:18). He turned from his pigpen, got up, dusted himself off, and began the journey home to his father's house, and what happens? When the father lays eyes on him, he runs to him. He runs to the boy, throws his arms around his neck, and kisses him with the kisses of forgiveness and the love of a father. The prodigal returned to the father. Why won't you return? Why won't you come to Christ in repentance? Why stay in your pigpen any longer? Why won't you come?

I stand here as Christ's own ambassador and I plead with you to come, *"Now then we are ambassadors for Christ, as though God did beseech you by us: we pray you in Christ's stead, be ye reconciled to God"* (2 Corinthians 5:20). Oh friend, be reconciled to God through His Son Jesus Christ. Why do you wait? Why don't you come? Your sin substitute is Jesus Christ. He paid it all. He took the Father's wrath upon Himself so you would not have to. Jesus died so you can live. Why won't you come and live? Jesus says, *"I am come that they might have life, and that they might have it more abundantly"* (John 10:10). Christ speaks of His own willingness for you to come and have this life that is freely offered in the pleas and invitations of the gospel, but you still will not come.

I would think that any sinner that heard all this would fly to God and Christ right now. That no matter how wicked you are, how sinful you are, how hard-hearted you are, you would be melted by the love of Christ towards you. Christ makes the invitation to poor sinners. Isn't that what you are, a poor sinner? Oh, will you not come? What will be your excuse when you stand at the Great Judgment and give reasons for your denial of Christ? Give excuses for your refusal of Christ and His pleas and offers and invitations for you to come to Him? What is your motive right now not to come to Christ and bow to Him and beg for mercy and grace? What is your reason that makes you unwilling to come to Him?

Christ's love is a very affectionate love. He invites you to the marriage feast. He calls you to the marriage supper of the Lamb. What a banquet awaits you in glory if you would only come to Him now. You can sit at God's table and sup with Him for all eternity. Why, why won't you come? *"Come ye to the waters ... come unto me, and drink"* (Isaiah 55:1; John 7:37), He beckons. He invites poor sinners to come to Him and drink. He plainly speaks of His willingness to receive you if you will but come. He bowed heaven and earth for you. He laid aside His royal robes of majesty to wear a rough-hewn garment, to go to a cross and bleed and suffer and die for you.

Listen to this incident in the life of Stephen Olford. He would often relate the following story on Christ's reception of sinners.

> Born in Africa to missionary parents, Stephen Olford grew up in the African bush in a humble little cottage. It was Christmas and young Stephen decided to sneak out of the cottage early that morning to go bag a goose for Christmas dinner. Before daylight, he left his parent's home quietly so not to awaken them. Into the darkness he walked with his rifle beneath his arm. Making his way to the gate he unlatched it but it made a squeak. He kept going into the dark bush to a distant field and a pond where he knew wild geese would be. Slowly he moved in the darkness but unfortunately his next step landed him into a treacherous bog of mire. He began to sink in the miry bog. As he held his rifle above his head with one hand, while frantically trying to extricate himself with the other, he realized he was in grave danger and sinking to his death. But unknown to him, the native servant of his father's house was awakened by the squeak of the gate and this African had followed him in the darkness without his knowledge. There stood the African as the morning sun began to break over the field. He was attired in a colorful robe of silk which was wrapped around his naked body. Quickly, the native began to unfold his cloak about him. It unfolded into one long piece of material and as he unfolded it he reached the garment over to the desperate Stephen Olford. Stephen grabbed it and hung on for dear life as he was pulled to safety.

Dr. Olford would often relate that this action of the African was like gospel of Jesus Christ in His reception of sinners. That Jesus stepped out of the glories of heaven to come to earth to rescue lost man who was sunk in the mire of sin. And in His great mercy He unfolded his royal robe of righteousness and reached it out to us to grab hold of. Jesus saves his people from their sins. Once we acknowledge our desperate condition and need of Him, Christ's welcome mat is out for all who come to Him.

He gave His all to gain your heart. Why do you keep your heart from Him? Oh, why is your heart so hard? Why won't you come now to the Christ who can save you? Whoever gave such an example of selfless love as Christ who gave His all for you? Do not blame Christ and say He is unwilling. No, it is you who is unwilling. Do not lay blame on Him that He cannot save you. He has already paid the price, the sacrifice has been made. Do not blame Him for His unwillingness to receive you; it is your unwillingness to receive Him. He wills but you won't. He calls but you won't listen. He says I would but you would not.

Christ weeps over you as He did over Jerusalem. Why won't you come? Will you not weep for yourself? His yoke is easy and His burden is light. His commandments are not grievous, *"My yoke is easy"* (Matthew 11:30), He says to you. Look unto Him. Look unto Him now.

Listen to Him, *"I, even I, am the LORD; and beside me there is no saviour"* (Isaiah 43:11). Again listen to Him as He declares, *"I am the LORD, and there is none else, there is no God beside me"* (Isaiah 45:5). Look to Jesus, *"Look unto me, and be ye saved, all the ends of the earth: for I am God, and there is none else"* (Isaiah 45:22).

All it takes is a look. See the revealed Christ and come to Him and surrender. You who are thirsty, you who are hungry, you who are weary, come to Him now; come to Him now and He will receive you. He will gladly receive you. The heart of the gospel is for the thirsty, the hungry, the weary. Come to Him now.

Look and live. Look and live.

> *As Moses lifted up the serpent in the wilderness, even so must the Son of man be lifted up: That whosoever believeth in him should not perish, but have eternal life.* (John 3:14-15)
>
> *My sheep hear my voice, and I know them, and they follow me: And I give unto them eternal life; and they shall never perish, neither shall any man pluck them out of my hand.* (John 10:27-28)

Oh friend, sell all that you have for the pearl of great price. *"Again, the kingdom of heaven is like unto a merchant man, seeking goodly pearls: Who, when he had found one pearl of great price, went and sold all that he had, and bought it"* (Matthew 13:45-46). Coming to Christ means that self is dethroned and another is enthroned there.

He is altogether lovely, Jesus is altogether worthy. Worthy is the Lamb, worthy is the Lamb. Come to Him, but you need no money for the pearl of great price. Listen to how free grace is, *"Ho, every one that thirsteth, come ye to the waters, and he that hath no money; come ye, buy, and eat; yea, come, buy wine and milk without money and without price"* (Isaiah 55:1).

Oh, the pearl of great price is yours for free, without price. Jesus has already paid the price, He paid your sin debt so that you can be reconciled to the Father. Jesus came down here so we can go up there.

Dear friend, I am through. I have presented and argued the case that Christ receives sinners, that He has a warm reception for them. If you do not possess Christ then go to your knees. Knowing about Him and having Him are two entirely different things. Eternity hangs in the balance. To possess Christ means He is yours and you are His. It means you are in a vital union with a living Lord. That's salvation.

Listen to these promises from the Word of God and the pleas from the heart of God to you. If you are without Christ, I implore you to ask God to give you the grace to do what they say, *"Seek ye the LORD while he may be found, call ye upon him while he is near: Let the wicked forsake his way, and the unrighteous man his thoughts: and let him return unto the LORD, and he will have mercy upon him; and to our God, for he will abundantly pardon"* (Isaiah 55:6-7). Remember those words, for He will abundantly pardon all who come to Him in true repentance.

Christ's reception of sinners is a fact. He will abundantly pardon. Oh friend, repent and come to Him now.

CHAPTER 9: THE KING OF GLORY OF REVIVAL

Bible Text: Psalm 24
Preached On: Tuesday, September 10, 2013

My message tonight is on revival. People often ask me what revival is. Revival is the manifest presence of God amidst His people whereby they are melted down under the awful solemnity of a holy God. Revival is when God shows up and takes the field and all human enterprise crumbles in importance and things of eternity grow in importance. Revival is when God cleans house, so to speak, when God purifies His people for a specific purpose, to bring Him glory. During a revival of religion, more people are saved than through years of steady evangelistic labor. Revival is harvest time.

We may ask, when do we need revival? We need revival when the people of God are no longer salt to a nation in moral decline. Salt is a preservative. The people of God, when rightly aligned to God, are a preservative against sin in the land, but when the people of God are out of step with God, then they cease to be salt and light in the very nation in which they reside, and instead of preservation, there is putrefaction, and sin abounds.

Listen, friends, revival is needed when the church and people have strayed from God in disobedience and disinterest in spiritual things. Revival is needed when the church is more interested in building her own campus than building churches in third world countries. Revival is needed when the people of God are content and satisfied with weak preaching. Revival is needed when we have more teachers in the pulpits than preachers. Revival is needed when our eyes are dry, our Bibles are closed, and our prayer life is stale. Revival is needed when our focus is ourselves and our families rather than the lost and perishing. Revival is needed if we have dry eyes when we pray. Revival is needed when the way we worship God is tainted with strange fire by adding worldly entertainments to sacred things. Revival is needed when our worship time in church is centered more on entertainers than on God. Revival is needed when there is a noticeable withdrawal of the presence of God. Revival is needed when there exists a great proportion of unconverted church members who have never been truly born again.

There was a time in America years ago when you could not join a church unless you demonstrated credible evidence of regeneration. We have many in our churches today who have never been truly converted and regenerated through the new birth. In seasons of revival, many unconverted church members come savingly to Christ, all to the glory of God. Revival is needed when the people of God are not heartbroken over the things that break God's heart, and revival is needed when Jesus is no longer our first love. However, there is a cost to seeing revival. What costs counts and what counts costs. Are we willing to pay the price of laying ourselves on the altar of sacrifice to see God move in our lives?

My message tonight is entitled "The King of Glory of Revival," for true revival is when the King of Glory steps in and takes the field. True revival is when Jesus is once again prominent and preeminent in our churches in the land. My text is found in Psalm 24. Let us turn there now and I will read it to us, for the pathway to revival is found in this great passage of God's holy Word.

> *The earth is the LORD'S, and the fulness thereof; the world, and they that dwell therein. For he hath founded it upon the seas, and established it upon the floods. Who shall ascend into the hill of the LORD? or who shall stand in his holy place? He that hath clean hands, and a pure heart; who hath not lifted up his soul unto vanity, nor sworn deceitfully. He shall receive the blessing from the LORD, and righteousness from the God of his salvation. This is the generation of them that seek him, that seek thy face, O Jacob. Selah. Lift up your heads, O ye gates; and be ye lift up, ye everlasting doors; and the King of glory shall come in. Who is this King of glory? The LORD strong and mighty, the LORD mighty in battle. Lift up your heads, O ye gates; even lift them up, ye everlasting doors; and the King of glory shall come in. Who is this King of glory? The LORD of hosts, he is the King of glory. Selah.*

There are four aspects to this passage which stand out in striking harmony: first, there is a walking mentioned with its conditions; then there is a standing spoken of with its requirements; then there is a seeking described by responsibility on our part; lastly, there is a receiving of a two-fold blessing from God. Each of these aspects of Psalm 24 are related to one another and are in perfect harmony with each other. If one of these is out of alignment, then it throws all of them out of alignment.

When you examine historical periods of revival, which I have done over the last few decades; when you study revival, you will often find great hindrances to revival and how those hindrances to revival were dealt with before revival broke out upon a church or nation. With God there is perfect harmony, and we must align ourselves to be in harmony with Him and His purpose in our lives. If we are out of step with God as individuals, then the church body will be out of step corporately, for it is the members of a church which comprise it. And, if the church is out of step with God, then there will be a great hindrance to seeing revival come in a national awakening.

Revival is a sovereign work of God. The wind blows where it will. We cannot produce revival on our own. However, we can set out sails to catch that wind when it does blow. This message tonight is on setting our sails, getting them properly aligned to catch these revival winds when God sends them. If we fail to align ourselves to God, He will bypass us and send revival to others. I cannot stress how critically important this is, friends. If we are off here, we are off everywhere.

For years, we have confused revival with evangelism. Evangelism is something we can do, revival is something only God can do. But we must pay attention to the four aspects mentioned in this striking passage from Psalm 24, for herein lies the pathway to revival.

Let us look at this first aspect mentioned in our text: there is a walking mentioned with its conditions. *Who shall ascend into the hill of the LORD?* One walks up a hill to get to the top. Often Scripture speaks of a relationship with God by the term "walking" as in *"Enoch walked with God"* (Genesis 5:22, 24). How is our walk with God? Are we out of step with God because of sin? Look at the conditions that are mentioned here in our text regarding walking with God and ascending that hill. *"He that hath clean hands, and a pure heart."* These conditions are two-fold as the blessings received are two-fold. These conditions speak of two relationships: one with people, and the other with God. Our relationship with others is like a horizontal beam. Think about a wooden telephone pole lying on its side and we must walk atop it in perfect balance or we will fall off. Think of that wooden beam.

This aspect of clean hands speaks of our horizontal relationship with others. A pure heart speaks of our relationship with God. That is the vertical beam. Picture a telephone pole standing upright in the ground. Our walk with God must be upright. We must maintain a right relationship with Him and this is the vertical relationship.

Now, take those two telephone poles, so to speak, the horizontal beam which is our walk with others and the vertical beam which is our walk with God. When these two are properly aligned they form a cross. For us to have power with God and influence with men, we must live crucified lives in complete harmony with the Lord Jesus Christ. If we are out of alignment in any area, our walk with men or our walk with God, then it is a hindrance to revival, both personal and corporate.

Let us take this aspect of the horizontal relationship in our dealing with others. What are some areas in our lives that can have a negative effect on our prayer life? Let me mention a few. Do you have an unforgiving heart toward another, living or dead? I say living or dead because we can harbor unforgiveness towards someone who has hurt us in the past, but they are now dead. Have we forgiven them? Or do we harbor resentment and hurt and unforgiveness towards that person? Do we have a person in our lives who is living, that when we think of them, or see them, we seethe with anger? Listen, unforgiveness is a sin. Confess it and go to God and ask him to give you the grace of forgiveness toward another and even toward yourself if necessary. This is a glaring hindrance to revival.

There is a golden thread that weaves its way through revivals, and if this purified thread is broken, it has been a bar to revival throughout history. That to which I refer is the golden thread of a forgiving heart toward others. When one researches the history of revival, it is plainly shown that several revivals began accompanied by a sudden manifestation of God's presence when Christians began to confess their sins of an unforgiving heart to one another.

Another area which can hinder our prayers and our ascending that hill of the Lord is this: have we told a lie? Our passage in Psalm 24 goes on to state, *"who hath not lifted up his soul unto vanity, nor sworn deceitfully."* The Hebrew word used means "fraud, deceit." Have we deceived someone with a lie or have we withheld a truth from them? Jacob stole Esau's blessing through deceit. God cannot tolerate deceitful weights and a false balance is an abomination to Him.

Is there something covered in your life by deceit? Is there a wedge of Achan's gold in your life? Oh, let the searching spotlight of the Holy Spirit penetrate your heart and conscience right now. Achan's sin affected the entire corporate body in the camp. People died because of Achan's deceit. This is serious business. Are you guilty? Go to God now and get things right in your dealings with others.

I vividly remember a time in my life that describes what I'm talking about. Many years ago I was playing racquetball with a Christian friend who was in my Sunday school class. When he learned we went to the same college, he asked me when I graduated. At the time, I had not yet graduated so I lied to him and gave him a year of my graduation. My pride was in the way and I lied. For an entire week I was disturbed in my spirit; I felt awful that I had lied to this man, telling him an untruth. Finally, I met him in the hall at church and walked up to him and said, "Look, I need to ask your forgiveness for something." He said, "What is that?" I then told him about the lie. He looked surprised but he forgave me. I had to get my relationship with him rightly aligned for my relationship with God to grow. My two beams had to be in proper alignment or my prayers would be hindered and my walk with God weakened.

So we must maintain a proper alignment in our dealing with others. This is the horizontal relationship. Now, let us go to our vertical relationship with God. Is there a sin in our life that we hug and refuse to give up? Is there something in our life that stands between us and our God? Oh friends, how important this aspect of the vertical beam is. Take a moment and think of the apostle Peter when he denied Christ in the courtyard. The text says he went out and wept. Think of how awful Peter felt when Christ was dead and buried in the tomb before his resurrection. For those three days, all Peter could think about was how he had denied his Master and Jesus was now dead and the last thing Peter did was to lie and deny that he knew Jesus.

When we sin, we are denying that we know Jesus. We are robbing God of his glory. When we sin, we are telling God to get out of the way, for we are going to have our way. Sin is this: *"All we like sheep have gone astray; we have turned every one to his own way"* (Isaiah 53:6). Sin is going our way when we know it isn't God's way. When we sin, we are like Peter denying Jesus in that courtyard and it's as if God is dead and in a tomb.

The great reformer, Martin Luther, was in a period of doubt and despair and his wife said to him, "Martin, is your God dead? You act and look as if God is dead." Well, that brought Martin Luther out of his despair and he quickly returned back to a vital walk with God. Is God dead in your life right now, because of your sin? Are you out of fellowship with God right now? Be honest.

Now, look at the difference in Peter when he realizes that the resurrected Christ is standing on the seashore that morning. Peter jumps in the water and cannot wait to get to Him. The resurrected Christ restores Peter to a vital love relationship with Him with His three questions, "Peter, do you love me?" Do you love Jesus? Jesus says, *"If ye love me, keep my commandments"* (John 14:15). The risen Christ can restore you back to a right relationship with Him. Go to Him now and get right with God, the God of your salvation.

So, these two aspects of walking must be in harmony with each other: our walk with others and our walk with God. The Christian life is lived via the cross. The crucified life is seldom preached on today but it's the only life to live in this world. If you want to have power with God, the self-life must be nailed.

Next in our text here is a standing spoken of with its requirements. When we are properly aligned in our dealings with others and our walk with God, we can access Him and stand in His presence and bring our petitions to Him but we must be in a right standing with God. Do you see how important this is?

Duncan Campbell was used mightily as an instrument of revival during the Lewis Awakening in Scotland in the Hebrides in 1949-1952. When he arrived on the island, some elders of the church met him and asked, "Mr. Campbell, are you walking with God?" Duncan carefully replied, "I can say this: I fear God." Do you fear God like that? Do you walk in a holy fear as you approach the Mount, the holy hill? Is your pride hindering your access to God? Listen, friends, I believe the number one sin in the church in America today is pride: pride in the pulpit and pride in the pew. This is our greatest hindrance to seeing revival in our day.

The next aspect of Psalm 24 is this: we notice there is a seeking described in our passage with a responsibility on our part. Seeking involves effort. Heaven is taken with violence. There is an importunity to prayer. There is a desperation of prayer. How desperate are we to see revival? How long are we willing to storm heaven with our petitions and heart-cries to move the heart of God and sue Him, so to speak, until He answers?

Listen to these next two verses, *"This is the generation of them that seek him, that seek thy face, O Jacob. Selah. Lift up your heads, O ye gates; and be ye lift up, ye everlasting doors; and the King of glory shall come in. Who is this King of glory? The LORD strong and mighty, the LORD mighty in battle."* Oh, listen, friends, when we properly align ourselves with God and seek Him in holy desperation, then the doors of heaven open to us and God comes in, the King of Glory steps in.

So, there is a seeking involved, but it depends on our standing with God as spoken of in our walk with God and our walk with others. The text says, *"the King of glory shall come in."* That is the God of revival, this King of Glory. When Christ is King in our lives and ruling on the throne of our heart, that's when God can move. Christ must reign on the throne of your heart. There is only one room on the seat of your heart. If you're sitting and ruling there, it's no wonder God has withdrawn His presence from you. There is only one who can sit there and that is the King of Glory.

We are bought with a price and that price was a bloody cross, for it was on the cross that the King of Glory died for sin. He took God's wrath upon Him and divine justice was satisfied. We cannot go to God by our own merits, but only by the merit of another, Jesus Christ. As believers, our Christian life must be in harmony with God and in harmony with man. If we are out of kilter with one or the other, those two beams just won't line up, and we will not have the access to God that we desire, or the blessings received that he wishes to bestow upon us.

And that brings us to the last aspect of this passage: the receiving of a two-fold blessing from God. *"He shall receive the blessing from the LORD, and righteousness from the God of his salvation."* When we are properly aligned to God, we can access the hill of the Lord, and be like those spoken of in the book of Hebrews in chapter 11 who are in the Hall of Faith. They are mentioned there because they obtained promises. When you walk with God in a close walk with Him, you will obtain the promises which He has made to you through his written Word. This is a two-fold blessing of revival and it is seen in this: firstly, the blessing received of a revived church living for eternity with apostolic fervency; and secondly, revival sends spiritual awakening in the land where many lost are saved, and they can then say of God that He is the God of their salvation. All glory goes to Him.

I truly believe that God wants to send revival to America but the church in America is out of alignment with the things of God. The church in America is out of alignment in her dealings with man, the horizontal beam. The church in America is out of alignment with her walk with God because of her pride and self-sufficiency. The vertical beam is out of alignment. There must be proper balance for God to work in the midst of man. There has to be a heavenly balance between these two beams; they must meet at the cross, for Jesus declared, *"If any man will come after me, let him deny himself, and take up his cross, and follow me"* (Matthew 16:24).

Let me ask you and be honest: Is your Christian life out of balance with your fellow man? Are you living in a lie? Are you bitter towards someone? Have you an unforgiving heart? Do you need to go and apologize to that person like I did to my friend in church? Do you need to make things right with man and with God Almighty? Are our relational beams lined up properly? There is a cost to proper alignment as they form that cross in our lives. The crucified life is the only life to live in this sin-soaked land and in our lost generation. Go to your knees right now and ask God to grant you what you need to be properly aligned to Him. Ask Him for the grace to do it.

The pathway to revival is found in our passage tonight. We are told what to do in the princely passage of Scripture which speaks of a King. Listen, *"Lift up your heads, O ye gates; even lift them up, ye everlasting doors; and the King of glory shall come in. Who is this King of glory? The LORD of hosts, he is the King of glory. Selah."*

Let me pray. *O Lord, O King of Glory, how our hearts are deceitful. Open our eyes, Great King, open our eyes so we can lift up our heads and seek you properly. Align our lives, Great God, in perfect harmony with Thy Holy Spirit. Open our eyes to see our sins. Open our eyes to reveal our unforgiving hearts and the deep roots of bitterness that have poisoned your Bride. Purify your people, Great God. Grant us the grace and repentance to turn from our sins and seek your face in holy desperation, for You are our only hope, the blessed hope. O Lord Jesus, rain righteousness upon the land once again through a national awakening. Wash the corruption and filth away with a mighty outpouring of Thy presence. Have mercy upon us, Great King. Come in, King of Glory. Come in, King of Glory. Come in and change us, cleanse us, align us to You for Your great purpose, I pray, before it's too late. Who is this King of Glory? The Lord of Hosts. He is the King of Glory. Blessed be His holy name.*

CHAPTER 10: TEN MISTAKES OF MODERN EVANGELISM

Preached On: Tuesday, July 30, 2013

When I was conducting my research on the First and Second Great Awakenings, I was shocked by the vast dissimilarity of the preaching in those days compared with the preaching of our day. I read the sermons of Jonathan Edwards and his contemporaries of the 18th century and then I studied the sermons of Asahel Nettleton and his contemporaries of the 19th century, and I noticed that God seemed to be pleased to bless the messages that were preached in those centuries with tremendous outpourings of His grace and revival and spiritual awakening. But, I look around today and all I see is deadness everywhere in the churches, and it's tied directly to the preaching of our day.

There's been a sad declension in the preaching of great doctrines of the Bible and evangelism in our day. We want to see God move in revival like He's done in former times, but the problem is, we aren't willing to preach the same messages that former men of revival preached. Part of this may be due to the fact that we're living in a day of great spiritual declension that knows little about vital Christianity. These are the days of the lukewarm church and, unfortunately, much of the preaching is lukewarm as well. It's neither hot nor cold, it's just room temperature because the pastor doesn't want to turn the temperature up in the room and upset any of his hearers. We invite a lot of people to walk an aisle and repeat a prayer but there is little evidence of true conversion in the churches in our day.

The problem with much of the evangelism is that we present a Jesus to people who aren't interested in Him because they feel they just don't need Him. Everyone needs Christ, but their eyes are blinded and they are dead in sin. Old time preachers knew how to use the Word of God to awaken sinners to their lost estate and ruined condition. After a sinner was awakened and convicted of sin by the Holy Spirit, then the remedy for sin was applied in the person of Jesus Christ. But today we offer the remedy to people who just don't realize they are sick and in need of it. We must realize that a sinner needs to be awakened before he can be converted.

But sadly, much of the preaching done today is shallow, and shallow preaching leads to shallow conversions, and shallow conversions lead to shallow congregations, and shallow congregations leave the devil alone, leave the lost astray, and lead the nation into moral bankruptcy. So, the end result of shallow preaching is a long line of people going straight to hell.

I don't blame the White House for the problems of our hour. I don't blame the courthouse for the problems of our day. Rather, I place the blame on the pulpits of our land that have conformed to the pagan society that they were meant to reach, and instead of preaching to the lost a pure gospel of the Son of God, the pulpits water down the gospel so it can be more easily swallowed. We have swallowed this diluted gospel which lacks true spiritual nourishment, and we are sunk.

This message is a call for the pulpits of the land to return to the old paths of preaching the great doctrines of the Bible whereby men are awakened to their sins and alarmed about their lost and ruined condition before a just and holy God. My message today is entitled "Ten Mistakes of Modern Evangelism." I will first list them and then elaborate upon each of them as we proceed.

1. Modern evangelism has tried to shrink God down to our size.
2. We have taken salvation out of the hands of God and placed it in the hands of men.
3. We fail to preach the gospel in its purity and proper order in preaching the doctrines of ruin, redemption, repentance, and regeneration.
4. There is a failure to show man his duty of repentance.
5. Modern evangelism has failed to preach the utter strictness and severity of the law of God.
6. We have failed to proclaim that man first has to be lost before he can be saved; a man needs to be awakened to see his need of Christ before the remedy can be applied.
7. Modern evangelism makes false converts by mistaking a physical act like walking an aisle and repeating a prayer as true conversion.
8. We have failed to warn sinners to flee from hell and to describe hell and its terrors.
9. We have failed to preach up the lordship of Jesus Christ.
10. Modern evangelism has miserably failed in its portrayal of what the Christian life is to a new believer; we paint it as all red roses and honey blossoms and neglect to inform our hearers about the demands of discipleship in following a crucified Savior.

Each of these ten mentioned items is of immense importance to the salvation of a soul. Things have gotten so bad in our country that when I visit churches, and I visit countless numbers of them all the time, I seldom hear what I consider to be a full presentation of the gospel message. In fact, I hear very little preaching. It's mostly teaching being done in our pulpits today; teaching informs, preaching transforms. It is little wonder that so few are being saved today in our land because of our meager attempts to preach the true gospel message to a generation of hell-bound sinners.

Mistake #1

Modern evangelism has tried to shrink God down to our size. I was sitting in a large Baptist church and the minister in the pulpit made the following remark. He said, "Friends, I can't wait to get to heaven because when I die and go to heaven I want to walk up to Jesus and grab his hand and shake his hand for all he has done for me." Well, I guess this seminary trained pastor was not familiar with the passage from the book of Revelation where the apostle John encounters a risen Christ and he falls down as dead. No, this foolish minister thinks Jesus is just his pal; he can just casually walk up to the Lord of glory, grab his hand like the hand of a deacon, and shake it because Jesus is just his buddy.

I'm afraid that this is the mentality of a majority in our pulpits today. Many have taken out their pocket knives and whittled out a god that suits them, a god they feel comfortable with, one they can worship according to their idea of him. They've tried to shrink God down to their level of reason to where He's on their level, He thinks like they do, He acts like they do. Why, He wouldn't send anybody to hell because He just isn't like that anymore.

Our evangelism today presents a god who is our size or smaller, a far cry from the reality of the living God of the Bible, the Ancient of Days, of whom the prophet Isaiah when he caught a glimpse of Him fell down as dead and cried out, *"Woe is me!"* (Isaiah 6:5). But the god of modern day evangelism doesn't make anybody cry out, "Woe is me!" because we have tried to shrink Him down to our size so He won't intimidate anybody. But look in your Bibles and see the Jews before Mount Sinai with God's presence upon it as the mountain quaked and trembled with all smoke and fire like a great furnace, a sight so terrible that even Moses could not endure it. There are very few pulpits all on a smoke today.

So, the first point is: We have tried to shrink God down to our size. Preachers of wiser days refer to God as the Almighty, or the Great God. Now we refer to Him on our terms and our level. This is a great mistake. We must preach an exalted view of the Almighty. Isaiah 57:15 declares, *"For thus saith the high and lofty One that inhabiteth eternity, whose name is Holy; I dwell in the high and holy place, with him also that is of a contrite and humble spirit, to revive the spirit of the humble, and to revive the heart of the contrite ones."*

Mistake #2

Mistake #2: We have taken salvation out of the hands of God and placed it in the hands of men. A favorite Bible verse of modern day evangelism is Revelation 3:20, *"Behold, I stand at the door, and knock: if any man hear my voice, and open the door, I will come in to him, and will sup with him."* Today's evangelist presents an impotent Jesus standing at the door of a man's heart unable to even turn the doorknob, waiting helplessly with his hat in his hand like an insurance salesman who's come to your front door. Will you let him in or not? But in reality when the Christ of the Bible saves a man, He enters in with authority and majesty. Man cannot save himself. Salvation comes from God. It is He who regenerates the heart through saving faith. Jesus declared, *"No man can come to me, except the Father which hath sent me draw him"* (John 6:44).

The orthodox revival men of the 18th and 19th centuries knew that salvation was of God, that man did not regenerate himself. Only God could transform the heart and He could give saving faith or withhold it and still be God. But, today's evangelist has taken salvation out of the hands of God and made it something you can do and it is something you can have any time you want it. I've heard preachers say, "Just open your heart and receive Jesus and He will come in."

Listen, friends, a dead man cannot open his heart. Only God can open the heart of man through regeneration. In Acts, we read of Lydia whose heart the Lord opened (Acts 16:14). God is sovereign in salvation, yet we must not fail to call lost sinners to come to Christ. George Whitefield used to beg lost sinners to fly to Christ.

Mistake #3

Mistake #3: We fail to preach the gospel in its purity and proper order. Men like Jonathan Edwards and Asahel Nettleton knew better than most of us today. They knew that the gospel must be proclaimed in its purity and proper order. God must be first magnified and exalted. The law must be preached to show man that he's a ruined sinner under a curse and unable to help himself or alleviate his misery, that a man must be awakened to his lost condition and perilous position outside of Christ. The only way to be reconciled back to an offended God is through the blood of Christ resulting in a repentant and humble heart.

We fail today to preach up the great doctrines of ruin, redemption, repentance, and regeneration. Our Puritan fathers knew better than these men today, for they knew that there was a preparatory work in the sinner's heart by the Holy Spirit who acted like a surgeon, bringing conviction and compunction upon the sinner's heart:

conviction of sin and an awareness of it; compunction, bringing a sinner to a place of humility over his sins and offending a holy Creator. Study the works of Thomas Hooker, John Shepherd, and Solomon Stoddard to learn more about the preparatory work in the process of salvation. We, today, have made numerous false converts because of our great ignorance of how the Spirit of God works upon the sinner's heart in the act of salvation.

Mistake #4

Mistake #4: Failure to show man his duty of repentance. One of the greatest heresies to plague the church in the last fifty to sixty years has been the "Only Believe Gospel" invitation which omits the necessity of repentance to come savingly to Christ. Jesus declared, *"Except ye repent, ye shall all likewise perish"* (Luke 13:3, 5). And thousands have entered hell from the neglect of this command.

The failure of modern day evangelism has been the neglect of the need of repentance in coming to Christ. How can one ignore God's Word which clearly states that God now commands all men, everywhere, to repent. If a man does not preach faith and repentance, he's just not preached the gospel.

We have failed as preachers to show man his duty of repentance and in the process we have cheapened the gospel and diluted it to be more pleasing to man. And, in the process, we have offended God. Sin is rebellion against God's authority and God will have no rebels in heaven. Unless one repents, they will indeed perish into a burning everlasting hell.

Brother preacher, we must open up the great gospel duty of repentance and show man his duty to repent toward God and be like the apostle Paul who declared that a Christian is one who comes to God exercising repentance toward God and faith in Jesus Christ. I fear that the "Only Believe Gospel" has filled our churches with unconverted sinners who are on the church roll but not on the Lamb's roll, the Book of Life. We must tell lost sinners it is their duty to repent now, right now, for you must repent in this world while the Spirit is striving with you, or you will repent in the netherworld of hell, but it will be too late then. The main reason you don't hear many sermons today on the need for repentance is that our theology today in evangelism is: God loves everybody, therefore, there is no need to repent; all you have to do is just come to Jesus and walk an aisle.

Listen, man is an enemy of God because of his sin nature and he lives in rebellion to all that God stands for, and a lost sinner must throw down his shotgun of rebellion and surrender to the King of Kings and repent. Jesus said, *"For I am not come to call the righteous, but sinners to repentance"* (Matthew 9:13). True gospel repentance involves turning from your sins and turning to God. Jesus never preached a sinning religion but a self-crucifying one.

Mistake #5

Mistake #5: Modern evangelism has failed to proclaim the utter strictness and severity of the law of God. Every man will be held up against the holy law of God and all will fail that test. All men must recognize that they are sinners and need a sin substitute in the person of Jesus Christ. All are the children of Adam and come into the world in a miserable state and ruined condition. The law of God brings a true knowledge and conviction of sin so every mouth will be stopped. The law must be preached in all its strictness and severity and be plainly presented and well understood in order for men to know their own character as sinners and to embrace the way of salvation through Jesus Christ.

When the law is effectively preached and understood in its true impact, the sinfulness of mankind revives the sinner to see he is wholly dead in trespasses and sin. The preaching of the law is used by the Holy Spirit to arouse a sinner out of his sleepy security by applying the divine law to the conscience. When God descended atop Mount Sinai, it was *"altogether on a smoke"* (Exodus 19:18). The threatening sounds of the law bring alarm to the unconverted, as he sees his proper standing as a law-breaker and guilty criminal before a holy and just God. The law of God is a slayer of the flesh, for all mankind has broken it through sin and all will be held accountable to the strictness and severity of the law of God when God judges the works of man in the future judgment.

Listen, friends, every person, when he will be held up against the utter strictness and severity of that holy law, will fail that test. All have broken that law. God must punish sin. That's the first message of the cross, that God is a God who punishes sin and when you believe that, you can come in with the second message of the cross which is the substitute for sin, Jesus Christ. But today we've got it all backwards. We present the remedy before people know they need it. God will pour out His wrath upon sinful man who has broken His law, and the only ones who will escape that punishment are those who stand, not in their own merit, but in the merits of another, Jesus Christ. Christ bore our sins on that bloody tree. We are law-breakers and deserve damnation, but as saved sinners we are under the blood and escape God's wrath for sin.

Men of older days knew better in regard to preaching the law. Both John Wesley and George Whitefield, even though they disagreed on their theology, preached the law before grace. Man must see that he is in need of a Savior before the remedy can be applied. But in our day, we present the remedy before a man even knows he's in need of it. We make false converts by the multiplied thousands by our weak preaching today, whereas George Whitefield always said, "A sinner must first be brought to Mount Sinai before he can be brought to Mount Zion." We must warn sinners about the strictness and severity of God's holy law because each will stand alongside it at the future judgment.

Mistake #6

Mistake #6: Man must become lost before he can be saved. This is the biggest fault of modern day evangelism—we just don't get men lost. Man must be awakened to the fact that he's lost before he can be converted. We foolishly tell people to believe John 3:16 and they will be saved, and they believe a verse and go to hell. And we get people to believe the fact of Christ's dying on a cross for us, but I fear many today just believe in the death of Christ rather than believing in the Christ who died.

Our evangelism is deficient and our watered-down presentation of the gospel is insufficient when it comes to saving men from sin. God must get a man lost before he can save him. Man must be brought to the place where he sees his ruined and hopeless condition apart from God. He has to be brought face-to-face with the reality that he is on the wrong side of God and under the condemnation of God and standing in a perilous position outside of Christ, that without saving faith, he is doomed to an eternal hell. Man must be awakened to his lost condition before he can seek the remedy in the person of Jesus Christ.

People just don't realize they are lost today, and when you offer them Jesus, or ask them to believe John 3:16, they just don't feel there's any need for Him because they are fine without Him. But a man must be awakened to the fact that he is lost and ruined without God in the world. God is against him because he is a sinner and a rebel and an enemy of God. God can cut him down any time and send him to hell and be a just God because He is a sovereign Lord and He will have no rebels in His kingdom.

You see, friends, once a man gets lost, then he has hope. Then he can become a seeker of the Lord. Once a man gets desperate for God and realizes his great need of Him in salvation, then that person enters the place of the person spoken of in the gospel. Once you realize you are lost and hungry for God and weary of your sins and thirsty for Christ, then you become a seeker and an object of grace, for the gospel is for the hungry, the weary, and the thirsty.

But today, we cast our pearls before swine and the Bible forbids us to do that. We offer Jesus to people before they see any need of Him. Our job as evangelists is to present the sinner with the law of God and inform him of his duty of immediate repentance; that God requires repentance from him. Then, and only then, once a person sees his need of Christ, do we tell them about the pearl of great price. We do it all backwards today. I repeat, we must preach the gospel in its purity and proper order so a man gets lost before he can be saved. A man must be awakened before he can be converted.

Mistake #7

Mistake #7: We tell people they are saved because they have walked an aisle or repeated a prayer. Conversion is not something we can do but it's something that God does for us. God changes the heart of stone into a heart of flesh. Conversion is when a lost sinner experiences change. He is a new creation. God has given him a new disposition of holiness through the Holy Spirit. We are not converted by walking an aisle or reciting the Sinner's Prayer. I can't even find that in my Bible. And our great mistake in today's evangelism is when we see a person do some physical act like that, we then walk up to them, slap them on the back, shake their hand and tell them they're now saved and a Christian.

But God says otherwise. In Titus 3:5 we read, *"Not by works of righteousness which we have done, but according to his mercy he saved us, by the washing of regeneration, and renewing of the Holy Ghost."* True conversion occurs when a person has a principle of spiritual life implanted within by the Holy Ghost. The implantation of this divine principle is called regeneration, and it is a supernatural act of God done in a person, whereby a sinner is actually turning from the power of sin to God. It's a principle of life which gives one spiritual knowledge of divine things.

True conversion means a very great change has happened in a man. The whole temper of the heart is quite altered and when the saving change takes place, a man has a new appetite. New appetites for spiritual things and things of eternity, for the Spirit of God has affected a change within the person, giving him a new disposition which is described by the following verse from 2 Corinthians, *"Therefore if any man be in Christ, he is a new creature: old things are passed away; behold, all things are become new"* (5:17).

He is now savingly united to Christ and has entered a vital union with a living Lord. But much preaching today just doesn't cover what true conversion is. You can just listen to some men in the pulpits and though they have a degree from a seminary, they lack the understanding as to how God saves a person by doing a work which He wrought upon the heart. Our error is that we foolishly tell people they are saved when we have no clue as to their true spiritual condition. Listen, brother preacher, only the Holy Spirit can tell a person he is now saved.

D. L. Moody knew better than the rest of us. The main reason Andrew Bonar agreed to work alongside and support Moody in his British campaign was the fact that Moody taught his workers the following: Moody told them, "Listen, when you meet with an inquirer in the Inquiry Room, never, ever, tell that person they are saved. Only the Holy Spirit can do that." You see friends, Moody knew better.

We base our judgment of their eternal security on a faulty system of their performing a physical act we have asked them to do. We ask them to walk an aisle or repeat a prayer and then we tell them, "Welcome to the family of God. You are now a Christian." When in reality, they may be joining the church because they are lonely, or they may be joining the church to make business contacts, or they may be joining the church because they just made a mere intellectual assent to an easy believe gospel, but they are not entering into an experiential knowledge of Jesus Christ whereby they're washed in the blood and born from above.

Let's not tell people that they're saved. Let the Holy Spirit do that. That's His job. The Bible in Romans declares, *"For as many as are led by the Spirit of God, they are the sons of God. For ye have not received the spirit of bondage again to fear; but ye have received the Spirit of adoption, whereby we cry, Abba, Father. The Spirit itself beareth witness with our spirit, that we are the children of God"* (8:14-16). Our job is to preach the full counsel of God, call men and women and boys and girls to repentance towards God and faith in Jesus Christ, and then let the Holy Spirit do His work.

Mistake #8

Mistake #8: We have failed miserably to warn sinners to flee from the wrath to come and preach up the terrors of hell to this lost generation. How many sermons on hell have you heard this year? How many sermons on hell did you preach this year? God used men like Jonathan Edwards and Asahel Nettleton because they preached on the doctrine of hell and warned sinners not to go there. Jesus spoke of hell and its torments. He said it was a place where the worm dieth not and a place of outer darkness where there is weeping and gnashing of teeth. Listen, friends, weeping speaks of great loss and anguish, and gnashing of teeth speaks of great anger and regret.

Old timer preachers used greatly of God always preached on the agonies of hell to awaken sinners and alarm them to their danger. They had to be shaken off their false security of being on a false bottom. But today we just quote John 3:16

and expound the love of God and fail to tell our hearers what the word *"perish"* means in that much quoted verse. Perish means to perish in an everlasting burning hell, to be an object of God's wrath for all eternity, to be separated from God forever and ever and ever and to perish in perdition. Go through your sermon notes of sermons you've preached over the last five years and look around for the number of times you've preached on the doctrine of hell. You may be surprised at your lack.

Hell is a place of torment, of great anguish, of terror. Hell is your worst nightmare come true and there is no waking up from it and no exit from its regions. It's a place of unquenchable fire and misery for all eternity. Hell is a very crowded place and someone is being cast there right this instant as you listen to the sound of my voice. If you could open the lid of hell and listen to the cries and shrieks of the damned, it would keep you awake at night. If you went to all the hospitals in your city and took every patient there off his pain medication and just let them scream in agony, it would keep your town up tonight. Imagine the terrors of hell and those there that want to get out and they cannot.

How foolish we are for neglecting to use one of the most effective weapons in evangelism, which is preaching on the doctrine of an eternal hell. Men like Edwards and Nettleton knew how to effectively wield the sword in evangelistic preaching and they spoke often on hell and warned their hearers not to go there. They believed if you could not be alarmed, you could not be saved. If you do not believe you're under the sentence of death from God's holy law, then you do not feel your need of pardon and you will not come to Christ that ye might have life. If a sinner cannot feel the awful conviction of this truth, then they cannot be pardoned, nor saved. God interposes to rescue the guilty sinner by arousing his guilty conscience and showing him the burning hell that awaits all those rebels of God who refuse to repent and believe on His Son.

Listen, hell is a reality and we must warn sinners not to go there. How dare you, brother preacher, be afraid to preach on hell because you're afraid of offending the people that are listening to you. No, you'd rather offend God. Please, warn men not to go there.

Mistake #9

Mistake #9: Modern evangelism has failed to preach the lordship of Jesus Christ. Just because a modern day movement occurred in our lifetime whereby a major seminary omitted the necessity of repentance and salvation and preached an "Only Believe Gospel" of heresy, we have swallowed it hook, line, and sinker and we're sunk. You cannot come savingly to Christ and be united to him in saving faith without surrendering to his lordship at the time of salvation. Our modern theology has made two things of this when it has always just been one. You don't come to Christ now savingly and then later on have a deeper experience of him and then surrender to his lordship to have a deeper walk. One of the most damning heresies of our day has been the omitting of the lordship of Jesus Christ.

He is a King, a Sovereign, and He will have none in His kingdom who are rebels against Him living in sin. You must throw down your shotgun of rebellion and surrender to the Almighty to come to Him savingly. You must bow to Christ and His lordship now, or you will bow to it a future day when He puts His foot on your neck. Jesus sits on a throne at the right hand of the Father and He earned that right by way of a bloody cross. He is a risen Lord. You must submit to Him in his present office. I fear many today in our churches have never seen a revealed Christ or heard His voice through saving faith. They've never seen the risen Lord and submitted to His authority in their lives. No, but they sure want a Savior who can write them an insurance policy against hell. They don't want to surrender to all His claims and rights on their lives through His lordship.

Jesus sits on the right hand of the Father and He reigns in glory as Lord and He earned that right by way of a bloody cross. You must take Christ where He is right now and He's a living Lord. Like I said, the biggest heresy of our day for the last fifty years has been the omission of the lordship of Jesus Christ. The devil has used this as a controversy in the church because the devil wants you to remain unsaved and in your sins and his servant, and this error has damned countless thousands. You must bow to His lordship now or He will place His foot on your neck and make you bow to Him then when His enemies become His footstool.

Mistake #10

Lastly, Mistake #10 of modern evangelism is: We have failed miserably in telling people of the demands of discipleship in following a crucified Savior. Rather, we paint salvation as all red roses and honey blossoms where your road will be smooth when you come to Christ. Rather, Jesus said, *"Foxes have holes, and the birds of the air have nests; but the Son of man hath not where to lay his head"* (Matthew 8:20). We offer a Jesus who is a problem solver; that once you come to Him and accept Him, you won't have problems anymore. He will fix your finances, He will heal your body, He will bless you with prosperity and health and happiness all your days. Rather, the gospel paints a different picture for the Christian. Listen to the words of Christ, *"If any man will come after me, let him deny himself, and take up his cross, and follow me. For whosoever will save his life shall lose it: and whosoever will lose his life for my sake shall find it"* (Matthew 16:24-25).

How many preachers did you hear proclaim the doctrine of the cross in the life of the believer? Who is preaching sermons on the crucified life today?

Becoming a Christian means life everlasting but it also means a present and daily death. Death to self, mortification of sins and self-denial. Galatians 2:20 declares, *"I am crucified with Christ: nevertheless I live; yet not I, but Christ liveth in me: and the life which I now live in the flesh I live by the faith of the Son of God, who loved me, and gave himself for me."*

Believers in other parts of the world who are persecuted for their faith know full well all the implications of following Jesus. They know that to become a follower of Jesus means at times to lose it all: it may be to lose your home, your friends, perhaps your family, even possibly to lose your very life. They have counted the cost in following a crucified Christ. They know that suffering and persecution for their testimony in Christ is part and parcel of becoming a Christian. So, they carefully weigh and count the cost before they make that decision to come to Christ and follow Him.

We in the West fail to preach up the life of discipleship for a new believer in Christ. The apostle Paul describes the Christian life as enduring hardship like a soldier, or striving as an athlete who strives to gain a victory, or as a farmer who labors dutifully and hard to bring forth fruit from the ground. The cross in the life of the believer must be preached once again.

These ten great mistakes of modern evangelism have done more hurt than good. We must faithfully preach the full counsel of God. We must preach the gospel in its purity and proper order. We must preach the great doctrines of ruin, redemption, repentance, and regeneration. We must warn sinners about an everlasting and burning hell that is prepared for all who die in their sins apart from Christ. We must awaken a sinner to his lost condition before we present the remedy, the great pearl of great price. We must preach up the lordship of Christ and show mankind the utter strictness and severity of God's holy law.

Perhaps the next generation of young preachers will be wiser than this generation and preach alarming messages to awaken the conscience to allow the Holy Spirit to convict of sin. Perhaps the next generation of preachers won't fear man and preach peace, peace, when there is no peace for the wicked. Perhaps this next generation of preachers will be wise enough to tarry until they are endued with power from on high so they will have unction and authority and enter a pulpit with the mantle of authority on them when they preach the great doctrines of the gospel.

Oh, we need a revival in our land today. Let the revival begin in our pulpits. Oh, pray that our pulpits will have a Holy Ghost revival. We need a revival of sound preaching. We need men on fire for God and who live for eternity.

O God, send us such men for this hour, I pray.

CHAPTER 11: THE POWER OF A HOLY LIFE

Bible Text: 2 Kings 4:8-9
Preached on: Tuesday, July 3, 2012

I'll never forget my next door neighbor when I was a teenager. He was a godly Christian man and he gave me my first Bible. He prayed for me. He was concerned over my lost condition. He invited me to church and he was my dear friend. This man always had a smile on his face and kind words of encouragement. When I think of him now, although over forty years have passed, the fragrance of his holy life lives on in my memory today. I'll never forget the power of his holy life which so influenced mine.

There is something special about a person who walks near to God in a life of holiness. The Bible speaks of a holy man of God in 2 Kings 4:8-9. This passage is about the prophet Elisha. Listen to how he is described: *"And it fell on a day, that Elisha passed to Shunem, where was a great woman; and she constrained him to eat bread. And so it was, that as oft as he passed by, he turned in thither to eat bread. And she said unto her husband, Behold now, I perceive that this is an holy man of God, which passeth by us continually."*

The Shunemite woman observed that the prophet Elisha, even in his daily activities, was a holy man of God and there was something different about him. He stood out from other men. She comments to her husband in so many words, "Look here, I see that this person is a holy man of God." There was something about the prophet Elisha that made him stand out.

If you recall, at the beginning of his public ministry, he walked with his mentor, Elijah. And Elijah said to him, *"Ask what I shall do for thee, before I be taken away from thee. And Elisha said, I pray thee, let a double portion of thy spirit be upon me"* (2 Kings 2:9). And all one has to do is read about the ministry of Elisha to see the miracles that God performed through this consecrated vessel of a man. Look at this list of miracles that God did through this vessel of His. He parts the Jordan River, he makes the Jericho spring drinkable, he sends bears to punish irreverent youths (pay attention, young people), he floods ditches to confuse the Moabites, he multiplies the widow's oil, the Shunemite woman bears a son and he resurrects the Shunemite woman's son from the dead, he purifies poison stew, he heals Naaman's leprosy, Gehazi is struck with leprosy, he floats a lost axe head, he gives special sight to the king's messenger, and he blinds the Syrian army. Did he not indeed receive a double portion of Elijah's mantle?

What impresses me more than all of these as to the mighty deeds of this man Elisha is this, listen to this passage from 2 Kings 13:20-21:

> *And Elisha died, and they buried him. And the bands of the Moabites invaded the land at the coming in of the year. And it came to pass, as they were burying a man, that, behold, they spied a band of men; and they cast the man into the sepulchre of Elisha: and when the man was let down, and touched the bones of Elisha, he revived, and stood up on his feet.*

That is an astonishing fact that Elisha's corpse had power to resurrect a life. You see, friends, the power of a holy life lives on. If you live a holy life unto the Lord, the influence of that life will live long after you've gone. The power of a holy life will live on.

My message today is entitled "The Power of a Holy Life," and I've been fortunate enough to know men of God who knew the power of living a holy life. Two men come to my mind as I speak to you now. Both of these men are in glory but they stood out for their lives of holiness. One was my mentor, Dr. Stephen Olford. He was known for the power of his holy life. Let me share this story with you about him. Dr. Olford was scheduled to preach at a church in Texas and a young seminary student who was to pick him up at the airport asked the pastor of the church to show him a picture of Dr. Olford so he would know how to recognize him. The pastor told this young man, "No need for that. Just go to the airport terminal and watch the people as they exit and look for a man who has God all over him." And sure enough, when the young man saw Dr. Olford emerge from the crowd, he recognized him instantly as a man of God. That's the power of a holy life.

Let me tell you about another man who had the power of a holy life and that man was Dr. Adrian Rogers. I'll never forget it, I had just dropped my wife and daughter off at a local restaurant in Memphis and it was raining and dark outside. I parked the car and got underneath my umbrella. It was raining so hard I could barely see in front of me. As I made my way to the door of the restaurant and finally opened it, there was a man standing in the light of the room and his arms were extended to greet me. And he hugged me and said, "Ernesto!" It was Adrian Rogers; he called me Ernesto. But the sensation I felt was as if I'd died and entered heaven and Jesus was greeting me and hugging me and calling my name. You see, Adrian Rogers made me think of Jesus because of the power of his holy life. Do you know people like that? That when you are around them they make you thirsty for Jesus? They model Jesus' will.

There are four aspects from this theme on the power of a holy life which I would like to look at in Scripture. First I will list them. We are called to be holy. We are commanded to be holy. We are changed so as to be holy. And we are consecrated by God to be holy vessels, to bring Him honor.

Let's look at the first one. We are called to be holy. This is how God describes a believer as found in Paul's letter to the Ephesians, 1:4, *"According as he hath chosen us in him before the foundation of the world, that we should be holy and without blame before him in love."* What a magnificent thought that before the world was even spoken into existence, that in the heart of God he chose us, elected us, *"that we should be holy and without blame before him in love."* What a staggering thought that in spite of the fact that we were enemies of God, alienated from him because of sin, even in spite of ourselves He chose us according to the good pleasure of His will. He chose us to be holy. We have here a synopsis of the entire gospel. The purpose of God and Christ was to undo and to rectify completely the effects of sin and the fall of man. This is plainly seen in the third chapter of the first epistle of John, *"For this purpose the Son of God was manifested, that he might destroy the works of the devil"* (3:8). See, holiness is an attribute of God. So to be holy is to be godly. To be a follower of Christ is to be Christ-like. Is that not what our Bible tells us? You cannot live in sin and still be a follower of Christ; it's impossible.

Amos 3:3 tells us, *"Can two walk together, except they be agreed?"* God is light; in Him there is no darkness. God told Abraham, *"Walk before me, and be thou perfect"* (Genesis 17:1). Our purpose in salvation is that we are to walk with God and enjoy His fellowship. So we are called to be holy.

The second aspect of this holy life is that we are commanded to be holy. Since holiness is an attribute of God, God Himself has declared, *"Be ye holy; for I am holy"* (1 Peter 1:16). We are commanded to be holy as followers of God. A life of holiness for a believer is not optional. You see, we err terribly in our pulpits by trying to divide the Christian life into separate experiences of salvation and then the deeper committal to Christ and the deeper life which is optional. There's no biblical basis for that. Jesus said to his disciples, *"If any man will come after me, let him deny himself, and take up his cross, and follow me. For whosoever will save his life shall lose it: and whosoever will lose his life for my sake shall find it"* (Matthew 16:24-25). You cannot call yourself a follower of Christ if you don't follow Him.

The apostle Peter knew the demands of discipleship. He counted the cost of following a crucified Savior. He gave up everything to follow Christ. As a Hebrew, Peter was kicked out of his church, so to speak, for following Christ. He was alienated from his family members for following Christ. He was persecuted and imprisoned for his testimony for Christ. And Peter eventually was martyred for his faith in Christ.

You see, the early church knew the cost of following Christ and the demands of Christ upon their lives. They knew full well the utter severity of God's holy law and that man must be judged by that law. No man will pass that test because we are sinners and we desperately need a substitute for sin, Jesus Christ, our Redeemer.

Peter knew the commands of Christ so he writes in his epistle, 1 Peter 1:14-17:

> *As obedient children, not fashioning yourselves according to the former lusts in your ignorance: But as he which hath called you is holy, so be ye holy in all manner of conversation; Because it is written, Be ye holy; for I am holy. And if ye call on the Father, who without respect of persons judgeth according to every man's work, pass the time of your sojourning here in fear.*

So we are commanded to be holy.

Next, as followers of Christ we are changed so we can be holy. You cannot live the Christian life and have victory if you're not truly born again. You must be washed in the blood and born of the Spirit to live the Christian life. How can one live a supernatural life, a life only given from above, if you are not saved. How can you be joined to the vine as a branch and abide in Him in a living union with a risen Lord if you are truly not regenerated? You cannot. Therefore, you must be born again. You see, a Christian is someone who has experienced change. When Jesus was here in his earthly ministry and he entered a village, those individuals who encountered him were changed.

Allow me to illustrate this by the story of John Wesley's conversion. John Wesley was known for his life of holiness. In 1735, John Wesley sailed to America as a missionary to the colony of Georgia. He came to convert the Indians. He was an ordained minister in the Church of England. But he had nothing but trouble here in America. He fell in love with a young woman and she fell out of love with him and he forbade her from taking communion. And her father, who was the sheriff, ran him out of town. You see, John Wesley was not saved when he was a missionary to America. He was unsaved. He was an ordained minister in the Church of England and a missionary. And he tried his best to live as a Christian but he couldn't do it because he was unsaved.

Looking back on his time in America, he wrote in his journal, "I went to America to convert the Indians but, O, who shall convert me?" Three years later, he came savingly to Christ in a meeting in London. Let me read you the words from his diary dated May 14, 1738.

> In the evening I went very unwillingly to a society in Aldersgate Street, where one was reading Luther's preface to the Epistle to the Romans. About a quarter before nine, while he was describing the change which God works in the heart through faith in Christ, I felt my heart strangely warmed. I felt I did trust in Christ, Christ alone, for my salvation; and an assurance was given me that He had taken away my sins, even mine, and saved me from the law of sin and death.

Did you notice that Wesley spoke of the change which God works in the heart? That is regeneration, where God takes a heart of stone and makes it a heart of flesh, whereby he gives us new life from above. We are a new creation and old things are passed away.

You see, friends, a Christian is someone who has experienced change. Allow me to contrast John Wesley with Pharaoh in the time of Moses. Moses appeared before Pharaoh and asked him to let the people of Israel go and to release them from their bondage. But Pharaoh refused. God then began a series of remedial judgments. Do you recall them? The river became blood, the land became infested with frogs, and so on. Pharaoh relented because of these judgments but only briefly. He reformed, so to speak, for a time, but then continued to cause Israel harm because Pharaoh was never altered. He was never changed. He died in his sins.

After each plague that God sent to Egypt, for a brief time Pharaoh reformed himself, but he never was changed. Reformation is something we do to ourselves; regeneration, on the other hand, is something God does in us. And regeneration means change. You are not born again without being regenerated. To be born again you must be a changed individual. You cannot live a life of holiness on your own steam. If you do, you will be doomed to failure because the human heart is deceitful and wicked because of sin. Salvation is a change which God works in the heart through faith. Then, and only then, can you live a life pleasing to God in holiness before Him.

Oh friends, please don't miss this, for to be off on this is a matter of eternity and where you will spend eternity, either in heaven or in hell. We are redeemed with the blood of Christ and by His death. We need a sin substitute. He has paid the price for our redemption with His blood.

Allow me to explain this word "redemption" as given by three words in the Greek language. See, the Bible tells us that Jesus came to save His people from their sins.

There is an incident in the life of John Sung, the famous Chinese evangelist. One day after Dr. Sung preached, another minister upbraided him. He said, "Dr. Sung, in your sermon today you told the audience that you sin every day. You erred in that remark, my brother. Don't ever say that again. Geniuses never preach the sinning religion." After that, John Sung never made that comment again. You see, a holy God expects his followers to be holy. I'm not speaking of being a Pharisee but inward holiness towards God.

Let me give you these Greek words that explain redemption in clearer terms. I once visited the ancient city of Ephesus and I took a tour to the excavated ruins. And there among the ruins was what was called an agora. An agora was an outdoor marketplace, kind of like a mall that we would know today. It was a marketplace where items were bought and sold; slaves were also sold in the agora. Now take that word spelled *agora* and make the word *agorazo*. You see in the Greek the word *agorazo* means redemption, and in the Greek, the word *agorazo* means that Jesus went into the marketplace of sin and bought us by His blood and with His death. That is redemption.

Now, add the little preposition *ex* in front of that word *agorazo*, and you have *exagorazo*. Ex means to take out of something, to remove something out of. So this word for redemption, *exagorazo*, means that Jesus not only entered the marketplace of sin and purchased us by His blood and with His death, but He removed us from the marketplace of sin. He set us free from its dominion.

You see, a saved person has experienced a double cure. That person is saved from the penalty of sin and is saved from the power of sin. To be saved means we're brought out of the kingdom of darkness into the kingdom of light and life. We are given a new heart and are changed so that we are no longer the servants of Satan but the bond slaves of Jesus Christ. Amen?

The power of a holy life should be seen in every follower of Christ. It should be seen in our testimony, our walk, our witness, and our daily contact with others.

THE POWER OF A HOLY LIFE

As the Shunemite said of Elisha as he passed by in his daily walk, she perceived he was a holy man of God.

Now here is the test. Can your spouse say of you that you are a holy man of God? Can your spouse say of you that you are a holy woman of God? Can your children say of you that you are parents who emulate a holy walk before God? This generation of lost teenage church members needs to see the reality of Christ in the lives of their parents. This would draw the teenagers to God, to see their parents really living lives of surrender to Christ in their daily walk with Him.

Let me proceed to our last point in the power of a holy life and that is: We are consecrated by God to be holy vessels to bring Him glory. As Christians, we are consecrated for His holy use and service. Your life is not to be lived selfishly. That is the world's way. You are bought with a price. Your time is not your own, your body is not your own, your money is not your own. Christ must be a complete Master. Jesus said, *"Whosoever will come after me, let him deny himself, and take up his cross, and follow me"* (Mark 8:34). Have you done it? God saved you so that He can use you.

Let me repeat that; God saved you so He can use you. He did not save you so you would be happy. He saved you so that you would be holy. The Bible gives us a clear warning from Scripture and if you ignore this, it is hell for you. The Bible says in the book of Hebrews, *"Follow peace with all men, and holiness, without which no man shall see the Lord"* (Hebrews 12:14).

You see, friends, the truest evidence of a saved life is a life of holiness. In fact, when God saves a person He gives that person a disposition for holiness. You have a new desire to live for Christ and you now hate your old sins. And because of the great mercy of forgiveness of sins, you now serve God with a new heart, striving after holiness and obedience toward Him. Why? Because when you were lost, you were ruled with a self-love. Sin is when love itself rules on the throne of your heart and everything else is subservient to your love of yourself. When you are saved, self is dethroned and Jesus is enthroned as Lord of your life. Everything now is subservient to Him. You hate sin, you avoid evil, you live for eternity and winning souls. Bringing others to Christ is a passion for you now because that's what Christians do. They're constantly witnessing for Jesus.

That Shunemite woman said of Elisha, *"I perceive that this is an holy man of God"* (2 Kings 4:9). Pastor, let me ask you a question, "Can your congregation say that about you?" You see, a congregation will often reflect their pastor. If you are a man of prayer, chances are they too will be a praying people. If you are constantly witnessing for Christ, they too will become soul winners by your good example. If you are a holy man of God, they too will thirst after holiness.

Robert Murray McCheyne was a Scottish pastor who was known for his holy walk with God. His favorite saying was, "O Lord, make me as holy as a saved sinner can be." McCheyne warned his congregation with the following words. Listen carefully to what he said, "Dear friends, you may have awakenings and lightnings, experiences, a full heart and prayers and many signs. But if you lack holiness you will never see the Lord. A real desire after real holiness is the truest mark of having been born again." McCheyne knew what it was like to have a close walk with God. He once told his friend, Andrew Bonar, that Jesus was nearer and more real to him than his closest family member.

One day an American preacher went to visit Robert Murray McCheyne's church in Scotland, and the sextant of the church took him around and showed him McCheyne's chair and the pulpit he preached from. The sextant told the visitor, "Here, sit in his chair. Now, put your face in your hands. Now weep. That's how holy McCheyne did it." He then took the visitor to the pulpit and told him to stand in it. Again, he said, "Now, put your face in your hands. Now, weep. That's how holy McCheyne did it."

Robert Murray McCheyne's memoirs have influenced thousands. In fact, to read his memoirs is to be like the corpse thrown into the grave of Elisha. For to read them gives life. The power of his holy life lives on.

I will close with the words of another holy man of God, J. Sidlow Baxter. This man maintained a close walk with God and he often gave this advice to any who desired to go deeper with God in a life of holiness. Here are Dr. Baxter's words: "What I give to Him he takes. What He takes He cleanses. What He cleanses He fills. And what He fills He uses."

Oh friends, don't ever underestimate the power of a holy life. You see, a life lived properly for God will leave a lingering fragrance behind it.

CHAPTER 12: WALKING WITH GOD

Bible Text: Genesis 5:24
Preached on: Sunday, August 5, 2012

A friend of mine related the following story to me. He said that one year he worked as a park ranger at Yellowstone National Park. He said something odd happened that particular year which baffled the park rangers. There were an unusual amount of deaths among the bears, and the park rangers could not figure out why these bears were dying. Finally, they discovered the answer to the strange deaths. It seems that the bears had grown so accustomed to the visitors to the park feeding them, that they had forgotten how to feed themselves. And a number of the bears had died of starvation. As I thought of that story, my mind went to the church, and how church members have grown so accustomed to being fed by others, that they, too, get spiritually starved because they don't feed themselves by a daily walk with God. A daily walk with God feeds us with bread from heaven. We are nourished, revitalized, and renewed every day through a vital walk with Him. God has honored those individuals who have made the sacrifice of having a consistent walk with Him. If you study the men and women whom God has mightily used, you will find a common denominator, and that is, each one maintained a close walk with God.

There is a story about George Whitefield, the great British evangelist. One evening Whitefield was entertaining some minister friends for dinner. Abruptly he stood and walked to the door, handing the men their overcoats and stating, "Now, see here, gentlemen, we forget ourselves. It is time to retire." One of the ministers complained it was only ten o'clock. To which Whitefield replied he had to be in bed for he had an urgent appointment at four in the morning. One of the ministers inquired, "To whom would you be meeting at such an unusual hour?" To which the great Whitefield replied, "Sirs, I am meeting the King at that hour. The King of Kings."

Whitefield's friend, John Wesley, was also an early riser and a man known for his life of holiness. Listen to this entry taken from Wesley's journal: "I, this day, enter on my 85th year and what cause have I to praise God? As for a thousand spiritual blessings. So for bodily blessings also. To my having constantly for above sixty years risen at four in the morning, to my constant preaching at five in the morning for above fifty years." You see, Wesley knew the benefits of walking near to God and God honored that.

When I think of walking with God, I am reminded of that antediluvian Enoch and how he walked with God. In Genesis, chapter 5, verse 24 it states, *"And Enoch walked with God: and he was not; for God took him."* You see, not only did Enoch enjoy walking with God, but God enjoyed the fellowship of Enoch's company. In fact, God enjoyed walking with Enoch so much, one morning as they were out walking, God took Enoch by the hand and he translated him so their fellowship would not be broken.

How many of us miss out and don't enjoy the spiritual benefits of walking with God? Rather, our walk with him is up and down like an elevator. One day we're on the top floor in the penthouse suite enjoying His sweet fellowship but then we get negligent, cease to maintain that daily walk with Him, and we end up down in the basement of despair. We must learn the discipline of a daily walk with God. Even Jesus rose early in the morning to spend time alone with the Father.

From the gospel of Mark we read, *"And in the morning, rising up a great while before day, he went out, and departed into a solitary place, and there prayed"* (1:35). Jesus spent time alone with the Father and so should we. We must keep a regular time of devotions and prayer, for those individuals that have a close walk with God are those rare individuals who know how to pray and gain the ear of the Almighty. Listen, God will always raise up an Elijah whose prayers impact a sleeping nation. The church in each generation has had individuals who live on their knees; whose prayers reach heaven with a holy violence. India had her Praying Hyde, China her Hudson Taylor, England her Puritans, Scotland her Covenanters, America her fiery E. M. Bounds. Voices which gained the attention of the throne room, startled angels, and shook the gates of hell, even making the demons quake and tremble with their desperate prayers.

When I wrote the authorized biography of J. Sidlow Baxter, I was given some of his personal effects by his widow, Iza. One prized possession is a poem of Dr. Baxter's which he typed on a little piece of paper which I have framed in my study. Sidlow Baxter rose at five o'clock every morning of his life to go deeper with God, and when he reached the age of 90 he rose at six o'clock every day to meet with his Redeemer.

Listen to this little poem that he wrote and catch the heartbeat of a man who panted after God like the deer panteth for the water brooks. Here are Dr. Baxter's words:

> That I may know Him, Ah, I long to know,
> Not just the Christ of far gone years ago.
> Nor even reigning on a heavenly throne,

WALKING WITH GOD

> Too high in distance to be really known.
> I long to know Him closely, this is how,
> Alive and in this ever pressing now.
> A living one within my heart this hour,
> Communicating His all-conquering power.
> Who now no longer lives for me apart,
> But shares His resurrection in my heart.

Sidlow Baxter knew the joy of a close walk with God, for to have that kind of walk with God is to live a supernatural life. It's like the apostle Peter, who by faith got out on the water and actually walked on the water for a few steps, until the wind arose and he took his eyes off his Master. But the lesson Peter learned that day was that he no longer wanted to live the natural life, and stay in the boat where it was safe; he wanted to get out on the water, and risk everything for God, and live the supernatural life. You see, friends, once Peter tasted a little of the supernatural life, the ordinary was no longer appealing to him. And that's how it should be with us. When we step out on faith and see God move and stay in close contact with Him through a deep walk, then we no longer want to live that mediocre life but a life that can only be explained by what God does through us—Jesus doing the impossible through us. Amen?

Let me share a personal story with you. I was going through a very tough, ongoing trial in my life and there seemed no way out of it. I began to go deep with God to find out what He was seeking to tell me at this particular time in my life. I needed to get serious with Him and spend some extra time with Him to hear what He was seeking to teach me. At this time, I was reading the book by David Wilkerson, *The Cross and the Switchblade*. I was impressed by a facet in Wilkerson's life. Early in his ministry he was a country pastor who spent the hours of midnight to 2:00 a.m. watching television to unwind and relax. One evening, God challenged Wilkerson to give that time to Him. The next day, Wilkerson sold his TV and never again replaced it. From that point forward, he gave God midnight to 2:00 a.m. and it was during this time of walking with God that God called David Wilkerson to New York City to minister among the teen gang members, eventually starting Teen Challenge. I realized that God did not reveal this wider ministry opportunity to Wilkerson until he chose to go deeper with God in a vital, daily quiet time.

While I had maintained a regular time for many years with the Lord, lately my devotional time was missing something. There was no sacrifice attending it. I would get up at different times in the morning, especially when it was more convenient for me, but the God of the Bible delights in sacrifice, for He sacrificed His only begotten Son for sinful man. Well, after reading Wilkerson's story, I made a covenant with God to rise at 4:30 every morning and give God the first part of each day, walking with Him. It is amazing how God has honored that time, how God has transformed my own life. I would not be preaching to you today, friends, if I had not been obedient to that deeper walk with Him.

Allow me to ask you a question. Picture in your mind that your life is over and you have died and gone to heaven. You are facing Jesus in light of eternity and your earthly time to serve Him has ended. Would you regret the fact that you did not spend more time walking with Him while you were on the earth? Will your heart be filled with remorse that you did not pursue Him in an all-out pursuit of Him? Friends, we only have one life and it will soon be past. Only what's done for Christ will last. Are we giving him our all-in-all, or are we giving Jesus our leftovers and giving the world our best? I plead with you to examine yourself and see if there is anything hindering a deeper walk with Him. I beg you to alter your life in such a way as to live more sacrificially for Him, especially in these last days, while you have breath in your body and a life on earth to live for Him.

There are both benefits to walking with God and conditions to walking with God. Allow me to explain. There are many benefits to walking with God. The good news is you don't have to be a scholar to walk with God. You don't have to have a Ph.D. to walk with God. You can be an ABC and walk with Him. Also, you don't have to be a rich man to walk with God. In fact, all the money in the world won't buy you a walk with God. Donald Trump can't buy a walk with God. It's the poor in spirit who walk with Him. And you don't have to be important to walk with God. You don't have to be a "somebody" to walk with Him. In fact, it is often the "nobodys" of life who walk most closely with Him. In past ages, it was the outcasts of the world who had the greatest walk with Him. The New Testament Christians were viewed as the enemies of the state. They were the refuse of society in society's eyes. The world has always viewed Christians as oddballs.

Listen to the following story. There was an old man named Hans and he was a farm hand to a wealthy landowner. Old Hans was a faithful employee of this rich man. One day the wealthy landowner was out riding his black stallion and surveying his vast property when he came upon old Hans. Hans was sitting on the ground eating his lunch. "Hans, how are you today?" asked the landowner. Hans replied, "Oh, it is you, sir. I'm sorry, I didn't hear you coming. I've grown somewhat deaf lately. I was just sitting here giving thanks to my Lord for the meal which He has given me today." The wealthy landowner glanced down at the meager meal of a hard piece of bread and a piece of fried pork that the old man was eating. The landowner commented, "Hans, is that the kind of food you are thanking God for? I would feel quite deprived if that were all I had for dinner." Old Hans smiled and replied, "God has been good to me. He has kept me employed on your farm these many years. I worked for your father for a long time before you were born."

Just then, Hans stood up and walked over to the man on the black stallion. Hans said, "Sir, may I share with you my dream that I had last night?" "Why, certainly," the rich man replied. "Well, sir, I dreamed about the heavenly gates of glory last night and I heard a voice speak to me in the dream and I feel I should share what the voice said because it may be a warning to you." "What did the voice say?" asked the rich man. Old Hans replied in a serious tone, "The voice said that the richest man in the valley would die tonight. Then I woke up. Sir, those solemn words were spoken so plainly I haven't been able to forget them since. I feel I ought to tell you. Perhaps it is a warning." The landowner's face grew pale but he tried to laugh it off. "Nonsense, you may believe in a place called heaven but I do not. And I certainly don't believe in any voice you heard from heaven. Good day, Hans."

With that, the rich man grabbed the reins of his black stallion and rode off in a cloud of dust. Hans shrugged his shoulders and went back to his lunch. But the rich man could not eat his fine dinner that evening. The lobster remained uneaten on his golden plate. Even his glass of champagne seemed bitter to him that night. He could not get those words of old Hans out of his mind—the words "the richest man in the valley shall die tonight." The landowner thought to himself, "Surely, I am the richest man in this entire valley for I own most of it, but that old fool, Hans, should've never told me his dream. But I won't let the silly words of an ignorant old man disturb me."

But soon the rich man felt ill, he had trouble breathing and finally in desperation he called for the town doctor. By the time the doctor arrived it was late and as he came up the steps to his stately home, the rich man seemed to be on the brink of death. But after the doctor thoroughly examined him, he could find nothing wrong with the desperate man. He gave the distressed patient a pill and told him to get some rest.

Suddenly, the doorbell rang. The rich man yelled out in a distressed voice, "Who could be calling at this time of night?" The doctor walked to the door and opened it. There stood a young farm boy and he was crying. "Sorry to disturb you, sir, but I must tell you that old Hans died suddenly this evening. I thought you'd like to know."

Yes, friends, the richest man in the valley did die that night, old Hans, who had a walk with God that no amount of money could buy. And to be rich toward God is to be the richest person in this life and the life to come. There are many benefits to walking with God.

Now let me mention the conditions to walking with God for there is no walking with Him without meeting these conditions. The first condition is you must be born again. There is no walking with Him unless you are born again. We cannot walk with Him unless we know Him experientially. We must have a regenerated heart to hear His heart. We must be born from above and washed in the blood.

Secondly, the next condition to walking with God is we are to follow Him. You cannot lead the way and expect God to follow you, unless you want to end up in the ditch like I've done time and time again in my life. We must look to Him and see where He is operating and then join Him in that work. To know where God is at work is to join Him in that work. But in order to do this, we must be able to do the next thing which is to hear His voice. The Bible tells us to, *"Be still, and know that I am God"* (Psalm 46:10). We are to be hearers and to listen to His voice.

My wife has a friend who will ask her, "How are you?" and when she answers, "Fine," the friend will say, "Well, enough talk about you, let's talk about me." And sadly that is how many of us approach our devotional time with the Lord. We just talk and talk and talk, never allowing Him a word in edgewise. You see, friends, a walk with God is not a one-sided relationship where we do all the whining and complaining and talking. It's hearing His voice and being obedient to that voice. We must be doers of the Word and get on our heart what's on His heart, and then in obedience carry out that work which He has given us to do in our lifetime, to reach this generation of lost sinners with the gospel of God's glory.

If you think a walk with God is just taking a few minutes to read your Bible or a page of the *Daily Bread* and then say a quick prayer and be done, you are short-changing yourself. You are cheating yourself out of the greatest opportunity of your life. You only have one life to live and you must spend it wisely for God and His glory. We must not only be available to Him, but we must be obedient to Him, and join Him in His work, and experience the high privilege of carrying it out through our lives by reaching this generation of hell-bound sinners who desperately need to hear the good news of the gospel of the Son of God. But how can we possibly be on track with Him if our life is not in a red-hot relationship with Him, spending time with Him and hearing His voice?

A walk with God will cost you. It costs to walk with Him. But many don't want to pay that price because it's too demanding and too deadly to self. John the Baptist said, *"He must increase, but I must decrease"* (John 3:30). But all the popular self-help books on the shelves of our so-called Christian bookstores say that self must increase, self must be empowered, self must be our center. That's not true. The Lord Jesus Christ should be ruling on the throne of our lives, not self. And this generation of self-centered, church-going, hell-bound sinners needs to hear about a God who demands repentance and obedience and holiness from His followers. The only way to have that kind of life is to have and maintain a close walk with God. Study the lives of the men and women in history who have walked with God and you will see the great personal cost on their lives of being living sacrifices for Him. Read the life of Rees Howells, who God mightily used in revival, and see what a close walk with God that dear man had. But listen to his words about how God dealt with him on a day-by-day basis. This is what he said,

> He was not going to take any superficial surrender. He put His finger on each part of my self-life and I had to decide in cold blood. He could never take the thing away until I gave my consent. Then the moment I gave it, some purging took place and I could never touch that thing again. It was not saying I was purged, and the thing still having a hold on me; no, it was a breaking and a Holy Ghost taking control. Day-by-day the dealing went on. He was coming in as God and I had lived as man, and what is permissible to an ordinary man, He told me, will not be permissible to you.

It costs to have a close walk with God because it kills every bit of flesh in us, and that is painful. We tend to shy away from the pruning knife, but it is the branch that is pruned which bears the greatest cluster of fruit. Listen to the words of Jesus in John 15:2: *"Every branch in me that beareth not fruit he taketh away: and every branch that beareth fruit, he purgeth it, that it may bring forth more fruit."* I call John, chapter 15, the pruning chapter, for to have a close walk with God means to be in a place of surrender to that divine pruning knife which continually cuts away any fleshly things that stand between us and a holy God. Jesus will prune us to use us in a way that brings glory to the Father. But we shrink from that pruning knife.

I remember preaching one evening to a group of pastors, and I was preaching from John, chapter 15, on the pruning knife. Well, God began to move in some of those pastors' hearts, and I saw conviction come upon their faces. When I was through, an older pastor approached me and he told me tenderly, "Tonight, I'm going home and I'm kneeling by my bedside and I'm going to ask God to get His pruning knife out on me and my ministry." That man was ready to get serious with God; that man knew it cost something to go deeper with God.

It costs us something to wrestle with Him for a lost and perishing world. We cannot hang on to anything that hinders our usefulness to God. We must depend on Jesus and Him alone and cease our self-reliance, for Jesus said, *"Without me ye can do nothing"* (John 15:5). But we try to get along without Him and all we do is create a mess of things, when we should stay connected to the main thing, the true vine, abiding in Him. Real intercession costs us something. I remember Leonard Ravenhill saying that he believed that a night of prayer gave him his heart attack; that it was that terrible wrestle with God which damaged his heart. But we don't want to believe that, let alone experience affliction for our intercession.

Listen, friends, when we wrestle with God in prayer, in intercession for a nation and the lost, we spend ourselves, and when we're through praying we are spent. To have a close walk with God means we feel like a wrung out dishrag when we are through praying because it costs something to wrestle with Him. And that kind of prayer life grabs hold of heaven, and with violence.

To have a close walk with God is to be Christ-like. One man who walked close to God was Stephen Olford, my homiletic mentor. One day I was meeting with him in his study, and when Dr. Olford entered, he looked exhausted and sunk down in his chair. He said to me, "Excuse me, brother, I must regather myself. I must re-gather myself. I just finished preaching and virtue has left me." When he said that, my mind ran to the Bible story of Jesus in the crowd of people, and they are pressing up against Him, and the woman with the issue of blood touches the hem of His garment. And He turns around and says, *"Who touched me? ... I perceive that virtue is gone out of me"* (Luke 8:45-46). Listen, preacher friend, to be Christ-like means that when we preach, virtue leaves us.

A close walk with God will give you power and an anointed ministry, but there is a cost and few are willing to pay it. That is why so few today have power in the pulpit; they are unwilling to pay the price of self-denial and sacrifice. They'd rather work on their golf handicap or sit in front of the TV until their eyes are as big as saucers and their brains are the size of a pea.

If you want to have a close walk with God then you must come to your own personal Jabbok. Jacob heard that his brother, Esau, was approaching with 400 men and this terrified him. He had cheated Esau out of everything worthwhile in life. He had stolen his birthright and his father's blessing. Now, here comes Esau seeking vengeance upon him. Jacob has his large family pass over the ford Jabbok so he can be alone and think out his plans for survival. Jacob—the cheat, Jacob—

the supplanter, is going to try to wiggle and finagle his way out of this mess, as he has done in past times, even in dealing with his uncle Laban. Jacob was so crooked he could hide behind a corkscrew, but now he is struck with terror that his brother is coming to finally give him what he deserves. And he paces up and down near the ford Jabbok. Then an angel jumps on him and wrestles with him. It is God wrestling with Jacob and through that long, tiring ordeal, Jacob finally begins to wrestle back with God. He says, *"I will not let thee go, except thou bless me"* (Genesis 32:26). And he hangs onto the angel until he gets a blessing. God changed Jacob's name that night from Jacob, the supplanter, to Israel, prince with God. But a night of wrestling with God affected him for the rest of his life. Listen to this passage of Scripture from Genesis, chapter 32 and how God dealt with Jacob that terrible night:

> *And Jacob was left alone; and there wrestled a man with him until the breaking of the day. And when he saw that he prevailed not against him, he touched the hollow of his thigh; and the hollow of Jacob's thigh was out of joint, as he wrestled with him. And he said, Let me go, for the day breaketh. And he said, I will not let thee go, except thou bless me. And he said unto him, What is thy name? And he said, Jacob. And he said, 'Thy name shall be called no more Jacob, but Israel: for as a prince hast thou power with God and with men, and hast prevailed.* (verses 24-28)

You see, friends, when Jacob finally got to the place in his life where he was sick and tired of being Jacob, it was then, and only then, that he had a breakthrough with God and experienced change. Notice the text says that God changed Jacob's name and God said that Jacob now had power with God and with men and had prevailed.

A close walk with God will cost you, but it will be the greatest time of your life. Living in the supernatural is the only way to live. How can so many of us live superficial lives when we serve such a supernatural God? Jacob now had power with God and man, but it cost him.

Look at verse 31 of chapter 32 of Genesis. It reads, *"And as he passed over Penuel the sun rose upon him, and he halted upon his thigh."* Jacob's thigh was put out of place in wrestling with God. He wore a mark from that day forth for the rest of his life. The very last scene we have reported of Jacob, he is dying in Egypt and leaning on his staff giving the blessing to his gathered children. He limped on a bad leg until the day he died. Every step he took, every turn he made, made him wince in pain for the rest of his days but he was a man whom God said of, *"As a prince hast thou power with God and with men, and hast prevailed."*

Is that the kind of walk with God you desire? Are you willing to pay the price? What costs counts and what counts costs. So few preachers today have power in the pulpit because they don't want the limp associated with a close walk with God; they just don't want to pay the price. How about you? Do you want a supernatural walk with God? Do you want to taste what New Testament Christianity really is like? Then go deeper with Him in a vital daily walk with Him. And I promise you, you will never regret it. You, too, will have power with God and man.

Let me close with a hymn entitled "Walking with God," written by the great British poet, William Halper. Listen to these wonderful words and be encouraged by them. To begin a closer walk with him so you can enjoy those benefits given to the saints who closely walk with Him. Listen.

> Oh for a closer walk with God,
> A calm and heavenly frame,
> A light to shine upon the road,
> That leads me to the Lamb.
>
> Where is the blessedness that I once knew,
> When I first saw the Lord?
> Where is the soul refreshing view,
> Of Jesus and His Word?
>
> What peaceful hours I once enjoyed,
> How sweet their memories still,
> But they have left an aching void,
> The world can never fill.
>
> Return, O holy dove, return,
> Sweet messenger of rest.
> I hate the sins that made thee mourn,
> And drove thee from my breast.
>
> The dearest idol I have known,
> Whatever that idol be,
> Help me to tear it from thy throne,
> And worship only thee.
>
> So shall my walk be close with God,

> Calm and serene my frame,
> So pure a light shall mark the road,
> That leads me to the Lamb.

Let us take these words of comfort to heart and ask the Lord to show us anything that stands between us and Him and then ask Him for the grace to remove it so we may have a closer walk with Him.

May God bless you, friends, and grant you grace as you pursue Him passionately for the rest of your days. All glory to His holy name.

CHAPTER 13: THE OUTPOURED WRATH OF A LONG-PROVOKED GOD

Bible Text: Zephaniah 1:14-18
Preached On: Tuesday, July 23, 2013

My message tonight is entitled "The Outpoured Wrath of a Long-Provoked God," for this message is a lamentation over the sad decline of America as a nation. A nation once favored by God, America has now become a nation which provokes God with its multiplied sins. America has a long history of doing good for the Lord. One can only look back to how God has favored America in times past with periods of revival and national spiritual awakening whereby thousands of individuals were the recipients of grace and light and life. God poured out spiritual blessings upon the people of America during the Great Awakening under the preaching of Jonathan Edwards and George Whitefield and a host of other God-sent men. Divine blessings were so plentiful in America back then that Benjamin Franklin said of the city of Philadelphia that when George Whitefield had preached there, it seemed as if the entire city was going religious, for there wasn't a house that he had seen that didn't sing hymns or have family devotions.

Like I said, America has been favored in times past with divine blessings from God which came in the form of national spiritual awakenings. Then God seemed pleased to raise up America and bless her with vast prosperity to where she was looked up to by all the other nations on earth. They looked upon her in amazement. It seemed as if God's hand was still on America even during the two World Wars where he allowed victory to overcome the enemies of America.

But America as a nation slowly turned her back on God. She began to be self-sufficient and proud. In the 1960s, America chose to remove God from the public school system. America then chose to legalize abortion and murder millions of babies. America chose to legislate God out of the courthouse and force him out of the White House. Sadly the church house also turned its back on God as they cheapened the gospel and became a worldly self-reliant church where the focus was on man, and his needs, rather than on God and His glory.

Also, the modern day church began a heresy which divided God. The modern church declared that the God of the Old Testament was a God of judgment. He was severe and revengeful and angry with the wicked, but the God of the New Testament was a different God. He was a God only of goodness, mercy, and love.

Many pulpits preached such nonsense, but the God of the Bible is a God of divine justice, for in the book of Nahum, we read, *"God is jealous,"* and *"the LORD revengeth, and is furious,"* and *"he reserveth wrath for his enemies"* (1:2).

But many believe that God is just a God of love, that He is more tolerant towards sin today, and that He is a more tolerant God than the God of the Old Testament. Listen to this verse from the New Testament found in 2 Thessalonians: *"When the Lord Jesus shall be revealed from heaven with his mighty angels, In flaming fire taking vengeance on them that know not God, and that obey not the gospel of our Lord Jesus Christ: Who shall be punished with everlasting destruction from the presence of the Lord, and from the glory of his power"* (1:7-9).

Listen, friends, God is a God who changeth not. God has been long-suffering and patient with America, but her sins have only multiplied, and she has defiantly shaken her angry fist in the face of a holy God. God's timetable is up for America. America, once greatly favored by God, is now a nation that has filled the cup of her iniquity and she is ready to be the recipient of the outpoured wrath of a long-provoked God, for the God of the Bible is a God who must punish sin. The Almighty is a jealous God who will defend His holy name.

My message tonight is about the outpoured wrath of a long-provoked God, and the text is found in the book of Zephaniah, chapter 1 verses 14 through 18. This passage of Scripture speaks of how an angered God pours out His vengeance upon a nation because of the grievous sins of the people who refuse to turn to God or heed His warnings to return to Him. God is provoked by their unwillingness to return to Him and He is incensed over the flagrant sins of the nation. The anger of a long-provoked God breaks out upon a people who are stiff-necked and rebellious, so that they become the object of the outpoured wrath of a holy God.

Turn in your Bibles to the book of Zephaniah and we will look at this passage tonight. Allow me to read it to you beginning in chapter 1 and in verse 14:

> *The great day of the LORD is near, it is near, and hasteth greatly, even the voice of the day of the LORD: the mighty man shall cry there bitterly. That day is a day of wrath, a day of trouble and distress, a day of wasteness and desolation, a day of darkness and gloominess, a day of clouds and thick darkness, A day of the trumpet and alarm against the fenced cities, and against the high towers. And I will bring distress upon men, that they shall walk like blind men, because they have sinned against the LORD: and their blood shall be poured out as dust, and their flesh as the dung.*

THE OUTPOURED WRATH OF A LONG-PROVOKED GOD

Neither their silver nor their gold shall be able to deliver them in the day of the LORD'S wrath; but the whole land shall be devoured by the fire of his jealousy: for he shall make even a speedy riddance of all them that dwell in the land.

The prophet Zephaniah was preaching a judgment sermon to the people of Judah and Jerusalem. Zephaniah was sent by God to pronounce a judgment message upon the rebellious people of God. You see, the Jews foolishly believed they could remain in their sins and turn their backs on God because they felt they were a people favored by God, therefore, they could sin all they wanted to and God would be okay with that. But the Jews were so far removed from the mind and heart of God, through their willful disobedience, that their perception of themselves was distorted, and they held a perverted view of God that ignored His holiness and hatred of sin. They believed themselves to be so greatly favored by God that they believed they would never be the objects of His wrath and divine displeasure.

I can make the same comparison with the people of America today. The so-called followers of God also believe themselves to be so favored of God that they would never dream that God would bring His displeasure down upon them. Why, the God they serve just wouldn't act that way. But the problem is that many in our land have a distorted view of themselves and a perverted view of God. Many claim the name of Christ, but do not walk in His statutes or display credible evidence of true conversion. They are undistinguishable from the pagan society in which they live. The God they claim to serve is a figment of their imagination, not the true and living God of the Bible, for the God of the Bible is a God who punishes sin. But many in the churches today just don't believe in that kind of God. Their God wouldn't send people to hell or punish sin. But the fact remains that God is a holy God who hates sin and must punish it.

When a nation has so turned its back on the God of the Bible and defiantly shakes its fist at God, then God turns and breaks out upon that nation with His fierce wrath and destroys it. Look at ancient Greece. Study ancient Rome. Study all the once great nations of the earth that have been reduced to rubble by earthquakes and fire from the hands of an offended God who could no longer tolerate the people, whom He created, to rebel against Him and defy His holy attributes with their flagrant lifestyles and grievous sins.

Listen, friends, the city of London was destroyed by fire on September 2, 1666, but notice the difference between the governments of the world back in those days and our governments today. Listen to how the people of London responded to the great fire of London, viewing it as a judgment from the hand of an offended God for their national sins. Listen to this statement made public by Parliament in the Act for the Rebuilding of the City of London. Listen to these striking words from the government of London in that day.

> And that the said citizens and their successors for all the time to come may retain the memorial of so sad a desolation and reflect seriously upon their manifold iniquities which are the unhappy causes of such judgments. Be it further enacted that the 2nd of September be yearly forever hereafter observed as a day of public fasting and humiliation within the said city and liberties thereof to implore the mercies of Almighty God upon the said city to make devout prayers and supplications unto him to divert the like calamity for the time to come.

Oh friends, can you imagine the British Parliament today issuing a statement like that? London has forgotten, in the ashes of history, to commemorate the 2nd of September each year as a day of fasting and humiliation.

I remember America right after the tragedy of 9/11. The churches were full. People were looking to God for answers. But then, gradually, people began to turn their backs on God again, and our government has turned its back on God since then too. This was a wake-up call for America but I fear most everybody went back to sleep. There was a time in our land when pastors were wiser and called the people of God to fast and pray when disasters hit our land. These men of God attributed the calamity with the just displeasure of God against the sins of the land. Pastors in the day of the great fire of London called their congregations to humble themselves before an offended Creator. One London pastor, the famous Puritan, Thomas Brooks, wrote a lengthy sermon stating it was God's displeasure with the people of London and their sins which caused the calamity and his sermon is over 300 pages long. No, today you will hear about a comfortable Christianity and a fun-loving Jesus who is alright with you living in your sins.

We see God's judgment among the people of God. There is a famine in the land today for hearing the Word of God, and there is a withdrawn presence of the manifest presence of God. But friends, is there any hope? Is it too late? Let's look at chapter 2 in the book of Zephaniah, beginning in verse 1, for in this passage is America's only hope of survival. Please listen to it carefully as I read it to you:

> *Gather yourselves together, yea, gather together, O nation not desired; Before the decree bring forth, before the day pass as the chaff, before the fierce anger of the LORD come upon you, before*

the day of the LORD'S anger come upon you. Seek ye the LORD, all ye meek of the earth, which have wrought his judgment; seek righteousness, seek meekness: it may be ye shall be hid in the day of the LORD'S anger. (verses 1-3)

What God is saying to his people is that a coming judgment can be averted if the people of the land turn back to God in meekness and brokenness and repentance. God declares that the nation is no longer desired and He is ready to destroy it, but, if the people turn back to Him in true humility, and humble themselves, and seek his face, then it may be they shall be hid from the falling judgment. Certainly, this has happened in history before. Look at ancient Nineveh and how they humbled themselves from the king down to the beasts at the preaching of the prophet Jonah. The entire populace averted the swift judgment of God. Instead of being destroyed, they were recipients of His mercy. If any nation in history needs to be studied more greatly today, it is ancient Nineveh, for it is a textbook pattern to avert coming judgment from an angry God. America should heed the biblical examples that stand out in history and do the same. Revival is America's only hope of survival.

But the church slumbers, and the sins of the nation increase at a rapid rate. What will it take to awaken the church and stir the nation? Listen, friends, the entire nation should be on her knees right now, begging God for mercy before it's too late. The churches should be open all night and the sanctuaries flooded and full with the weeping, broken people of God crying out to God for their nation and people. The carpets in our sanctuaries should be soaking wet with our tears but alas, they are dry as dust, as dry as the blood described as dust in our passage tonight. The very blood of the church in America has run cold towards God and the things of God. God's sort of justice hangs over this nation like the sword of Damocles, ready to descend without a moment's notice. God's Word declares, *"God is angry with the wicked every day. If he turn not, he will whet his sword; he hath bent his bow, and made it ready"* (Psalm 7:11-12).

America, unless we repent, we will be brought face-to-face with the outpoured wrath of a long-provoked God. He is whetting his sword and his bow is bent and pointed at the heart of our nation. Heaven help us. May God have mercy on us all.

CHAPTER 14: THE HEART THAT CARES FOR THE SOULS OF MEN

Bible Text: Romans 1:16
Preached On: Saturday, January 5, 2013

I heard the late Manley Beasley relate the following story:

> There is a certain cliff in Mexico where you can stand and gaze down at a certain village of Mexican workers. These people work down in the riverbed in their corn patch, and there they grow their corn. When the corn is ready to harvest they shuck it, and after it dries out, they'll take it and grind it. They'll grind it into corn meal and make tortillas, and then take these tortillas down to the open market and sell the tortillas for a few pesos. They put the pesos away, come back out to their houses, and there they will live off of lizards. They'll go out among the rocks and catch these huge long lizards and they'll eat those lizards. They save that corn money for a special day, a special day when they will start a pilgrimage to a wooden statue of Jesus up in the mountains.

> The terrain to that statue is so bad that most of the people have to crawl on their hands and knees a couple of miles and by the time they get to that statue they are bleeding all over. Standing beside the statue is a priest and that priest is saying, "Now, if you love God, give to him because you show your love to God by giving." And those people will reach into their little bags and purses and pull those pesos out, stained in their own blood and drop that money into a slit in the top of the head of that wooden Jesus.

> Then the priest prays and when he is finished, the priest will yell, "You have not given enough. Look, Jesus is sad. He is crying." And all the time there is another priest hidden in that hollow statue with a little hand pump. He will pump water to where it comes out of human made tear ducts so that the statue is crying. And there those people will give all they have, crawl down that mountain and go back to eating lizards, growing their corn to make more tortillas to get more pesos to go and give to a dead god that cannot move or hear. And they are sincere, honest, and sacrificial in their

service to this idol which they serve.

Dear friends, this message today is a burden on my heart for I fear that we today, with our brand of evangelism, have committed two crimes. The first is that we have gotten out our pocket knives and have whittled out ourselves a little wooden Jesus who we can serve on our terms. And the second crime we have committed is that we have taken salvation out of the hands of God and placed it in the hands of man.

Many today present a Jesus that does not resemble the God of the Bible. We sneak up on people and catch them unawares and get them to accept this Jesus, without telling them of any demands of the Lord Jesus Christ on his followers. We fail to mention that to have Jesus means you must have him as Lord, and that he requires repentance towards God, and faith in Him. When we truly are saved, self is dethroned and another is enthroned there, with all His rights and claims on our lives. To be saved means a life of surrender to our Master, and utter obedience to His commands in a life of discipleship where we take up the cross and follow Him. But we, I fear, have diluted the true gospel message to make it more palatable and acceptable to man. And, sadly, many professing Christians today have no regular evangelism to the lost at all.

My message today is entitled "The Heart That Cares for the Souls of Men" and my text is from Luke chapter 10, verse 2, *"Therefore said he unto them, The harvest truly is great, but the labourers are few: pray ye therefore the Lord of the harvest, that he would send forth labourers into his harvest."*

Like I said, this message is a burden upon my heart, for the days in which we live are the end-times. These are the last days and the night is far spent. It's been estimated that eighty-three people a minute die apart from Christ. Do the math and that comes to almost 5,000 people an hour. That means each and every day 120,000 people enter a Christless eternity. That's over 800,000 people a week who perish without Christ. Every month that adds up to three million people falling into the torments of hell. Think of that. Over three million souls a month fall into hell and its agonies. Do you realize that through the course of a year over forty million people populate the regions of hell? Let ten years go by and another 400 million souls are shut up in hell to scream in agony.

Now think in your mind about all the generations since the time of Adam and add up all the hordes of people who have died apart from Christ and occupy hell right at this moment, and it's not hard to see that hell is a very crowded place. Right this minute somewhere on this planet over eighty people are dying and landing in hell.

THE HEART THAT CARES FOR THE SOULS OF MEN

Let me ask you, when was the last time you shared the gospel with someone? When did you last witness to a lost soul? Was it today? Yesterday? Last week? Last month? Think about it? Who was the last person you shared your faith with? When was the last time you handed out a gospel tract and told someone about the love of Christ towards sinful man? Has a year passed without your witness to another? When was the last time you told somebody about the free grace of God? When last did you tell a fellow sinner about the mercy, pardon, and eternal life offered in the gospel of the Son of God? When did you tell them about Jesus and the heart that cares for the souls of men?

If you are a Christian then you are an ambassador for Christ and it is your duty to carry the treasure of the gospel and tell others about this good news. You are to go out to the lost sinners and invite, entreat, require, command, and compel them to come in. It is your duty to tell others about the pearl of great price. Jesus said, *"The harvest truly is great, but the labourers are few"* (Luke 10:2).

The time is short. Your life is but a vapor that appears for a little while and then disappears. How you have spent your time on this earth will impact eternity. All that will matter when we stand before the judgment seat is how many sinners we shared the gospel with and how faithful were we to the Lord Jesus Christ. "Only one life, 'twill soon be past. Only what's done for Christ will last."

This message today is an alarm to awaken you to your duty as a believer in sharing your faith with others, and it is a call to share that faith with the full counsel of God, and call men and women and girls and boys to repentance and faith in Jesus Christ.

You, friend, should have a heart that cares for the souls of men. If you don't, and call yourself a Christian, then repent now and ask the Lord of the harvest to send you into his harvest field with the gospel of the Son of God. Your pocket or purse should be loaded with gospel tracts and they should be handed out throughout the day. The fact you don't hand out gospel tracts may reveal that you do not like rejection, so you don't hand out tracts. But Christ suffered rejection while in the flesh and he hung naked on an ignoble cross for sinful man.

How can some today call themselves a church when the carpet in their sanctuary isn't stained with the tears of broken-hearted Christians praying over the lost in their community? That's your only business, to bring in the lost. Why are you here? Why did Christ save you? Are you living a self-centered life or a selfless life spent for others? How can you keep Christ to yourself and not share Him with others? How would you have come to Christ had not someone told you about Him? A heart that cares for the souls of men lives so that others may live.

When you stand at the bema seat and your life is reviewed by the One who has eyes of fire, what will your life reflect? Will it be the gold, silver, and precious stones of a life lived on the full stretch for God? Or will you stand there knee-deep in the ashes of a wasted life and bend over and scoop up those ashes and place them into his nail-pierced hands?

I grieve over the fact that I failed to witness to a man who worked on my house. I was too preoccupied to share the gospel with him. A month later I was reading the newspaper and his face stared out at me from the obituary column. He was a young man who died suddenly and I failed to tell him about Jesus and how he came down to earth so that sinners could go up to heaven. That man's face still haunts me. Oh friends, when we get to heaven how we will wish that we witnessed more for our Savior. Never miss an opportunity to share the gospel with others, to invite them in.

There is a story about D. L. Moody which I can't get out of my mind. Moody was in Chicago preaching to his congregation and he ended the service without giving a public invitation. Rather, he told them to go home and think about it and they would talk next week about what to do with Christ. But next week never came for many in his congregation perished that dreadful night. It was 1871 and the night of the terrible Chicago fire when the entire city became an inferno and thousands lost their lives.

Listen to Moody's words about his deep regret of not giving a gospel invitation that terrible night:

> What a mistake. I have never dared to give an audience a week to think of their salvation since. If they were lost, they might rise up in the judgment against me. I remember Mr. Sankey singing and how his voice rang when he came to that pleading verse, "Today the Savior calls, for refuge fly, the storm of justice falls, and death is nigh." I have hard work to keep back the tears today. Twenty-two years have passed away and I have not seen that congregation since, and I will never meet those people again until I meet them in another world. I have asked God many times to forgive me for telling people that night to take a week to think it over. And if he spares my life, I will never do it again. One lesson I learned that night which I've never forgotten and that is when I preach, I press Christ upon the people then and there.

Oh friends, there are so many missed opportunities each day where we fail to share the story of the good news of the Son of God. You never know if your witness today will plant a gospel seed, or water another seed already planted, or that you will be the one to lead a soul to Christ after others have paved the way.

There's a story about a stewardess who was being witnessed to by a passenger on a plane and she replied, "You are the seventh person to tell me about Jesus this month." She went on to accept Christ from that recent gospel witness. The next week, on 9/11, she was on a plane that went down.

You never know how important your witness for Christ may be to a person. You may not have the reward of seeing the fruit of your witnessing, but you are planting seeds. You may be number five or you may be number seven in that person's conversion. It's always worthwhile to share Christ with others. *"For whosoever shall call upon the name of the Lord shall be saved. How then shall they call on him in whom they have not believed? and how shall they believe in him of whom they have not heard? and how shall they hear without a preacher?"* (Romans 10:13-14). Think of how you came to Christ. Someone told you about Him either from the pulpit or from the pew. Oh friend, ask the Lord to give you a heart that cares for the souls of men.

I have given up many a night to go door-to-door in neighborhoods sharing the gospel. I have had the blessing of an active tract ministry for years. Handing out tracts is a wonderful way to tell others about the love of Jesus Christ who came to save sinners. A pen ministry is also a wonderful way to spread the good news of the gospel. Gospel literature will work while you are asleep.

Not only is it our duty to tell about the love of Christ, but we must preach the full counsel of God. With all the claims of Christ, we must point sinners to the cross and preach about Jesus, our sin substitute, who cares for the souls of men. And we must warn men to flee from the wrath to come, and that repentance is necessary to true salvation. We must show poor sinners that Christ is Lord and anyone that desires Him must submit to Him as Lord. They must throw down their shotgun of rebellion and surrender to the lordship of Jesus Christ on their lives. Self must be dethroned and Christ enthroned there. For to be a follower of a crucified Christ, we must take up our cross and live crucified lives, all to the Father's glory.

Listen to this story. There's a big Baptist church in Memphis, Tennessee, and one of the former pastors was R. G. Lee. He is known for preaching a famous sermon called "Payday Someday." Well, there was a member in Dr. Lee's congregation, an attorney who had to be out of town on business frequently, but no matter where this lawyer went he made sure to catch a train back to Memphis on Saturday night so that he could listen to R. G. Lee preach on Sunday. He loved to hear that man preach. Well, this lawyer got cancer and he was in the hospital dying and he called for his pastor to come to his bedside. Dr. Lee entered the hospital room whose window overlooked the Mississippi River. The lawyer told R. G. Lee, "I want you to know how much I've enjoyed your preaching through the years and I never missed a Sunday if I could help it. I lie here dying with only a few weeks left to live and I want to reprimand you, sir, for never telling me how to be saved. You never preached the cross to where I could see it. You never put the blood out there where I could reach. I am dying and I will die in my sins and I chastise you, sir, for your lack of preaching the true gospel."

R G. Lee left that man's hospital room with his head down, feeling berated and guilty as charged. It was now dark outside as he walked down to the banks of the Mississippi River. There he got down on his knees in the mud, getting his white suit pants dirty in the process, while he dipped his hands in the muddy river. He knelt there awhile reflecting on what this dying man had told him, and right there and then he promised God from that point forward, he would preach the cross and the blood, and he changed his message that night. In three weeks time there was a move of grace at that church, and three blocks of downtown Memphis were shaken with revival.

You see, the heart that cares for the souls of men will be honest with them. The heart that cares for the souls of men will not dilute the gospel to make it more palatable to sinners. The heart that cares for the souls of men will preach Christ and Him crucified. The heart that cares for the souls of men will speak the ruin, redemption, and the need for repentance and regeneration.

Oh friends, those Mexican farmers served a dead wooden Jesus because they were ignorant of the true gospel message of grace. Those farmers needed someone with a heart that cares for the souls of men to share the good news of the gospel of the Son of God with them. But there are so many false gospels today and not enough true witnesses for Christ to declare the true gospel. That's why it's so important for each of us to actively witness for Christ on a daily basis and tell poor sinners about Jesus who cares for the souls of men so much that He hung upon a bloody cross for sinful man. We are to invite, entreat, require, command, and compel the lost to come in. We are not to be silent followers of the Lamb but vibrant and active witnesses for Him who loved us enough to die for us.

The apostle Paul declared, *"For I am not ashamed of the gospel of Christ: for it is the power of God unto salvation to every one that believeth"* (Romans 1:16). The power of His glory and His grace is seen in the conversion of sinners. Let us be like Paul and not be ashamed of the gospel of Christ, because when we fail to be witnesses for Christ, we fail in our duty to proclaim him to our generation. The apostle Paul had a heart that cared for the souls of men. Paul was a Christ-intoxicated man who could not live unless he preached the gospel. Let us follow in his footsteps and boldly proclaim the gospel of the Son of God to this lost and perishing generation. Your witness today has impact more than you'll ever know this side of eternity.

Let me close with the following story which highlights our duty to be daily witnesses for Christ Jesus.

> D. L. Moody was a soul winner long before he became a famous evangelist. Moody was converted in the back room of a shoe store in Boston where he worked as a clerk. He was a teenager at the time. His Sunday school teacher had a great burden for him and he nervously made his way down that street and went on a God-sent errand that day to witness to young Moody. God did his work that day in D. L. Moody's heart and his life was never the same again. Soon after his conversion, Moody moved to Chicago and there he began to share Christ with every citizen in that great metropolis. He refused to go to bed at night without sharing his faith in Christ.
>
> One night, he got into bed around midnight and he realized he had not witnessed to a lost soul that day. It was drizzling rain outside but Moody got up out of bed, put on his coat, and went through the night. There was a man leaning on a lamp post and Moody walked up to him and asked him if he were a Christian. The man was offended and cussed Moody out and called him "crazy Moody." That was the nickname that the citizens of Chicago gave Moody because he would stop anybody on the street any time and ask them if they were a Christian and share his faith.
>
> Well, after Moody asked the man if he were a Christian, the man flew into a rage, doubled up his fists and cursed Moody, who replied, "I'm very sorry if I have offended you." "Mind your own business," roared the man. "That is my business," Moody replied as he walked away into the night going home to his bed.
>
> Several nights later there was a knock on Moody's door, it was around 2:00 a.m. Moody got up to answer the door and to his astonishment there was the man who had cursed him for talking to him about Jesus as he leaned against the lamp post. Moody

asked him, "What do you want at this late hour?" "I want to become a Christian," was the reply. "I'm very sorry," said the man. "I haven't had any peace since that night you spoke to me. Your words have haunted and troubled me. I couldn't sleep last night and I thought I would come and get you to pray for me." That man accepted Christ that night and then asked Moody what he could do for Christ. Moody put him to work in the Sunday school until the Civil War broke out and that man was one of the first to be shot down, dying on the battlefield.

Oh friend, how can you keep the gospel to yourself? How can you not weep over the lost around you? Where are your prayers and your tears and your testimony to a dying world? Be like Moody and commit to sharing the gospel with others each day. These are indeed the last days and hell fills with the lost each hour. Ask God to make you a soul winner for Him. Pray that the Lord of the harvest will give you a heart that cares for the souls of men.

Pray with me as we go to God right now. *O King of Glory, you died for me, you have a heart that cares for the souls of men. Forgive me for not telling my generation about your great love for sinful man. O Lord, give me an ounce of Moody. Lord Jesus, give me, I pray today, a heart that cares for the souls of men. Help me to weep over them. Help me to reach them with your gospel. Help me to be a soul winner for thee. While I have breath in my body, let me proclaim you to my fellow man. Grant me this I pray right now, in your holy name, Lord Jesus. Amen.*

CHAPTER 15: THE SOLEMN ASSEMBLY

Bible Text: Joel 1:10-15
Preached on: Wednesday, February 27, 2013

It was an autumn day in New England when I stood at the grave of Asahel Nettleton, a man greatly used of God as a human instrument of revival during the Second Great Awakening. I stood in front of that brown mossy tombstone, and as I reflected upon his mighty ministry I sensed the awful solemnity of a holy God. I believe the one factor missing in the American church today is the absence of the awful solemnity of God—God in authority, God in His sovereignty, God Himself manifesting His presence. We must ask ourselves, why? Why has God withdrawn his presence from the American church in our day? Why does our once great nation lie in such wickedness and such great abomination and call evil good and good evil? Why has the church lost her power? Why has she lost her authority? Where is the holy fire emanating from our pulpits in our land today? Why has the flame gone out? The answer to these "whys" lies in the fact that we, as a people of God, have grieved the heart of God through our own personal and corporate sins.

Listen to the words of the great Puritan divine, John Owen, as he described England in his day: "When a sinful church or people have passed the utmost bounds of divine patience and forbearance, they fall into such abominable crying sins and provocations as shall render the utmost vengeance beneath their desserts."

So Josephus affirms of this generation after they had rejected and slain the Lord Christ, "That they fell into such a hell of provoking abominations that if the Romans had not come and destroyed them, God would have sent fire and brimstone upon them from heaven as he did on Sodom."

I believe the current crisis in the church in America is that the glory has departed. There is no felt presence of God among us. Our situation is similar to the people of God as described in Ezekiel chapter 8:7-12:

> And he brought me to the door of the court; and when I looked, behold a hole in the wall. Then said he unto me, Son of man, dig now in the wall: and when I had digged in the wall, behold a door. And he said unto me, Go in, and behold the wicked abominations that they do here. So I went in and saw; and behold every form of creeping things, and abominable beasts, and all the idols of the house of Israel, pourtrayed upon the wall round about. And there

> *stood before them seventy men of the ancients of the house of Israel, and in the midst of them stood Jaazaniah the son of Shaphan, with every man his censer in his hand; and a thick cloud of incense went up. Then said he unto me, Son of man, hast thou seen what the ancients of the house of Israel do in the dark, every man in the chambers of his imagery? for they say, The LORD seeth us not; the LORD hath forsaken the earth.*

That is the sad picture of the church in America today, elated with her personal and corporate sins, and hiding behind a thick cloud of incense saying, *"The Lord seeth us not."* But the eyes of the Lord do see the hearts of men; nothing is hidden from His eye. The church sleeps a sleep of death.

Listen to the wise comments of another Puritan, Thomas Brooks:

> When a man is in a deep lethargy if you pinch him with pincers or prick him with needles, he feels it not. If you scorch him, he cries not. If you threaten him, he fears not. Or if you speak to him fair, he regards it not. And now, this is the condition of such that are in a spiritual lethargy. Let the judgments of God be denounced and let the terrors of the law be preached, they tremble not. Let the flames of hellfire flash upon their souls, they regard it not for they are sermon-proof and judgment-proof and hell-proof.

The only remedy for a people of God who have departed from the heart of God is that they return to God in a time of Solemn Assembly. A Solemn Assembly is needed when there is a general decline of spirituality in the land, when wickedness is commonplace, and when there is little distinction between the church and pagan society. When God has withdrawn his presence from among His people, it is time to call the people of God back to Him in urgency. Now is the time in America for the churches in our land to sit in sackcloth and ashes and to weep before the porch and the altar as seen in the book of Joel.

Listen to this striking passage from Joel chapter 1 and verses 10-15:

> *The field is wasted, the land mourneth; for the corn is wasted: the new wine is dried up, the oil languisheth. Be ye ashamed, O ye husbandmen; howl, O ye vinedressers, for the wheat and for the barley; because the harvest of the field is perished. The vine is dried up, and the fig tree languisheth; the pomegranate tree, the palm tree also, and the apple tree, even all the trees of the field, are withered: because joy is withered away from the sons of men.*

THE SOLEMN ASSEMBLY

Gird yourselves, and lament, ye priests: howl, ye ministers of the altar: come, lie all night in sackcloth, ye ministers of my God: for the meat offering and the drink offering is withholden from the house of your God. Sanctify ye a fast, call a solemn assembly, gather the elders and all the inhabitants of the land into the house of the LORD your God, and cry unto the LORD, Alas for the day! for the day of the LORD is at hand, and as a destruction from the Almighty shall it come.

America, a once Christian nation, is now ripe for destruction from the Almighty and it shall soon come. The great burden of this should be on the church in America to fast and pray and weep over the sins of the land. But she cannot because of her own pitiful condition. The church itself needs to be roused and awakened from her slumber. Before she can pray for her country, she must first pray for herself, to repent of her personal and corporate sins and plead mercy unto God in true repentance and humility and brokenness before the Ancient of Days whom we have so greatly offended with our multiplied sins.

If God would return to His church in revival, and flood our sanctuaries with His presence, then the teenagers would flock to the house of God and have a real encounter with God. In a time of true spiritual awakening, thousands of teenagers could be swept into the Kingdom of God and saved.

So we see first this great need of a Solemn Assembly to call upon the Lord to forgive us our sins and then to heal our land. The need is great indeed at this late hour before the return of the Lord Jesus Christ. The hour is late, the day is at hand. It will either be total ruin and destruction for America, or great national revival will occur which will strengthen and revitalize the church and infuse it with apostolic vitality, and thousands upon thousands will be converted and swept into the kingdom of God. Oh friends, pray for the latter, that God will send a mighty outpouring of his Spirit upon our land to revive His people and show forth His glory to defend His holy name.

Now that we are in need of this Solemn Assembly and understand the great desperation of it, let us examine the nature of a Solemn Assembly. Just what is it? It's a time of weeping and fasting and humbling ourselves before an offended Creator. It's a time of brokenness over our sins, a time of confessing our sins and forsaking our sins corporately in the house of God. It's a serious and solemn time, night after night, where the people of God sit in the sanctuary of God, humble themselves under God and seek cleansing from Him and forgiveness of sins. It's a time where the people of God get right with God, where the leaders of the people lead this assembly and weep over the withdrawn presence of God because of the sins of the people of God. It is a time where a cry is made unto God.

The best way I can describe the solemn scene is to recommend a serious reading of Psalm 80. This Psalm is a plea to God for restoration of the people of God. Allow me to read this Psalm and then comment upon it in regard to the nature of a Solemn Assembly. Here now is Psalm 80; pay close attention to the petitions in it made unto God.

> *Give ear, O Shepherd of Israel, thou that leadest Joseph like a flock; thou that dwellest between the cherubims, shine forth. Before Ephraim and Benjamin and Manasseh stir up thy strength, and come and save us. Turn us again, O God, and cause thy face to shine; and we shall be saved. O LORD God of hosts, how long wilt thou be angry against the prayer of thy people? Thou feedest them with the bread of tears; and givest them tears to drink in great measure. Thou makest us a strife unto our neighbours: and our enemies laugh among themselves. Turn us again, O God of hosts, and cause thy face to shine; and we shall be saved. Thou hast brought a vine out of Egypt: thou hast cast out the heathen, and planted it. Thou preparedst room before it, and didst cause it to take deep root, and it filled the land. The hills were covered with the shadow of it, and the boughs thereof were like the goodly cedars. She sent out her boughs unto the sea, and her branches unto the river. Why hast thou then broken down her hedges, so that all they which pass by the way do pluck her? The boar out of the wood doth waste it, and the wild beast of the field doth devour it. Return, we beseech thee, O God of hosts: look down from heaven, and behold, and visit this vine; And the vineyard which thy right hand hath planted, and the branch that thou madest strong for thyself. It is burned with fire, it is cut down: they perish at the rebuke of thy countenance. Let thy hand be upon the man of thy right hand, upon the son of man whom thou madest strong for thyself. So will not we go back from thee: quicken us, and we will call upon thy name. Turn us again, O LORD God of hosts, cause thy face to shine; and we shall be saved.*

Now, let us apply this 80th Psalm to the Solemn Assembly and how to seek God in a desperate time of prayer. Notice first that this Psalm is a prayer for the ear of God, *"Give ear, O Shepherd of Israel."* Our prayers must rise up to the throne room of the Almighty and gain His attention, they must stir Him.

THE SOLEMN ASSEMBLY

Secondly, it is a prayer that acknowledges a high and lofty God. Our time of Solemn Assembly will be futile if we continue to maintain a low view of God, to have a God that we have shrunk down to *our* size and placed on a human level. God is the One that dwellest between the cherubims.

Thirdly, it is a prayer for backsliders to be turned back to God: turned back in a right relationship with Him. Notice the text *"turn us again."* When the people of God have grieved the heart of God with their sins of pride, arrogance, self-reliance, and presumptuous sins, it is time to seek God and beg for mercy. All we can do is beg for mercy and ask God for the grace and repentance to turn us again.

Notice the people spoken of in the Psalm acknowledge their need to be turned again. Until you admit and acknowledge your sins and agree with God about what *He* says about them, call them what *He* calls them, when you get serious with God and confess your sins, He will get serious with you.

Notice the fourth thing; it is a prayer asking God to turn back from His anger toward His estranged people. A shut-up heaven is a result of unrepentant sinning people. Without true repentance even our prayers anger Him. *"O LORD God of hosts, how long wilt thou be angry against the prayer of thy people?"*

Now notice the fifth thing; it is a prayer reminding God what He has done in former times, *"Thou hast brought a vine out of Egypt: thou hast cast out the heathen, and planted it."* This is reminiscent of the prayer of Moses before God upon Mount Sinai, when the people of Israel had sinned grievously against the Lord with the golden calf. Moses intercedes on their behalf, lest an angry God destroys them. Moses reminded God of how He had delivered His people from Egypt, and now His very name would become a reproach to the enemies of God if He chose to destroy them after He had so miraculously delivered them.

The sixth thing to make note of in this Psalm is the fact that it is a prayer recognizing the remedial judgments of God upon His estranged people, *"Why hast thou then broken down her hedges, so that all they which pass by the way do pluck her?"* The judgments increase in severity if the people do not repent.

And finally, it is a prayer for God himself to look down from the heavens and see His people in their distress calling out to Him; to the One who can save them, *"Return, we beseech thee, O God of hosts: look down from heaven, and behold, and visit this vine."*

In a time of Solemn Assembly when the people of God are honest with God about their sins, when they turn from their wickedness and confess their sins to Him, when they humble themselves and in brokenness and contriteness seek His face, and plead with Him to look down, and come down, then that is the kind of prayer that reaches the heart of God.

But our desperation must match our perspiration in this time of seeking God in repentance. We must be transparent and acknowledge the fact that we have grieved His presence away from among us. Then, and only then, can we pray for our nation that God will bless this great nation of ours once again. But first the people of God must re-enter a right relationship with God for Amos 3:3 states, *"Can two walk together, except they be agreed?"* We cannot go our own way and expect God to follow; we must realign ourselves back to Him.

A time of Solemn Assembly can certainly be such a time for such a time as this. Brother pastor, what is the reason that you are not in sackcloth and ashes in your sanctuary right now? Why are you not leading your people in nights of desperate prayer in a time of Solemn Assembly? Do you not need revival, or are you afraid that if God sent revival to your church it might change the dynamic of your status quo?

Friends, let us seek God in a serious time of prayer and fasting, for this is the most critical hour in the history of our nation. If we, the people of God, do not turn back to God, we will not witness revival in our day and our nation will be destroyed and our way of life eliminated. The pathway to revival is lined with the prayers of the people of God crying out to Him in desperation to show Himself strong. Let me ask you a question; are you willing to realign yourself to the heart of God? If not, then don't complain about things, if you're not willing to do anything about it.

Let me pray. *O Great God, we as a nation have sinned against thee. Heavenly Father, we as your people have sinned against thee. O Lord of glory, hear our prayer, look down and come down. Give ear to us once again. Come down in your manifest presence once again. Stir us, O God, to lay hold of you in nights of desperate prayer. We plead with you, O Lord God of glory, to come again and pour out your Spirit upon our land. Send a mighty revival, a spiritual awakening that will grip this nation with eternity and the God of that eternity. Move as you've done in former times. O Lord, come save the teenagers of this land, this lost generation of churched teenagers who've never seen a real vital encounter with the living God. Come, O great King, and with a mighty outpouring of your Holy Spirit, let them sit in your presence and be melted down under the awful solemnity of a holy God to where their hearts are broken up and hearts of stone are made hearts of flesh. Offer your great glory. Do it again. We pray this, O Lord, hear our prayer. Look down and come down once again. Amen.*

CHAPTER 16: WEARING THE ARMOR OF GOD

Bible Text: Ephesians 6:10-18
Preached on: Wednesday, January 2, 2013

At the Pastor's College in London the great Charles Spurgeon would host a weekly lecture whereby he would call upon one of his students and ask them to preach a message for the entire faculty and student body. On one such occasion, a young student was preaching on the subject of the armor of God from Ephesians chapter 6. The young man's eloquence was such that as he described the Christian's armor, you could almost hear the click and the clank as each piece of armor was put on. Then when he had finished his great oratory, with the shield of faith in one hand and the sword of the Spirit in the other, he called out, "Now, where is the devil?" In the back of the room sat the famous Spurgeon who cupped a chubby hand to his face and replied, "He's inside the armor."

Today our subject is the armor of God and wearing the armor of God and the strategies of Satan to disarm and thwart the believer. Satan is our great adversary and enemy of our souls. He will use any tactic to disarm us and to get us to take our eyes off of Christ, our Redeemer. The apostle Peter warns us about this great enemy of the Christian, *"Be sober, be vigilant; because your adversary the devil, as a roaring lion, walketh about, seeking whom he may devour"* (1 Peter 5:8).

My message today is not just an exposition of the passage found in Ephesians chapter 6 on the armor of God. It is an exhortation for us to be sober, to be vigilant against the wiles of this great deceiver who aims at your very soul. If you are a sincere believer who is washed in the blood and born of the Spirit, then you are a target for the evil one who will stop at nothing to deceive you if he can, and have you stumble and fall, thereby robbing God of His glory. For when we sin, we rob God of His glory. Oh friends, how delicate this chapter in Ephesians is to our understanding of our adversary and how to withstand him with the armor of God.

Today, we will examine the passage on the armor of God found in Ephesians chapter 6 where the apostle Paul describes the reality of the Christian's warfare with the enemy and in the necessity of being prepared for battle by wearing this protective armor. It is my prayer that you will receive something from this message to enable you to be better prepared and armed against this great adversary and that you will experience victory over him as a Christian in full armor.

Listen to Paul's admonition to the Christian as we read this text beginning in verse 10 as the Word of God declares:

> *Finally, my brethren, be strong in the Lord, and in the power of his might. Put on the whole armour of God, that ye may be able to stand against the wiles of the devil. For we wrestle not against flesh and blood, but against principalities, against powers, against the rulers of the darkness of this world, against spiritual wickedness in high places. Wherefore take unto you the whole armour of God, that ye may be able to withstand in the evil day, and having done all, to stand. Stand therefore, having your loins girt about with truth, and having on the breastplate of righteousness; And your feet shod with the preparation of the gospel of peace; Above all, taking the shield of faith, wherewith ye shall be able to quench all the fiery darts of the wicked. And take the helmet of salvation, and the sword of the Spirit, which is the word of God: Praying always with all prayer and supplication in the Spirit, and watching thereunto with all perseverance and supplication for all saints.*

In this passage the apostle Paul makes mention of our enemy and the reasons why we need the armor of God to withstand that enemy. But before we continue with this message, there are two books I highly recommend to you in regard to the Christians warfare. One is *The Christian in Complete Armor* by the Puritan, William Gurnall. It is a big book and I advise you that you read a portion of it every day for your benefit. The other book is also by a Puritan writer, Thomas Brooks, and it is a shorter book. It is entitled *Precious Remedies Against Satan's Devices.* Get that book at all costs, friends, and study it; for to have knowledge of how Satan comes against us is one of our best defenses against him. When you are engaged in a battle, you must know your enemy's strategies to withstand and defeat him.

One of Satan's greatest weapons against the Christian is discouragement, particularly a Christian minister. He will attempt to discourage you, to get you to take your eyes off of God and onto yourself, to focus on your discouraging situation and through that get you into despondency. We must be on the watch against this enemy of our soul and be wise to his stratagems. If Adam and Eve fell into sin in a perfect environment without having a depraved nature, how easy a target are we, who live in a fallen world and who have an Adamic nature within.

Our reliance upon God, our faith in the Scriptures, and our submission to the Holy Spirit is our only hope. Those are the three keys to victory: reliance upon

God, faith in the Word of God, and submission to the Holy Spirit of God. For if Satan can get us to be self-reliant, we will be indifferent to the things of God. If Satan can get us to doubt God's Word, then we lose our sure foundation. If he can get us to grieve or quench the Holy Spirit with sin, then that affects our walk with God.

If I could open a portal of hell and let you peer into the shadows of the sufferings of the damned, it would shock you to realize just how much Satan hates mankind, how much malice he has towards any man who follows Christ, and how desperate he is to ruin your testimony and rob God of the glory due Him. Satan wants to ruin you, destroy you, devour you.

Oh friends, how we must stay in an unbroken fellowship with the lover of our soul, the Lord Jesus Christ. How badly we need to stay in a moment-by-moment sensitivity to the Holy Spirit in us. As believers, we are called to lives of holiness unto the Lord.

Robert Murray McCheyne, the greatly used Scottish pastor, would cry out to the Lord, "O Lord, make me as holy as a saved sinner can be." This should be our heart cry as well. That's what I am, a saved sinner. I do not profess any doctrine of perfection. The only perfect man who ever lived was Jesus Christ. I do know that as a redeemed sinner, although I may make imperfect tracks along the way, I am on the way. I am kept by a holy God. I do not believe in antinomianism. We should endeavor to live holy lives unto God in obedience to His commands and under the lordship of Jesus Christ.

I remember a story I read about John Sung, the God-owned Chinese evangelist. John Sung was preaching in a province in China and an American missionary heard Sung say in his message, "I sin every day." That evening, this American missionary approached John Sung and rebuked him. He said, "Dr. Sung, you erred in your comments today. You told your hearers that you sin every day. My dear brother, Jesus never preached a sinning religion. Please, don't ever say that again." John Sung took that man's advice. And it's true, God is holy and He calls us to be holy. Satan hates a holy God and his enmity is raised against any follower of Christ who endeavors to live a holy life unto God.

This is why the armor of God is so critically important to the Christian. We will now look at each piece of the armor and how to put it on and wear this armor of God. We are to take the whole armor of God and wear it, so it is vitally important that we know what each piece is, and what its provision is for us, so we will withstand in the evil day. Resist him and he will flee from you. We are told to be strong in the Lord and the power of His might. The battle is the Lord's. We are to turn to Jesus for help in this military engagement where we wrestle, not against flesh and blood, but with principalities, powers, rulers of darkness. When Jesus was tempted of Satan in the wilderness, he answered Satan with the Word of God. We should immerse ourselves with the Word of God daily, saturate ourselves with it as a weapon and defense against the evil one. Jesus kept pointing Satan to the Word of God. We should point Satan to Jesus through the Word of God.

The first part of the armor spoken of is the girdle, or belt, of truth. This speaks of the Word of God being wrapped around us securely. We are to be garrisoned with the truth of God's Word. In China, the believers there are walking Bibles. They have memorized so much Scripture that they can recite entire books of the Bible. We in the West have many more rich resources to study God's Word at our disposal than many other nations, but many believers are bankrupt with their knowledge of the Word of God because they spend such little time in it. Scripture memory should be a priority with us each day. Set a goal to memorize parts of your Bible. This will enable you to have a strong belt of truth firmly around you to stand against Satan and his devices against you. Jesus should be our example here, in how he withstood the attacks of Satan in the wilderness with the sure Word of God. Remember the word of the Psalmist who said, *"I rejoice at thy word, as one that findeth great spoil"* (Psalm 119:162).

The next piece of armor is the breastplate of righteousness. The breastplate secures the heart. We are told in the book of Proverbs, *"Keep thy heart with all diligence; for out of it are the issues of life"* (4:23). We must guard the inward man and keep a strict watch over the defilement of sin. We must be a clear, unobstructed mountain stream. Just like a mountain stream runs down to the valley with clean water, we must remain unobstructed vessels so that the Holy Spirit can flow through us with no impediment or hindrance. The heart is deceitful above all things. How easy it is for our heart to be swayed. How easy it was for the Israelites to forsake God and turn to other gods as they turned their backside to Him.

Oh friends, our hearts should be guarded; guarded from the lusts of the flesh, the world, and the devil. It is so important to put on this breastplate of righteousness as the breastplate secures the heart. It is the righteousness of Christ who is our breastplate. The righteousness of Christ in us is our best weapon against the attacks of the enemy upon us.

The next piece of armor is shoes of the preparation of the gospel of peace. In Old Testament times, military armor consisted of shoes of brass, so that a soldier would not step on a sharp stick and injure himself and thus be unable to march or fight. Satan lays traps, snares, sharp sticks, before us in the hope that we will be caught in an unguarded moment, and injure ourselves and our usefulness to God.

So we must be watchful where we walk and how we walk in the Christian life. Our walk is our testimony to others. Psalm 1 declares, *"Blessed is the man that walketh not in the counsel of the ungodly, nor standeth in the way of sinners, nor sitteth in the seat of the scornful"* (verse 1). Because our walk is our testimony to the world, we must walk worthy of the Lord to be witnesses for Him with the preparation of the gospel of peace.

The next piece of armor mentioned in our text is the shield of faith. Oh friends, how mighty is the shield of faith, and it is our defense against the enemy. How much ground the enemy can have against us if our faith is weak! This shield of faith is our best defense against the attacks of Satan. Faith activated with a firm stance on the Word of God is a shield of defense against the fiery darts of the wicked one. How wonderfully does Galatians 2:20 point us to the shield of faith: *"I am crucified with Christ: nevertheless I live; yet not I, but Christ liveth in me: and the life which I now live in the flesh I live by the faith of the Son of God, who loved me, and gave himself for me."* The exchanged life is the Christian armor. Christ in us, the hope of glory.

The next piece of armor for us to wear is the helmet of salvation. The helmet of salvation is to be under the blood of Christ; under the protective blood of Christ. The helmet covers the vulnerable areas of the head and protects it. As we put this helmet of salvation on, we must ask the Lord to guard today our ears—what we hear, our thoughts—what we think. Ask Him that all of our thoughts be taken into captivity to Christ. Ask Him to place a guard over our eyes as to what we see throughout the day, that our eyes won't lust after the world or things of the flesh. Ask Him to put a guard over our lips so we won't speak deceit or be unkind with our words to others, so we won't grumble or complain about our present situation in life. But in all things give thanks to the Lord who saved us.

The last piece of armor is both proactive and defensive, which is the sword of the Spirit, the Word of God used as a weapon and as a defense. It is the Holy Spirit who renders the Word of God effective and powerful as a two-edged sword. How we must hide the Word of God in us on a daily basis by the memorization of it and dwelling upon it and meditating upon it.

But the spiritual glue which holds it all together and keeps the armor in force continually, please don't miss this, *"Praying always with all prayer and supplication in the Spirit, and watching thereunto with all perseverance and supplication for all saints."* A person's prayer life in the closet is the best defense against the enemy of our souls. You are only as good as you are on your knees before God in prayer. Constant prayer is both a defensive and offensive posture. Job found relief when he prayed for his friends. Our intercessory prayer life is the buckle that secures the whole armor of God. The importance of a daily quiet time is essential to our walk with God and our best defense against the enemy. For to be in a vital love relationship with Jesus Christ, which grows more intimate and more red-hot every day, is a high wall and bulwark against sin.

A close walk with God is the best remedy to avoid sin. Having a regular time of prayer every day is essential to keeping a watch over our own deceitful hearts and a look-out against the enemy of our souls. But my, how we fail to emphasize the importance of prayer in our day. The weekly prayer meeting is the spiritual engine of the church, but how many churches today are out of gas when it comes to vital prayer. Prayer breaks down spiritual strongholds, delivers the oppressed, and sets the captives free.

I am reminded about a painting in a Spanish art gallery. In the painting, there's a farmer who is in the position of prayer. There in the background is a church steeple in the distance and evidently the bell has rung in the village for a time of prayer. This farmer is kneeling in his field, his straw hat lies beside him, and he has put down his farm implements to lay hold of God in a time of prayer. If you look carefully at this oil painting, in the distance there's an angel who is just taking up the reins to a team of mules and is making a fresh furrow in the soil. And at the bottom of the painting is a brass plate with three words written on it and they read, "No time lost."

Do you see, friends, all of heavens resources are at our disposal when we pray? There is no time lost? Everything is gained when we pray. Oh, if we would only believe that and make time for prayer it would revive our churches and transform the lives of our congregations in our communities. A praying church is an effective weapon in the hands of God. A prayerless church is a laughing-stock to the world. It is a vital prayer life that girds the armor of God and secures it in the life of a believer. Don't ever forget that. Your walk with God is everything in the Christian life. Ask the Holy Spirit to point out in your life any chinks in your armor. Perhaps you are not spending enough time in the Word of God and with the God of the Word. You've become lax there and you're suffering for it. Make sure every piece of armor is secure so you don't step on a sharp stick, stumble, and fall.

Lastly, we must remember to keep on the whole armor of God and not get lazy or lax or let our guard down. We must not fail to put on every piece of the armor each and every day. A soldier in battle needs to have all his military gear on and secured. And he also needs to be aware of the tactics of his opponent. Ask the Lord for the necessary grace to succeed in spiritual warfare for our battle will not end until we ourselves finish the race that's set before us.

> *Wherefore seeing we also are compassed about with so great a cloud of witnesses, let us lay aside every weight, and the sin which doth so easily beset us, and let us run with patience the race that is set before us, Looking unto Jesus the author and finisher of our faith; who for the joy that was set before him endured the cross, despising the shame, and is set down at the right hand of the throne of God.* (Hebrews 12:1-2)

May you wear the full armor of God, friend, as you look unto Jesus for the grace to live the Christian life in a way that brings honor to Him and glory to the Father. I hope this message has been of some help to you as we keep looking at Him.

We thank you, O God of glory, that you have provided us with the armor of God. We thank you for the Spirit of God who guides us and quickens us to live for thee. And we thank you, Lord God, for your dear Son, Jesus, who gave himself for us as a ransom to reconcile us back to you. Help us to wear the armor securely as we face the battle each day and may we bring you honor and glory with our lives as we serve you today. I pray these things in the strong name of our Lord and Savior Jesus Christ. Amen.

CHAPTER 17: WHERE A TREE FALLS IT SHALL LIE

Bible Text: Ecclesiastes 11:3
Preached on: Sunday, August 19, 2012

King Solomon was the wealthiest man who ever lived. In fact, he had so much money he could've stuffed Donald Trump in his shirt pocket. King Solomon was also the wisest king who ever lived. And he wrote an entire book of the Bible, Proverbs, which is chock full of wisdom for us today. But the book of the Bible that stirs me the most from his pen is the book of Ecclesiastes. It is written from the perspective of an older man looking back on his life and how he lived it, and reflecting on what was significant or foolish in it. For when I read the book of Ecclesiastes it makes me reflect on my own life and how much of it I wasted in sin and in the foolishness of this world.

King Solomon looked back on his large life and saw how he had sought the pleasures this world had to offer. But he found no pleasure in them. He chased after wealth and discovered there was no pleasure in wealth. In fact, he envied the man who worked with his hands, who had nothing, but who could sleep well at night because he didn't have to toss and turn and worry over losing his wealth.

In his reflections on life, King Solomon came to the conclusion that there is one fate for every man, and that is death. Death comes to the rich and poor alike. It is no respecter of persons. He sums up his thoughts in the last two chapters of this book. And he ends it with a vivid description of a funeral procession. This is found in chapter 12:1-7.

> *Remember now thy Creator in the days of thy youth, while the evil days come not, nor the years draw nigh, when thou shalt say, I have no pleasure in them; While the sun, or the light, or the moon, or the stars, be not darkened, nor the clouds return after the rain: In the day when the keepers of the house shall tremble, and the strong men shall bow themselves, and the grinders cease because they are few, and those that look out of the windows be darkened, And the doors shall be shut in the streets, when the sound of the grinding is low, and he shall rise up at the voice of the bird, and all the daughters of musick shall be brought low; Also when they shall be afraid of that which is high, and fears shall be in the way, and the almond tree shall flourish, and the grasshopper shall be a*

burden, and desire shall fail: because man goeth to his long home, and the mourners go about the streets: Or ever the silver cord be loosed, or the golden bowl be broken, or the pitcher be broken at the fountain, or the wheel broken at the cistern. Then shall the dust return to the earth as it was: and the spirit shall return unto God who gave it.

King Solomon saw that the very best this world can offer is but futility; it is sand. That no matter how much we achieve in this world on human terms, it is all but dust that will blow away. And the memory of our life will soon be forgotten. The Bible tells us that our life is but a vapor that appears for a little while and then disappears as the morning mist. And wise old King Solomon saw that he spent much of his life as a fool. He saw that he began well but he ended poorly. He had vast wealth but he ended up poor in the things that matter for God. He saw the futility of pleasure and wealth and the brevity of life and the stark reality that all men will have to face death, and after that the judgment.

For it has been said as soon as we leave the cradle we commence our funeral march to the grave. For eventually we all die and every man's spirit returns to God who gave it. And it returns to God for judgment. For man's spirit returns to God who gave it, and I repeat, it returns to God for judgment. But the verse in the book of Ecclesiastes which cries out to me the loudest and stands the blackest on the white pages of my Bible is verse 11:3. Let me read it to you: *"And if the tree fall toward the south, or toward the north, in the place where the tree falleth, there it shall be."*

And that, friends, is the title of my message today, "Where a Tree Falls It Shall Lie." Our sermon today is on the doctrine of regeneration, and you are like that tree when it falls. For the fate of man is fixed at death. You will either die in your sins and drop into hell and its torments, or you will rest in the merits of Christ and be under His blood and enjoy the benefits of His presence in glory. But, I repeat, the fate of man is fixed at death. For where the tree falls, there it shall lie.

Death may shortly come to you and suddenly cut you off without warning as it often does, and you will fall to the ground in death like that tree. And whatever your position is, whether in Christ or outside of Christ, where the tree falls, there it shall lie. You may believe you have many good years left on earth but the very breath in your lungs is put there by God. And He can remove it at any instant. A car accident, a heart attack, a sudden tragedy can cut you off and send you into another world, either a place of joy and peace, or a place of misery and flames. I

WHERE A TREE FALLS IT SHALL LIE

repeat, God is the giver and sustainer of life and He can snatch it from you at any moment.

I was in a hotel in Edinburgh, Scotland, and I stepped into the shower. And the next thing I knew I was lying on a concrete floor almost unconscious with my wrist broken and my head injured. God could've removed me easily that day. I no sooner stepped into that slippery bath tub, which was a death trap, that I was pitched right out of it on my head.

Listen to the Word of God. *"Surely thou didst set them in slippery places: thou castedst them down into destruction. How are they brought into desolation, as in a moment!"* (Psalm 73:18-19).

I slipped suddenly that morning and without warning. Listen, again, to the Word of God which declares, *"To me belongeth vengeance, and recompence; their foot shall slide in due time: for the day of their calamity is at hand, and the things that shall come upon them make haste"* (Deuteronomy 32:35).

King Solomon speaks in Ecclesiastes of how death can suddenly come upon a man. *"For man also knoweth not his time: as the fishes that are taken in an evil net, and as the birds that are caught in the snare; so are the sons of men snared in an evil time, when it falleth suddenly upon them"* (9:12).

America has become one of the most dangerous nations to live in. Sudden death is everywhere. You can be sitting in a movie theater and be murdered. You can be sitting on an airplane and be blown up. Something noxious can be in your very next meal and kill you. No matter how healthy and active you may be now, a sudden calamity can end your life without warning, and if you were to die today, your fate is fixed at death. Death will eventually come to you and cut you down. And you will be like that tree in an unchangeable state for all eternity. For a man's character is unchangeable at death. For where a tree falls, there it shall lie.

Allow me to present to you two godly Bible commentators who wrote wisely on this text of where the tree falls, there it shall lie. Both these men are on the opposite theological poles but they both come out at the same place on their commentary on this text. I speak of John Wesley and John Gill. One was an Arminian, the other a Calvinist. But whichever side your theology falls, if you die and you are not the subject of regeneration, you will be cast into hell whether you are a Calvinist or an Arminian. You must be born again. Where a tree falls, there it shall lie.

Listen to the words first of John Wesley taken from his commentary on Ecclesiastes, chapter 11 and verse 3. Wesley comments: "Therefore, let us bring forth the fruits of righteousness, because death will shortly cut us down, and we shall then be determined to unchangeable happiness or misery, according as our works have been."

Now listen, friends, to the words of John Gill on the same verse of Scripture. Dr. Gill writes:

> As when a tree is cut down, let it fall where it will, there it abides, and is no more fruitful; so when a man is cut off by death, as he was then, so he remains; if a gracious and good man, and has done good, he is like a tree that falls to the south, he enters into the paradise of God, the joys of heaven; and if not a good man, and has not done good, he is like a tree that falls to the north, he goes into a state of darkness, misery and distress.

Both these Bible scholars, Wesley and Gill, though they disagreed on their theology, both came out at the same place here on this verse in Ecclesiastes because both men believed in the doctrine of regeneration. When John Wesley was finally converted after living a life on a false foundation, as an ordained minister with the Church of England, his heart, he says, was strangely warmed. Listen to what he wrote in his diary dated May 14, 1738.

> In the evening I went very unwillingly to a society in Aldersgate Street, where one was reading Luther's preface to the Epistle to the Romans. About a quarter before nine, while he was describing the change which God works in the heart through faith in Christ, I felt my heart strangely warmed. I felt I did trust Christ, Christ alone, for salvation; and an assurance was given me that He had taken away my sins, even mine, and saved me from the law of sin and death.

Wesley knew right then he had experienced a change which God gives in regeneration, and both these men understood the doctrine of regeneration even though they differed on their theology. They both knew the heart had to be changed and they both state in their commentaries on Ecclesiastes 11:3 that when we die, we die in that state and it's unchangeable. For as he was, so he remains.

The book of Revelation speaks of this, in chapter 22, verse 11. Listen, friends, *"He that is unjust, let him be unjust still: and he which is filthy, let him be filthy still: and he that is righteous, let him be righteous still: and he that is holy, let him be holy still."* In other words, where a tree falls, there it shall lie.

WHERE A TREE FALLS IT SHALL LIE

Jesus said that a follower of His was one who does the will of God. And here in Revelation 22, verses 14-15, we have more on this thought. *"Blessed are they that do his commandments, that they may have right to the tree of life, and may enter in through the gates into the city. For without are dogs, and sorcerers, and whoremongers, and murderers, and idolaters, and whosoever loveth and maketh a lie."*

You can't predict when a violent storm will hit your neighborhood and knock down one of your trees. And you can't boast of tomorrow because you may die tonight and when death comes to you it uproots you whatever spiritual state you are in. When you die where you spend eternity is determined. For where a tree falls, it shall lie.

There is no imaginary place called purgatory where the good Catholics go to twiddle their thumbs until they can be prayed out or bought out by those here below. No sir, in eternity it is either heaven or hell. And if you are truly regenerated and born again you will go to heaven, but if you have never been the subject of a work of grace upon your heart, you will die in your sins no matter how good a church member you have been all your life. Your record of church service won't help you then, it won't matter how much you tithe or how often you prayed. Your unregenerated heart will reveal your true state.

Jesus said the fruit of a man's life reveals the condition of his heart. Jesus compared men to a tree which produces either good or bad fruit. And by their fruits you shall know them. Jesus said this:

> *Either make the tree good, and his fruit good; or else make the tree corrupt, and his fruit corrupt: for the tree is known by his fruit. O generation of vipers, how can ye, being evil, speak good things? for out of the abundance of the heart the mouth speaketh. A good man out of the good treasure of the heart bringeth forth good things: and an evil man out of the evil treasure bringeth forth evil things.* (Matthew 12:33-35)

This use of the imagery of a tree by the Word of God to speak to the man's life is striking. A tree is true to its character. It will not produce what it is not. An apple tree cannot produce figs. And a fig tree cannot produce oranges. The fruit of a tree is a product of its nature. And the fruit of your life is a product of your nature, whether you are a servant of sin and unchanged, or you are a subject of grace and regenerated. You are what you are, friends, and if you are cut off tragically and suddenly today, you will die as you are. For where a tree falls, it shall lie.

I have often seen death in my life. My two childhood pals both experienced sudden death while they were in their 20s. One died on a motorcycle. He had gotten into an argument with his wife and jumped on his motorcycle and turned the corner and split his head open on the curb. My other friend was on his way to work in a snowstorm and his automobile was hit head on and he died instantly. Neither one of them thought that day was to be their last. They were both young and in good health. They had their whole lives before them. But sudden death cut them off. And where a tree falls, it shall lie.

My mother lay dying in the nursing home, my mother who made me quit going to church when I was a teenager. She made fun of those Christians and made me quit attending their services. She lived to be an old woman of 97 and she lay dying in the nursing home. The staff in that nursing home had to dope her up at night to keep her quiet because her shrieks and screams kept the other patients awake. My mother faced death and it terrified her. She resisted God right up to the very end. I would visit her and ask her if she wanted me to pray for her or if she wanted a chaplain to come and pray with her. And she'd say, "No, it doesn't work." I would read her a get well card from a Christian friend and I would say to my mother, "Here is a card from your friend and she is praying for you. Here is her prayer." And my mother would interrupt me and cut me off with the harsh remark, "Don't tell me about that." And she would cuss and say, "Just tell me who the card is from." Like I said, they had to dope her up at night so she wouldn't wake up the other patients with her shrieks and cries. My mother eventually died, and where a tree falls, it shall lie.

My father was an agnostic all his life. He seldom darkened the door of a church. He was a selfish, self-centered man who lived only for himself. When he died, he didn't leave me or my mother any life insurance or any money. All he left me was the change on his dresser. And I took that change to McDonald's and it wasn't even enough to buy me lunch. When it came time for him to die, he was alone in the hospital with the doctor beside him. The doctor called me to tell me my father had died. And the doctor's voice trembled as she told me how horribly he had died. Where a tree falls, it shall lie.

I have been to many a funeral and I've heard many a minister say nice words over the deceased. I have yet to hear a funeral service where the minister says, "Old Joe is now in hell." No, it's always, "He's in a better place now. He's not suffering anymore. He's at rest." But if old Joe died in his sins, even if he was the chairman of the deacons, he is going to suffer the torments of an everlasting hell. For when we die, we die as who we are and if our character is outside of Christ our long church record of service won't be of any help to us then. It won't matter how many missions trips we went on, how many doors we knocked on to share the gospel, how many gospel tracts we handed out, how many prayer meetings we attended, how many Sunday school classes we taught, or how many choir rehearsals we sat in on. If our hearts are not regenerated, when we die, we die in our sins. For where a tree falls, it shall lie.

A truly born-again person is Christ-like. Jesus said, *"If you love me, keep my commandments"* (John 14:15). A true Christian has a holy disposition in him planted there by God and a regenerated heart through a work of grace. A person in whom God has worked a change in the heart has a principle of holiness in his life. That principle of life is within. The Holy Spirit resides in the life of a real Christian. And it is that power of a holy life which marks out a true follower of the Lamb. For without holiness, no one shall see the Lord.

If you can sleep at night with known sin in your heart, you are apart from Christ and will die in your sins. Only those who are born again from above and washed in the blood of the Lamb are truly saved. This is the demarcation line between heaven and hell. If you are not living a holy life unto God, you are not in the Lamb's Book of Life. If you claim to be a Christian and Jesus is not your Lord, if you still sit on the throne of your life and you have not enthroned Jesus there as the Lord of your life, you are a rebel against a holy God and no rebels are allowed in heaven. Here hope of heaven is a hole in the wall and you might as well try to climb to heaven on a rope of sand. You can buck that, resist that, and fight that, but you can't fight God and win. He will be your Lord, complete Master, or he will damn you to hell for eternity. He will have no rebels in heaven.

If you have not the power within to live a holy and righteous life, you are unrighteous still. And if you die tonight, you will remain in that condition for all eternity. If you have not surrendered your all to the Christ who gave His all for you, then you are deceived and sit upon a false foundation. If you are a long-time church member and your heart is not regenerated, you will die and be cast into hell even if you are the minister of the church. For where a tree falls, it shall lie.

Oh friends, don't be deceived. I know of what I speak. For I was a lost church member for years. I rested my salvation on the fact that I walked an aisle as a teenager and made a public profession of Christ. For years I faithfully served my church in many capacities. I conducted door-to-door evangelism. I taught Sunday school. I witnessed. I handed out tracts on a regular basis. I prayed. I read my Bible. And I was lost. Lost. Lost. I sat on the throne of my life, not Christ. Christ was not my complete Master although I was a church member of good standing. I had a point of rebellion in my life. And God will have no rebels in his kingdom. I had yet to throw down my shotgun of rebellion and submit to the claims of Christ on my life. I still wanted to maintain control in a certain area of my life. And I stuck a stake in the ground with a sign on my heart which said, "Keep off, God." It was a "keep off the grass" sign. I told God to keep off this area of my life, that I would take Him every other way and have Him except this way. And God will always cross us at our point of rebellion if we are to be saved. And he crossed me and saved me. He almost had to kill me to do it, but he saved me.

We live in a day where they say we can be saved and still hang onto our sins and still go to heaven and many have swallowed that hook, line, and sinker. And we are sunk. We still sit on the throne of our lives and tell God what He can touch and what He may not and call that salvation. Heaven help us!

Hell is populated hourly with decent church members who died with an area of their life in rebellion to God. And where a tree falls, it shall lie.

But listen, friend, if you have an area of your life where you have put a stake in the ground and a sign that reads "keep off," where you have told God to keep His hands off this area of your life, it is hell for you. And if you died this instant, your character would determine your final destiny forever and ever. You can be the pastor of a church and if you have a point of rebellion in your life, where you've told God to keep His hands off, then face the fact, pastor, all is not well with your soul. Your ministry license won't do you any good in hell. For where a tree falls, it shall lie.

No one knows the hour that death will visit them. There will be a day when your name will be in the obituary page of the paper. There will come a time when your name is written on a death certificate. There will come a day where a slab of stone covers your grave with your name upon it, with the date of your death. There is no escaping death when it comes, for it comes to all men, rich and poor, all alike as King Solomon said. There will come a day when your spirit goes back to the God who gave it and it will go to Him to face judgment and you will be held up against the utter severity of God's holy law which requires perfection from all men.

You are a sinner because of the condition you are in from the fall of Adam. You were born with a ruined nature and you drink iniquity like water because that's the kind of a person you are. You sin because you are a big sinner and as you were held up against the holy law of God you will fail the test and be sent to hell and its torments. For if you cannot lay hold of the righteousness of Christ through His shed blood where He is your sin substitute, then you will stand before God on your own merits and God's holy law will kill you and you'll be sent to hell like the tree whose character determines the fruit it produces. So too your character will determine your destiny as to how it falls, to the north or south. For to be truly saved means you have a vital union with a living Lord and are born from above and washed in His blood. Oh friend, don't rest your hope of heaven on a past experience, but on a present relationship with Jesus Christ. We are not saved by merely believing on the fact of the death of Christ but believing on the Christ who died.

Many of you have heard preaching all your lives. You have been in church for much of your life. But please listen to the following story very carefully. There is a big Baptist church in Memphis, Tennessee, and one of the former pastors of this church was R. G. Lee. He is known for preaching one of the most famous sermons of all time. It's called "Payday Someday." There was a point in Dr. Lee's ministry early on when there was a member in his congregation, an attorney. And this attorney had to be out of town a lot on business, but no matter where this lawyer went, he made sure to catch a train back to Memphis on Saturday night so he could hear R. G. Lee preach the next morning.

Well, he loved to hear Dr. Lee preach. And this lawyer one day got cancer and he was in the hospital dying and he called for his pastor to come to his bedside. Dr. Lee entered the hospital room whose window looked out on the Mississippi River. And the lawyer told R G. Lee this; he said, "I want you to know how much I've enjoyed your preaching through the years. And I never missed a Sunday if I could help it. I lie here dying with only a few weeks left to live and I want to chastise you for never telling me how to be saved. You never preached the cross to where I could see it. You never put the blood out there where I could reach it. I am dying and I will die in my sins and I chastise you, sir, for you lack a preaching the real gospel."

R. G. Lee left that man's hospital room like somebody just kicked him in the stomach. His head was hung down low and he felt berated and he also felt guilty as charged. It was now dark outside. As he walked down to the banks of the Mississippi River there he got down on his knees in the mud and dipped his hands in that muddy river getting his white suit pants dirty in the process. And right there and then he promised God from that point forward he would preach the cross and the blood and he'd change his message that night. And in three weeks time there was a move of grace at that church and three blocks of downtown Memphis were shaken with revival.

You may be sitting under a pastor who doesn't preach the cross and the blood and the need for repentance to be saved. You may have come into the church under that kind of weak preaching. Someone may have spoken peace to you when there was no real peace within. Deep down, if you are honest with yourself, you know all is not well with your soul. When the devil crooks his finger at you it is like a magnet that draws you, for he has a hold on you, for you are still in his kingdom although your name is on the church role. You have never experienced the new birth. You are not a subject of grace. You do not possess a regenerated heart. You are sick in your sins. You are tired of your up and down life. But you are hungry for God, you feel a great need for Christ, you know you are a sinner and that your good works won't save you. You may have been resting on a past experience and a record of service instead of a real faith in Christ. You sense that the roots of your tree are rotten and bad and if you were to topple over in death right now your character is as rotten as that tree fallen toward the north and hell. The Bible declares that when a man comes to Christ through an exercise of repentance towards God and faith in Christ, he's saved. You now want what you presently haven't possessed and that is Christ. You thirst but you've yet to be satisfied. I have good news for you, friend, the promises of the gospel are for the weary, the hungry and the thirsty.

Listen now to the following invitations of the gospel:

> *Come now, and let us reason together, saith the LORD: though your sins be as scarlet, they shall be as white as snow; though they be red like crimson, they shall be as wool.* (Isaiah 1:18)

> *Ho, every one that thirsteth, come ye to the waters, and he that hath no money; come ye, buy, and eat; yea, come, buy wine and milk without money and without price.* (Isaiah 55:1)

> *Seek ye the LORD while he may be found, call ye upon him while he is near: Let the wicked forsake his way, and the unrighteous man his thoughts: and let him return unto the LORD, and he will have mercy upon him; and to our God, for he will abundantly pardon.* (Isaiah 55:6-7)

> *Look unto me, and be ye saved, all the ends of the earth: for I am God, and there is none else.* (Isaiah 45:22)

> *And as Moses lifted up the serpent in the wilderness, even so must the Son of man be lifted up: That whosoever believeth in him should not perish, but have eternal life.* (John 3:14-15)

> *If any man thirst, let him come unto me, and drink. He that believeth on me, as the scripture hath said, out of his belly shall flow rivers of living water.* (John 7:37-38)

And the Spirit and the bride say, Come. And let him that heareth say, Come. And let him that is athirst come. And whosoever will, let him take the water of life freely. (Revelation 22:17)

Listen, friends, Jesus invites those weary ones to come to Him. *"Come unto me, all ye that labour and are heavy laden, and I will give you rest. Take my yoke upon you, and learn of me; for I am meek and lowly in heart: and ye shall find rest unto your souls"* (Matthew 11:28-29).

Listen to this last verse, friend, for it speaks of what we've gone over today in this message on the doctrine of regeneration. Your heart has to be regenerated, friend, if you're going to spend eternity with Christ forever. Listen, *"He that believeth on the Son hath everlasting life: and he that believeth not the Son shall not see life; but the wrath of God abideth on him"* (John 3:36). Where a tree falls, it shall lie.

CHAPTER 18: UNCTION IN PREACHING

Bible Text: Luke 3:16
Preached on: Thursday, December 27, 2012

In 1770, when George Whitefield was preaching in the fields of Exeter in New England, he addressed a crowd of 4,000 who had assembled in the open air to hear him preach. As he made his way to the makeshift pulpit he paused, clasped his hands together, looked heavenward and commented, "I will wait for the gracious assistance of God for He will, I am certain, assist me once more to speak in His name." Minutes passed while the great Whitefield stood there in silence, waiting on the divine empowerment from on high. George Whitefield knew full well that he had no power in the pulpit apart from the unction of the Holy Spirit.

In the gospel of Luke, chapter 3 and verse 16, it describes John the Baptist as he answers the people whether he was the Christ or not. We hear him state: *"I indeed baptize you with water; but one mightier than I cometh, the latchet of whose shoes I am not worthy to unloose: he shall baptize you with the Holy Ghost and with fire."*

Dear friends, there is a distinction spoken of here in Scripture of a baptism of water and a baptism of fire. Men mightily used of God knew the difference in regard to this baptism with fire—men like George Whitefield, Charles Spurgeon, D. L. Moody. Each knew they needed divine assistance from on high when they preached. They needed this holy fire of God, this element in preaching called, "unction."

A pulpit without unction is merely a platform which dispenses information with no transformation. No transformation occurs in the hearts of the people without unction. A pulpit without unction is operated by personality and human methodologies. That kind of preaching may entertain, absorb, and inform, but it does not penetrate into the sin-laden heart of man. There may be laughter, enjoyment, and encouragement from that kind of preaching, but there is no conviction of sin and transformation of a heart from a heart of stone into a heart of flesh. Unction is the divine power which takes the Word of God and makes it like a hammer which breaks the rock in pieces.

After his resurrection, Jesus appeared to his disciples and admonished them to preach after this fashion: *"And that repentance and remission of sins should be preached in his name among all nations, beginning at Jerusalem. And ye are witnesses of these things. And, behold, I send the promise of my Father upon you: but tarry ye in the city of Jerusalem, until ye be endued with power from on high"* (Luke 24:47-49).

This is the answer to power in the pulpit. We are instructed to tarry before God until we, too, are endued with power from on high. Every gospel minister and witness for Christ should seek this enduement from on high that comes in the form of unction upon the preacher.

Let's look at a clear description of what unction is, taken from the pen of a man mighty in prayer, E. M. Bounds. Listen carefully to how he describes what unction in preaching is. He writes:

> Unction is simply putting God in his own word and on his own preachers ... It is that which distinguishes and separates preaching from all mere human addresses. It is the divine in preaching ... This unction comes to the preacher not in the study but in the closet. It is heaven's distillation in answer to prayer. It is the sweetest exhalation of the Holy Spirit. It impregnates, suffuses, softens, percolates, cuts, and soothes. It carries the Word like dynamite, like salt, like sugar; makes the Word a soother, an arranger, a revealer, a searcher; makes the hearer a culprit or a saint, makes him weep like a child and live like a giant; opens his heart and his purse as gently, yet as strongly as the spring opens the leaves. This unction is not the gift of genius. It is not found in the halls of learning. No eloquence can woo it. No industry can win it. No prelatical hands can confer it. It is the gift of God—the signet set to his own messengers. It is heaven's knighthood given to the chosen true and brave ones who have sought this anointed honor through many an hour of tearful, wrestling prayer ... it takes a diviner endowment ... to break the chains of sin, to win estranged and depraved hearts to God, to repair the breaches and restore the Church to her old ways of purity and power. Nothing but this holy unction can do this.

How true those statements of E. M. Bounds are. How absent is the mark of unction in our pulpits today. In the words of another, "There may be crowds but there's no Shekinah." Where, oh where, is the man of God today with the power of God upon him in a baptism of fire? Where is the gripping preaching that grabs the heart of the listener and grips with eternity and the Christ of that eternity? Why do so few today possess this element in preaching called unction?

UNCTION IN PREACHING

I submit to you that few today feel they need it. They are quite content to operate their churches on present methods as long as the congregation is content and the church campus is growing. Why rock the boat with preaching that may upset someone? But preachers of old knew they could not have any eternal impact upon their hearers apart from having this divine anointing upon them as they preached the gospel of the Son of God.

D. L. Moody was no great orator, and he was an uneducated man, but he sought the anointing of the Holy Ghost and it transformed his preaching to such a degree that he could preach in any major city like London, Glasgow, and Edinburgh, and hold 10,000 hearers at a time, for a month at a time. His preaching could literally shake a city for God. Moody knew about this anointing. He speaks about it in his own words.

> I was crying all the time that God would fill me with his Spirit. Well, one day in the city of New York—oh, what a day! I cannot describe it, I seldom refer to it; it is almost too sacred an experience to name. Paul had an experience of which he never spoke for fourteen years. I can only say that God revealed Himself to me, and I had such an experience of His love that I had to ask Him to stay His hand. I went to preaching again. The sermons were not different; I did not present any new truths, and yet hundreds were converted. I would not now be placed back where I was before that blessed experience if you should give me all the world—it would be as the small dust of the balance.

Another preacher mightily used of God was C. H. Spurgeon. He knew the necessity of having this power from on high upon him. Spurgeon taught his students at his Pastor's College the following on this holy subject of unction:

> Our hope of success and our strength for continuing the service lie in our belief that the Spirit of the Lord rests upon us. To us as ministers, the Holy Spirit is absolutely essential. Without Him, our office is a mere name. Unless we have the Spirit of the prophets resting upon us, the mantle which we wear is nothing but a rough garment to deceive. We ought to be driven forth with abhorrence from the society of honest men for daring to speak in the name of our Lord if the Spirit of God rest not upon us. If we have not the Spirit which Jesus promised, we cannot perform the commission which Jesus gave.

Spurgeon knew full well where his power in preaching lay. It came from on high from an anointing of the Holy Spirit.

When I recall my homiletic mentor, the great Dr. Stephen F. Olford, I remember his power in the pulpit. Stephen Olford knew the necessity of having unction from God before he entered any pulpit to preach before men. I was in his study with him one day and he looked tired. He sank in his chair and remarked to me, "Give me a few moments, brother. Give me a few moments to gather myself. I must re-gather myself. I just finished preaching and virtue has left me."

That brought to my mind the time when Jesus was walking in a crowd of people and the woman with the issue of blood touched the hem of his garment and this account in the gospel of Mark declares, *"And Jesus, immediately knowing in himself that virtue had gone out of him, turned him about in the press, and said, Who touched my clothes?"* (5:30). Let me ask you, brother preacher, when you preach to others can you say afterwards that virtue has left you?

Dear brethren, we must distinguish between popularity and power. To be a popular preacher without unction is one thing, to have power on high is altogether quite another. Allow me to illustrate. I was with Dr. Olford on another occasion and he was telling me the following story. There was a popular preacher within the Southern Baptist Convention years ago. And this man was filling every big pulpit in the convention with his big personality. But Dr. Olford told me that years ago this man came to him privately and asked him to help him on the topic of having the anointing of the Holy Spirit. But the man never followed up on his request. Years later, this man was a big gun, a big preacher in the SBC. One day, Stephen Olford wrote this man a letter and in that letter he said, "My dear brother, I see you have found popularity but where is the power?"

That's the secret, friends. There is a vast distinction between popular preaching that informs and entertains and one that has power to transform the heart through conviction of sin and awaken a sinner to his lost condition before God. Why is this element of preaching so rare today? I believe it's because the cost involved to attain it is so high. As E. M. Bounds said, "It is found in the closet of desperate prayer and waiting upon God." Few today want to take the time or make the sacrifice to shut themselves up with God alongside their own River Chebar and wait upon God until they, too, are endued with power from on high. What costs counts and what counts costs.

The anointing of God on a man is not a casual occurrence but one in which heaven must be stormed with a holy violence until the petition is given from on high. Let me ask you, friend, have you ever sought this anointing? I do not mean speaking in tongues. I mean to have an anointed ministry with which, when we preach, we grip others with eternity and the God of that eternity. Preaching that startles, awakens, convicts, converts the sinner from the kingdom of darkness into the kingdom of light and life. Preaching where the preacher has the baptism of fire spoken about in the gospel of Luke.

Oh friends, how this would transform the pulpits in our land today. If the blessing was sought more often and gained by those who storm heaven for it, preaching by men of God aflame with the fire of God, preaching that stirs a congregation, preaching that transforms, preaching that alarms and awakens, that grips the heart and the conscience of sinful man.

One man who was used greatly during the Second Great Awakening was the great evangelist, Asahel Nettleton. Nettleton understood the need for unction and the power it had over his hearers. When I was conducting my research for my biography on Nettleton, I spent a great deal of time at Hartford Seminary going over his personal papers of how God had moved in revival under his anointed preaching. Here's one man's account, a pastor friend of Nettleton's who had a pastorate in Lennox, Massachusetts. Dr. Shephard gives this account of the effectiveness of Asahel Nettleton's preaching and how unction attended Nettleton's preaching and its effect upon his hearers. Listen to his comments.

> His preaching was soon attended with a divine blessing and was undoubtedly instrumental of a revival of religion in Pittsfield and several other towns in the vicinity. You ask, "What were the characteristics of his preaching? And in what did its chief excellencies consist?" I answer, his labors consisted principally in preaching the Word. He was eminently a man of prayer, that he entered the pulpit directly from the mount of communion with his Maker. No one would readily doubt, who was witness of his holy calm, the indescribable, the almost unearthly solemnity and earnestness of his manner. The joy in which his heart seemed to be filled with a contemplation of the love of Jesus in giving his life a ransom for sinners marked his preaching and imparted an unction and the uncommon energy to his eloquence. When he spoke of the glories of heaven, it was almost as if he'd been there himself. When he made his appeals to the sinner, he made them with a directness which placed before him, as in a mirror, his utterly lost state. It seemed at times as if he was about to uncover the bottomless pit and invite the ungodly to come and listen to the groans of the damned.

That kind of preaching is what we lack in our land today. We have grown accustomed to the churchianity of our day and the meager attempts to convey divine truths without the divine anointing.

Oh friends, will you not get alone with God and shut yourself up with the Ancient of Days until you are endued with power from on high? It may take a week, it may take months, but lay hold of God until he imparts His Holy Spirit upon you in a baptism of fire. Then see the transformation in your preaching and in the hearts of your hearers all for His great glory.

CHAPTER 19: HELL-SHAKING PRAYER

Bible Text: James 5:16
Preached on: Wednesday, May 15, 2013

I believe the main reason we are not seeing revival in our land today is a lack of fervent prayer. I believe that our pulpits are powerless and without influence because there is no influential prayer life behind them. I believe a man is only as tall in the pulpit as he is long on his knees in continued prayer. The spirit of antichrist is in the land and society crumbles all around us and the church seems powerless to do anything about it. And I believe the answer can be traced back to the day that the American church threw the weekly prayer meeting out the window and replaced it with programs and entertainment. The powerhouse of the church is the engine of prayer and I'm afraid today that too many of us have run out of gas.

My message today is entitled "Hell-Shaking Prayer." For I believe in my heart that if the people of God got on fire for God and laid hold of Him in nights of desperate and prevailing prayer, we could push back the powers of darkness in our communities and usher in a Holy Ghost revival that would shake this nation from coast to coast with its hell-shaking prayer.

My Bible says in the book of James, *"The effectual fervent prayer of a righteous man availeth much"* (5:16). The key phrase in that sentence is *"righteous man."* Too few today pursue a life of holiness unto the Lord. Too few today give up their sports and entertainments and devote that time to prayer.

I was standing in line at the dry cleaners the other day and the man ahead of me was all excited about our local basketball team. And as he talked about it, he knew all the names of the players and what shots they'd made and he almost leaped off his feet as he described it with such excitement. I'll bet the average church member today could tell you all about their favorite sports team or favorite television program but they couldn't name the Ten Commandments or name more than five of the twelve disciples of Christ, much less quote large portions of Scripture to you. Why? We today in the church in North America are consumed with our idols and care little about the perishing world around us. The proof of this is the time spent on indulging our pastimes and passions as opposed to the time spent on our knees and in our Bibles.

It's been said that your average pastor only spends ten minutes a day in prayer. I'll bet he spends more time than that at the practice range at the golf course working on his handicap when he should be working on his sanctification. But a desperate life of prayer costs something. There is a price to be paid and few want to pay it.

When Jacob wrestled with the angel of God all night it cost him physically for the rest of his life because he walked with a limp. Every step he took made him wince in pain. But because of that desperate night of prayer, God changed his name from "supplanter" to "prince with God." I believe Leonard Ravenhill's heart attack was due to a night of desperate prayer. He even said so himself.

Listen, friends, what costs counts and what counts costs. If we desire to have prayer lives which move mountains of resistance and shake the gates of hell, then we must stay on our knees in brokenness and importunity until the answer is gained.

Jude speaks of praying in the Holy Ghost, *"But ye, beloved, building up yourselves on your most holy faith, praying in the Holy Ghost"* (verse 20). To pray in the Holy Ghost means that you first must be anointed by the Holy Ghost, filled with the Holy Ghost, and sensitive to the Holy Ghost. For to pray in the power of the Spirit means unobstructed access to the Almighty, influence to gain his attention, and power to attain answers to our pleading petitions. For praying in the Holy Ghost storms the portals of heaven with violence, shuts up the heavens from rain, and makes fire fall upon the drenched altar of sacrifice. It makes kings tremble and kingdoms shake. For a man praying in the power of the Holy Ghost has the ability to shake strong cities off their foundations and the potential to send mountains tumbling into the sea, to startle the very angels of heaven and rattle the red-hot gates of hell.

A man full of the Spirit and anointed with the Spirit and praying in the Spirit knows no resistance, has no opposition, fears no earthly mortal, and conquers all unearthly enemies. For praying in the power of the Holy Ghost is the essence that makes prayer effectual and fervent. As the apostle declares, *"The effectual fervent prayer of a righteous man availeth much"* (James 5:16). For a righteous man to be praying with fervency and heat in the Holy Ghost is to have great influence upon one's generation and avail much for eternity.

Listen to the story that a pastor shared with me one day while I was having lunch with him. He was a pastor from Glasgow, Scotland, and he told me that he and some other pastors in the city grew concerned over the growing evil in their community. Drug use was on the rise, crime had increased, and out-of-wedlock pregnancies among teenage girls had literally skyrocketed. He told me that there used to be a city banner that was prominently displayed throughout the city of

Glasgow which read, "Let Glasgow flourish in the Name of the Lord." But some godless civic leaders decided to change the city's motto to "Let Glasgow flourish," leaving out the name of the Lord. When that happened, the city began to fall into a moral tailspin and evil increased daily.

Well, this pastor and his minister friends decided to do something about it, so they decided to meet on a weekly basis to pray for their city. They gave up their social lives to commit this time to prayer, pleading with God to make a difference in their community. After some months of desperate prayer by these dedicated men, they began to see a difference in the life of their city. Crime decreased, drug use decreased, and out-of-wedlock pregnancies decreased. This little band of men laid hold of God in such prevailing prayer that eventually they pushed back the powers of darkness in their community.

You see, when the light of the gospel grows dim through watered-down preaching and lack of prayer, then a vacuum is created, and that vacuum is soon filled with darkness. Why can't you in your city, in your community, band together with some other believers and commit to one another and God that you will give up your social lives and your entertainments to desperate prayer until you see God move in a mighty way?

If we can make a difference for God in our city and if enough prayer warriors emerge in other cities, this entire nation could be moved for God. The result would be that there would be so much hell-shaking prayer going on that this very nation would begin to tremble under the influence of God and His Holy Spirit. This is the way to revival. But, oh friends, a desperate life of prayer is a sacrifice and you must be prepared for it. God may have you in a trial right now to turn it into a vital place of influential prayer for Him.

When God allows us to go through a trial or storm, He has a larger purpose in view. He often brings us to places of brokenness where we become like the broken alabaster box. For to be broken alabaster boxes means to have a fragrant life pleasing to the Lord. We become better prayer warriors through trials, and our faith is tested and increased through these tribulations.

For a prayer life that grips the attention of the heavenly throne room is not built beneath calm, sunny skies, but shaken during dark, sorrow-filled nights. A serious prayer life is hammered out on the anvil of pain and anguish, desperation and despair, when hope hangs on a tattered thread and all human resources are gone. There, and only there, does the answer to the request come. Here is where the vital prayer life commences which gains the cupped ear of the Almighty, as He leans over to listen more intently to the pathetic sobs and anguished heart-cries which in desperation reach out and grab hold of His robe of righteousness and do not let go until the answer is attained. To become a person of prayer is to be a shrill, holy note which continually rings the ears of angels and rattles the gates of glory.

A true prayer life is not born out of comfort and prosperity, but through trials and adversities. In your leanness, you will learn to lean upon Him. Though you're rolling on stormy seas, you will learn how to effectively storm heaven's portals for deliverance. When friends fail, disappoint, and desert you, you will seek and find favor with your faithful friend, Jesus. A desperate life of prayer shakes the gates of hell and influences our generation, all for the glory of God. Do you believe that? I do. A strong prayer life will make you fear God and not man.

John Wesley said the following, "Give me one hundred men who fear nothing but God and hate nothing but sin and I will shake the gates of hell." And he did just that. We can do it too, friends. Wesley was just a man, and a short one at that, but he was long on prayer and he stood tall in the pulpit because of his mighty prayer life.

Oh friend, I beg you to fall to your knees and confess your lack of prayer to God. Be honest with Him and ask Him to help you redeem the time in your generation to show you the foolishness of your favorite pastimes and the wasted time consumed on them. It is time to put away our idols and lay hold of God for this lost and perishing generation of hell-bound sinners and hell-bound unconverted church members.

Dear brother pastor, if you want power with God and influence over man, go to your knees and stay there. Ask God to make your very bones afire for Him, to where you can ignite others with your holy life of prayer and powerful preaching. This is a call to the pulpits in our land to take back this land for God and for our children and our grandchildren. Go to your knees, fall on your faces, beg God above heaven and earth on our behalf to pour water upon this dry, thirsty land of ours today.

Let me pray. *O Great God, you are the Ancient of Days. You are holy and you are worthy to be praised. Give us the grace, O Lord, to seek thy face in desperate and prevailing prayer. Give us the power of your Holy Spirit to pray in the Spirit so that kingdoms will be shaken for thee. O Great God, forgive us for our selfish enterprises, our wasted time spent on useless things, things that don't matter, things that you see as dust in light of eternity.*

Help us, Lord Jesus, to be persons of prayer, mighty persons of prayer that you empower to perform your purpose. Help us to shake the very gates of hell with such power that we push back the darkness in our communities and usher in your presence in a Holy Ghost revival that will grip this nation with the awful solemnity of your presence.

Come, O Lord, and take the field in a great revival of religion, I pray. Come pour your Spirit upon this dry and wasted land. Come save our children. Come save our grandchildren. Come, Lord Jesus, and once again permeate our sanctuaries with your presence and your preeminence. I pray in the strong name of Jesus Christ our Lord. Amen.

CHAPTER 20: ISN'T JESUS WONDERFUL!

Bible Text: Revelation 2:1-5
Preached On: Sunday, July 29, 2012

Recently I was driving down the road and in front of me was a car with its left turn signal on. It blinked and blinked but the car never turned. The car just kept driving for miles in that direction. There's a passage of Scripture which illustrates this, it's in Revelation 2:1-5:

> *Unto the angel of the church of Ephesus write; These things saith he that holdeth the seven stars in his right hand, who walketh in the midst of the seven golden candlesticks; I know thy works, and thy labour, and thy patience, and how thou canst not bear them which are evil: and thou hast tried them which say they are apostles, and are not, and hast found them liars: And hast borne, and hast patience, and for my name's sake hast laboured, and hast not fainted. Nevertheless I have somewhat against thee, because thou hast left thy first love. Remember therefore from whence thou art fallen, and repent, and do the first works; or else I will come unto thee quickly, and will remove thy candlestick out of his place, except thou repent.*

These are stern words from the Lord Jesus Christ to His church in Ephesus. Notice how He acknowledges the fact that these church members were busy for the Lord, *"And for my name's sake hast laboured."* These church members were not lazy or negligent in their service for God. Quite the contrary, they were model Christians in this regard. They fought for truth, stood against evil, and exercised patience as they labored for their Lord. But something happened in their lives of which they were unaware. They were like the driver of that car, driving down the road, unaware that their turn signal was on. You see, they had turned away from God in their affections and they didn't even know it. But Jesus noticed it.

Jesus is more concerned about our love for Him than our service to Him. He wants us to maintain an intimate love relationship with Him. And when we grow cold toward Him, it grieves His heart. Decay often begins in the closet—meaning that our love relationship with Jesus often dries up from a lack of a vital daily quiet time and an utter reliance upon Him. Don't misunderstand me here, you can get up early and faithfully read several chapters of your Bible each day and still grow cold towards Jesus. You can be zealous in your work for Him and still lose your love for Him. I'm speaking of a daily tryst with the Lover of our souls where, when our alarm clock goes off, we jump out of bed and quickly go to our place of devotions because we cannot wait to get into His presence, to hear His voice, to share our troubles with Him, and to get on our heart what is on His heart. Unfortunately, it's easy to grow cold in our love toward Him by being too occupied in our service to Him.

There's a story about Duncan Campbell which illustrates this. Duncan Campbell was in his study early one morning preparing a sermon on the Holy Spirit which he was going to preach to a group of ministers at a convention. From up in his study he could hear singing downstairs in the parlor. It was his 16-year-old daughter's voice and she was happily singing a hymn. He went downstairs to listen to her. He asked her, "Lassie, what is there to sing about so early in the morning at six o'clock?" She came over and sat in his lap and explained, "Oh, Daddy, I have just spent an hour with Jesus. Isn't Jesus wonderful, Daddy?" Duncan Campbell felt like a knife had been stabbed through his heart. That remark stunned him because, at that point in his life, Jesus wasn't wonderful to him. It broke his heart and he went back upstairs to his study, threw himself down on the floor and wept for his lack of love for Jesus. Here he was, a settled pastor preparing a sermon on the Holy Spirit to preach to a bunch of ministers and Jesus wasn't wonderful to him.

Oh friends, how easy it is to become distracted with our service to the King, to the neglect of the King. Jesus wants us in a red-hot relationship all the time. We must do everything we can to maintain the embers on the altars of our hearts so that we do not grow cold in our affections to Him. Let me ask you a question right now, Is Jesus wonderful to you today? Is your love for Him as deep as it was when you first came to know Him, or have you become like the Christians in Ephesus who have left their first love?

Notice in our text in Revelation that Jesus tells his church in Ephesus to, *"Remember therefore from whence thou art fallen, and repent."* To fall out of love with someone is a terrible thing. When a marriage begins to fall apart, it's usually because one of the partners has begun to grow cold towards the other in their affections. And soon they forget what it was that even attracted them to that person in the first place. When they were first dating, they couldn't wait to get into the other person's presence and be with them. But now their love has grown cold toward that person who was once held dear.

ISN'T JESUS WONDERFUL!

Do we not do the same to Jesus? We tell Him, "Look, Lord, I'm just too busy to spend time with you right now. This ministry project is consuming me and I'm on a deadline. I'll spend more time with you tomorrow." But tomorrow comes and we're still too busy to walk in the garden with Him. Remember that old hymn, "In the Garden"?

> I come to the garden alone,
> While the dew is still on the roses ...
>
> And He walks with me,
> And He talks with me,
> And He tells me I am His own;
> And the joy we share as we tarry there ...

You know, we're just too busy for Him today. We don't have time for Him because we're too busy serving Him. Jesus said to his disciples, *"Abide in me, and I in you"* (John 15:4). That word "abide" in the Greek is "meno." It means to dwell, to linger, to spend time with Jesus. But we're too busy for that.

I am reminded of a story I heard about Billy Graham. Mordecai Ham was the evangelist who led Billy Graham to the Lord. And eventually the two evangelists became friends. One day, Billy Graham went to visit Mordecai Ham to ask his advice about ministry. Billy said, "Mordecai, what advice can you give me?" Mordecai Ham looked him in the eye and replied, "Billy, don't ever lose your sweetheart love for Jesus."

Let me ask you, have you lost your sweetheart love for Jesus? Is He your sweetheart right now? If not, what has come between you and Him? Has your love for Him grown cold through the lack of a vital daily quiet time with Him? Are we just too busy to spend time with Him? Are we like Martha who was preoccupied with many things when we should be more like Mary who sat at the feet of Jesus and was mindful of the one thing needful?

Remember this, both service and worship are necessary but they must have their proper order. Worship must precede service. Also, our affections can grow cold toward Jesus through discouragements or disappointments. We can allow our hearts to harden from someone who has hurt our feelings and this may affect our love for Christ. Even disappointments in ministry can make our hearts grow cold towards Jesus if we're not careful. We must take everything to Him. Peter tells us: *"Casting all your care upon him; for he careth for you"* (1 Peter 5:7).

We just don't believe that Jesus really wants to spend time with us, but He does. He looks forward to spending time with us. It is like the story about the boy and his dog. You see, this boy had a bird dog that just loved being with him. It was summertime, and every day as that boy got up, he would go out to the porch of his family's farm and there that dog would be waiting for him. They would run together through the fields, or the boy would jump on his bike and the dog would playfully run beside him. Every day, as that boy got up, there that dog would be sitting on the front porch wagging his tail ready to spend the day with his favorite master. But, one day, the boy met a girl who lived on a neighboring farm and when the boy got up in the morning, he couldn't wait to go visit that pretty red-headed girl. He would get annoyed at that dog if it tried to tag along with him. Finally, in anger he threw a stick at that dog one day and told it to scoot. The dog hung its head and backed away. The boy no longer needed his faithful friend. Another had captured his heart and affections.

How is it with you and your faithful Friend? Has another captured your heart? Jesus waits every day for you to spend time with Him. He actually looks forward to it. He is waiting for you now. He misses you. Listen, all Jesus wants from us is us. He wants you. He loves you so much He hung on a cross and died for you. Why has your love for Him grown cold? What has come between you and God? Has your turn signal been on for a while, signaling the fact that you have turned away from God and your affections for Him?

Notice from this passage in Revelation that Jesus states three things we must do if we find ourselves in this cold-hearted position. First, we are to remember from where we have fallen. At what point did our sweetheart love for Jesus begin to wane? We are to recall how it used to be between us and Jesus. Remember the early love we had for Him for saving us? We are to go back and not only recapture that love, but each day stoke it like a fire and make sure the fire never goes out again.

Next, Jesus says we are to repent in brokenness over our lovelessness towards Him. The next thing we must do is go back and do the first works. Do the things that kept us in a red-hot love relationship with Jesus. Keep a regular daily quiet time. Live in obedience to Him and spend time in His presence getting on our heart what is on His heart. Spend more time on our knees and in our Bibles. We are commanded to do the first works.

Then, Jesus issues a warning for those who do not comply and who remain in this loveless state. He says, *"Or else I will come unto thee quickly, and will remove thy candlestick."* He will set us aside. Instead of being useful to Him, we are useless to Him until we are willing to comply with those things which He has mentioned. I know some pastors who have let their ministries steal their love from Jesus and Jesus has set them aside. Oh, they still have a church and people still come, but there is no power there. They are like Samson who awoke out of his sleep and said, *"I will go out as at other times before, and shake myself. And he wist not that the LORD was departed from him"* (Judges 16:20). I know men in pulpits who are relying on their personalities to keep a crowd because they no longer have power from on high. So things are substituted to make up for the lack. They may have crowds attending their ministries but they have no power. Their turn signal is blinking and they don't even know it.

And I know churches that have moved away from the heart of God and have not retained a vital love relationship with Jesus through brokenness and humility. Their pride has crippled their usefulness to reaching the lost in their community. Jesus has removed their candlestick. Their doors are open, but on top of their building is a blinking turn signal that advertises the fact that the glory has departed and they are completely unaware of it.

Lord, help us! When will we awaken and realize how far we have moved away from God? When I think of walking with God, my mind goes to Enoch and how he walked with God, how God was pleased with him. God enjoyed walking with Enoch so much He translated him to glory so they could continue their uninterrupted fellowship.

Listen, friends, I can hear a man preach and within ten minutes tell you if he has a close walk with God or not. And I can listen to a man pray and tell you within two minutes whether he has a close walk with God. We're only as good as our walk with God. That is the one thing in life you cannot fake. You cannot fake a walk with God. You're only fooling yourself.

Let me share an incident which happened to me and it illustrates why we need to maintain a close walk with God every day through a vital love relationship with Him. I was at a week-long conference and every day was a spiritual high. I was busy in the Lord day and night and enjoying those mountain top experiences. But what usually follows a mountain top? A valley of despair. At the end of this particular conference, I had to be at my office early the next morning and I rushed my daily quiet time. I did not meet God that morning because I was in a hurry. And while I was in my office that day, I sinned. On my drive home, tears streamed down my face as I cried out to God, "O Lord, how could I sin like that after the week I just had with you? How could I do that?" Then a certain passage of Scripture was brought to my mind from Exodus 16, where the Israelites had manna to eat, but when some of the people stored up the manna, when they hoarded it for the next day, it grew worms and stank. As I pondered that passage a voice spoke to my heart. Not an audible voice but that still, small voice which speaks to the believer. You know of what I speak. Anyway, I heard God telling me the following, "You cannot live today on yesterday's experience of me. You must come to me fresh every day for your portion." And that is so true. God wants us to stay in a red-hot love relationship with Him. We must spend quality time with Him every day, seeking His face and hearing His voice.

But there is a cost to staying in a close walk with God. My late mentor Stephen Olford used to say, "What costs counts and what counts costs." But we don't want to pay the price and that is why we lack power. God wants us to stay hot on His trail and hear His voice so we can join Him in His work. God does not want us to slow down and go easy like D. L. Moody almost made the mistake of doing.

When the evangelist D. L. Moody reached the age of 50, he developed heart trouble. This was confirmed by a leading physician in London where he was preaching at the time. He took the doctor's orders to slow down and before embarking for America, he sent a cable to his friend in Chicago, R. A. Torrey. He informed Dr. Torrey that he had decided to cancel his fall campaign on the advice of his physician. And he ordered Torrey to make the necessary cancellations to the fall meetings at the upcoming World's Fair in Chicago. On his way back to America, the ship he was on began to sink. His teenage son, Will, was on board with him and this added to his concern. At one point in the dark night as the ship was sinking, the captain informed the passengers all they could do was to await their doom. All hope seemed to be gone. Moody went below deck to pray in his cabin. Miraculously the ship just faltered for a few days at sea until another vessel came to its rescue.

The key here is, listen to what went on in Moody's cabin as he wrestled with God that dark, terrible night. During the long hours Moody wrestled with his soul. He heard, as it were, the voice of His Lord. "Were you ready to let up, to go slow? Then I will take you to myself. You are of no use to me unless you are on the out-and-out." Moody said of this incident, "No one knows what I passed through as I thought that my work was finished and that I should never again have the privilege of preaching the gospel of the Son of God. And on that dark night, the first night of the accident, I made a vow that if God would spare my life and bring me back to America, the World's Fair campaign should be undertaken with all the power that He would give me." From that point on, Moody signed his name "D. L. Moody OO." Once a British minister asked him, "Mr. Moody, I sign my name D. D. for

Doctor of Divinity. But why do you sign your name OO?" Moody smiled and replied, "I am D. L. Moody, OO—out-and-out for Him."

That is how God wants us to be, on the out-and-out for Him, constantly pursuing Him in a red-hot love relationship with Jesus, the lover of our souls. We need to be on the out-and-out for Him. God uses those individuals who are on the full stretch for God. Look at the men and women in history who God has used—each shared a common denominator. They were each on the out-and-out for Jesus Christ.

Listen, the apostle Paul, Luther, Wesley, Whitefield, Knox, Edwards, Spurgeon, and Moody each shared a common denominator of fire in their belly. They were each so eaten up with the gospel, thirsty for Christ, and filled with the Holy Ghost, that they could not stand idly by while others perished. They saw nothing but eternity, worshipped a holy God, and served a risen Christ. Living not for earth or its gains, but living only for heaven and its rewards. When they preached, they linked the devil with sin and the cross with salvation. They preached hell and its fire and Christ and Him crucified. Not one of them feared king, queen or pope. And not one of them sought the compliments of men.

We have an admonition of Scripture to *"occupy till I come"* (Luke 19:13) and be proactive for Christ. So we need to remain in a close love relationship with Jesus and every day receive our marching orders from Him. To fail to do this is to risk being sidelined or to have our candlestick removed for our disobedience in not loving Him enough. He gave His all for us. We should give our all for Him.

I believe the real reason why we sometimes leave our first love is that we have lost the wonder of what He has done for us by redeeming us. The agony of the cross no longer brings tears to our eyes. We no longer weep over the lost and perishing. We have lost sight of how God was in Christ reconciling the world to Himself. We fail to ponder over the fact that Jesus hung on a bloody tree and the nails in His hands and feet which fastened Him to that cross were hammered into innocent flesh because of our rotten sins. He bore the penalty of sin as our substitute and suffered the scandals of the cross on our behalf. And as we peer into the heart of the Father, as He turned His face away from His beloved Son because He could not look on sin, we see just how much our salvation cost. It cost everything.

Oh friends, if we could only recapture the wonder of what Christ has done for us it would drive us to our knees in brokenness and repentance. You see, our trouble is that we just don't love Him enough. Pray that God will grant you the necessary grace to recapture your sweetheart love for Jesus because He is wonderful. He is always wonderful. Isn't Jesus wonderful? Is He wonderful to you?

CHAPTER 21: THE ROOT OF SIN

Bible Text: Luke 3:7-9
Preached On: Tuesday, August 6, 2013

Let me precede this message with a warning. It is greatly important how you listen to this message as Satan does not want you to hear this.

A minister's job is twofold when it comes to preaching. Preaching should afflict the comfortable, and comfort the afflicted. This message should bring comfort in the sense that it will help you better understand why you sin and hopefully help you to mortify the sins of the flesh. My message today is entitled "The Root of Sin," for when John the Baptist came preaching, he preached nice little messages that didn't disturb anybody. Oh, I'm sorry, I got him confused with preachers of our day. No, John the Baptist preached such disturbing messages that it cost him his head.

Listen to his remarks taken from the gospel of Luke in chapter 3, verses 7-9: *"Then said he to the multitude that came forth to be baptized of him, O generation of vipers, who hath warned you to flee from the wrath to come?"*

Now, that is "felt need" preaching, isn't it? He calls them vipers and warns them to flee from the wrath to come. Then he says:

> *Bring forth therefore fruits worthy of repentance, and begin not to say within yourselves, We have Abraham to our father: for I say unto you, That God is able of these stones to raise up children unto Abraham. And now also the axe is laid unto the root of the trees: every tree therefore which bringeth not forth good fruit is hewn down, and cast into the fire.*

Now listen, friends, we are going to address this aspect of taking an axe to the root of the tree and I'm going to dig up and uncover the root of sin in our lives. How can you be a Christian and sin? How can you in the morning have a quiet time with the Lord and in the afternoon on the same day fall into sin? Why is your life at times like an elevator where one day you are on the top floor in the penthouse suite of victory and the next day you are down in the basement of despair? Why does the same sin seem to plague you? Are you not saved? Are you saved? What is going on in your life when sin breaks out violently and takes you by force? We know, that as believers, Jesus came to save us from our sins. We also know that in the work of redemption, Christ paid our sin debt on Calvary and set us free from not only the penalty of sin, but from the power of sin. If that is true, which it certainly is, then why do we still sin?

Hopefully, this examination today will be of some help to you. You will need to take out a piece of paper and a pen or you can write this in the margin of your Bibles, whichever is more convenient for you. We are going to write out an acrostic using the word "sin," for we are going to break down sin today and get to the root of it so we can root it out, root it out of our lives. Are you ready with your pen and paper?

Now, write the word "sin" vertically in the form of an acrostic leaving ample room alongside each letter and leave space between each letter for notes. So, on a piece of paper you should have a capital S with a blank space, then beneath that a capital I with a blank space beside it, then beneath that a capital N with a blank space beside that. Are you with me?

We're going to get to the root of why we sin, for a true Christian is no longer under the dominion of sin. He's been placed in a different kingdom with a different ruler, King Jesus. Yet the influence of sin still is at war with our spirit, and it'll be that way until we go to glory and enter our state of glorification whereby we are finally free from the presence of sin. But until then, we are being sanctified by the Holy Spirit to mortify our sinful deeds of the body and to put them to death via the cross as seen in Galatians 2:20. *"I am crucified with Christ: nevertheless I live; yet not I, but Christ liveth in me: and the life which I now live in the flesh I live by the faith of the Son of God, who loved me, and gave himself for me."*

Let me ask you, how many messages have you heard this year on the cross in the life of the believer? Probably not very many because if you speak on that theme you will have to address the ugly topic of sin head on, and few wish to do it.

Well, let's look at your acrostic which you wrote down on your piece of paper. Beside the letter S write the word "satisfaction." Now, listen closely, if you look hard enough and are willing to examine yourself under the searching spotlight of the Holy Spirit, you will often find that the sin you struggle with has a much deeper root than appears on the surface. If we fail to properly examine ourselves after we sin, with the express purpose to avoid that sin in the future, then we will merely confess that sin over and over again without ever truly turning from it with true repentance and with a proper understanding of why we did it.

You see, the reason I had you write that word "satisfaction" alongside the letter S is because when we sin, we are telling Jesus that we are not satisfied in

THE ROOT OF SIN

Him. We sin because we do not have satisfaction in Him for all things in our life. We sin because, somehow, we have become dissatisfied with Him. Perhaps our dissatisfaction with God lies in the fact that the promise that God previously gave us, through his written Word, is not being answered. It's not coming true as you planned. God is not fulfilling that promise right now in your life and you are both impatient and unbelieving. You are not waiting God's time for Him to answer that prayer or promise, and your faith is failing in this regard. You do not doubt His ability to answer that prayer, but you are doubting His desire to answer it, even though He's already spoken to you through His holy Word.

The breakdown is not with God but with you, so you rebel and sin and your actions tell God you are not finding total satisfaction in Him. You are looking to another to satisfy you and to gratify you right now. Perhaps you have a wayward child and you feel God is not answering your prayers for that child to be saved. Perhaps it is a health issue and you find no relief. Perhaps it is a financial crisis that is pressing you into despair and seemingly there is no way out but down. Perhaps you are a pastor who is troubled by a deacon or member of your congregation and every time you see that person you seethe with anger. Perhaps your present sin problem is directly related to your unforgiving heart. You have a root of bitterness toward another and you literally cannot stand the sight of them any longer.

When we sin, we are telling God that our satisfaction is no longer in Him, that we are not satisfied in Him or with Him. Eve ate the fruit of the tree and gave it to her husband, Adam, to eat, and they both fell in monumental sin because they said in their minds and heart that God wasn't enough. Even though they were in paradise and in His very presence, still He wasn't enough. They wanted more; they just weren't satisfied with Him.

Often when we sin, we just confess that particular sin that we are struggling with and it keeps coming back to haunt us time and time again. Oh, it may be several months before it raises its ugly head and manifests itself in our conduct and lives, and we weep and cry and say, "Oh God, how did I do that again? Why did I lose my temper like that? Why did I fall into that grievous sin again?" And we confess the sin but fail to go deeper and search for the root of why we are sinning. The sin itself is just an outward thing or a response on our part to a temptation. We must go deeper to locate the real reason why we sin. Then, do as John the Baptist urges, and take an axe to the root of the tree, so that we will be better equipped spiritually next time to see the danger ahead of time and ask the Holy Spirit's aide in mortifying that sin in our lives.

Satan loves to see you sin. It makes you appear that you are still his captive. It allows him to have further access to you. Sin allows Satan to accuse you before God, for he is the accuser of the brethren. Satan wants you to sin because it sidelines you from Christian service, like an athlete who is benched and kept from playing the game. Satan wants to ruin your testimony for God and ruin your witness for Christ. He wants to rip you and tear you and devour you with sin. That is his weapon of choice. But as we put on the armor of God, as found in Ephesians 6, we learn about Satan's devices and how to fight the battles against him in our earthly bodies while we live here on earth.

But we must get to the root of our sin and dig it up and burn it, so to speak, as rotten wood is dug up and burned. So, remember this, when we sin, we are telling God that we are not satisfied in Him. We are not satisfied with our current situation or circumstances, and when we do that, we can easily fall into sin. We are telling Jesus that He is not our entire satisfaction.

This is the first word of our little acrostic on sin. Our satisfaction must be in Christ Jesus and not our present circumstance. Now, alongside the next letter, the letter I, write the words "I will." In the book of Isaiah it pictures Satan in rebellion to God. It is found in the passage of chapter 14 beginning in verse 12. I want us to listen to these five instances of Satan rebelling against God with his defiance of "I will." Listen:

> *How art thou fallen from heaven, O Lucifer, son of the morning! how art thou cut down to the ground, which didst weaken the nations! For thou hast said in thine heart, I will ascend into heaven, I will exalt my throne above the stars of God: I will sit also upon the mount of the congregation, in the sides of the north: I will ascend above the heights of the clouds; I will be like the most High. Yet thou shalt be brought down to hell, to the sides of the pit.*

And I say to that a big Amen. But notice here we have the five "I wills" of Satan. He will ascend above God for he is not subject to God any longer. He says, "I will do as I will." And when we sin, we are doing the same. We are saying to God, "God, get out of the way. I will have it my way." For also in the book of Isaiah we read, *"All we like sheep have gone astray; we have turned every one to his own way"* (53:6).

You see, sin is going our way when we know it isn't God's way. It is putting our will above His will for us. We are, in essence, shouting at the top of our voice to God, "I will have it my way!" That is outright rebellion. Your problem isn't just

THE ROOT OF SIN

your rotten sin, it's your stinking will. So we sin when we are not satisfied in Jesus, when we exalt ourselves above God and we turn our own way over His way for us. That is sin.

The last letter of our acrostic is found next the letter N. Beside the letter N, write the word "neglect." Sin is a neglect of another thing. Sin is a neglect of a duty. Sin is a neglect of time with God and humility in prayer. Sin is a neglect of witnessing to the lost. Sin is a neglect of reading the Word of God because we like our football games and basketball games and entertainments over the things of God. Neglect of God is sin and it eventually will break out in some gross sin, either through your disposition, your temper, or your lust. When we neglect our time with God a vacuum is created, and that vacuum will be filled with something other than God, and it will more than likely turn to sin.

One of the greatest dangers of a Christian is to not be thankful to God or neglect to be thankful to God for mercies received and graces given. It is a grievous sin to God, and this sin uncovered and unearthed will eventually break out in sins of passion and gross sins. Neglect may be your biggest fault right now. Neglect of God and neglect of His will in your life. Neglect of obedience to what He has revealed to you and said to you.

Listen, I was having lunch with a businessman whose career was up and down, usually more down than up, and I asked him what he did before he got into that line of business. Suddenly he looked sad and confessed to me that God had previously called him into the ministry as a young man but he did not want to be poor, so he chose a profession where he could make money. His neglect of what God wanted for him was disaster in his life. He eventually was fired even from this job.

I was discipling a man who was having marital problems. His life at that time was utter chaos. He was successful in business but his marriage was a failure. It was falling apart. I probed him and asked him what he originally did before he got into that career. His face fell when he told me he had been a pastor but he quit the ministry because he needed more money. He wanted money over being a pastor. Neglect of what God had for him in life had put him on a road of family ruin.

Neglect is sin. Let me ask you a question, has God called you to the mission field and you didn't go? Has God called you repeatedly into full-time ministry and you still haven't surrendered? Has God told you to do something and you have neglected to do it and you wonder why you fall so readily into sin?

I repeat, the root of sin must be unearthed. It must be dug up and examined under the light of the Holy Spirit and the Son of Righteousness. You will stand amazed at the difference in your life if you will only heed this warning, for if we look deep enough into our behavior, especially our sinful behavior, we will often find one or more of these three things in our little acrostic today.

S is for satisfaction.

I is for "I will."

N is for neglect.

For you see, dear friend, sin is all three of these. When we are dissatisfied with our life and circumstance that God has sovereignly placed us in, when we are dissatisfied with our unanswered prayers or not realized promises from God, then we tell God, "I will find satisfaction in another." So we sin.

When we exalt ourselves and say, "I will do this thing over God's will. I will even do this though I know it is not God's will for me to do this. I'm going to do it anyway." That's grievous sin.

When we neglect to visit a widow or give to missions, neglect our duties that God has called us to do, we sin. And worst of all, when we neglect God Himself by replacing Him with the things of this world, then we fill up our lives with superficial things that give no real lasting satisfaction because only Jesus satisfies. Only Jesus satisfies.

Get to the root of your sin problem and you will make great progress in your sanctification. Listen to God's voice from the book of Isaiah which declares:

> *For thy Maker is thine husband; the LORD of hosts is his name; and thy Redeemer the Holy One of Israel; The God of the whole earth shall he be called. For the LORD hath called thee as a woman forsaken and grieved in spirit, and a wife of youth, when thou wast refused, saith thy God. For a small moment have I forsaken thee; but with great mercies will I gather thee. In a little wrath I hid my face from thee for a moment; but with everlasting kindness will I have mercy on thee, saith the LORD thy Redeemer.* (54:5-8)

That, friends, is the kind of God we serve. All glory to His holy name.

CHAPTER 22: AMERICAN CHURCH BUFFET

Bible Text: Hosea 4:17
Preached On: Friday, August 16, 2013

When somebody is searching for a church today, they usually ask the following questions to the church secretary or pastor: Do you have a youth program? How many ball fields do you have? Do you have a fitness center and does it have basketball courts? Do you have a contemporary music program at your church and a good worship band? Do you have recovery groups for the divorced and drug-dependent? Do you have yoga classes? Do you have Zumba dance classes? In other words, a typical American family looking for a typical American church today approaches it like they do a buffet line in a restaurant with a smorgasbord of choices. In essence, they are saying, "Before I join your church, let me see a menu and look over it to see if you can service my family the way I want you to."

So, for the last several decades, the American church has bowed to consumer demand and has provided all the above-mentioned delicacies to attract new members over their competition. We have become the American Church Buffet to the point where if the consumer says they want a yoga class, we give it to them, for if we don't, they may leave and go to another church that offers it. The American church has become a fitness center, sports complex, house of entertainment. After all, Jesus said, "My house should be a house of entertainment." Isn't that what he said? That's what we think he said. That's what we pattern our churches after.

I wonder what Jesus would say to the typical American church today. Would he stand on the outside of it and declare, *"It is written, My house shall be called the house of prayer; but ye have made it a den of thieves"* (Matthew 21:13). Listen, friends, selling out to the world is spiritual whoredom. Listen to how God views his people when they depart from Him and fall into spiritual whoredom. Listen to this from the book of Hosea, *"And the LORD said to Hosea, Go, take unto thee a wife of whoredoms and children of whoredoms: for the land hath committed great whoredom, departing from the LORD"* (1:2).

You see, much of the American church has sold itself to the world by bringing in the idols of yoga (which is Eastern philosophy), Zumba dancing (which is erotic gyrations), and worldly entertainment (which is spiritual harlotry).

Listen to how the Jews departed from the living God as seen in Hosea 4, beginning in verse 9:

> *And there shall be, like people, like priest: and I will punish them for their ways, and reward them their doings. For they shall eat, and not have enough: they shall commit whoredom, and shall not increase: because they have left off to take heed to the LORD. Whoredom and wine and new wine take away the heart. My people ask counsel at their stocks, and their staff declareth unto them: for the spirit of whoredoms hath caused them to err, and they have gone a whoring from under their God. They sacrifice upon the tops of the mountains, and burn incense upon the hills, under oaks and poplars and elms, because the shadow thereof is good: therefore your daughters shall commit whoredom, and your spouses shall commit adultery.*

Now, listen to what God says in verses 16-17: *"For Israel slideth back as a backsliding heifer: now the LORD will feed them as a lamb in a large place. Ephraim is joined to idols: let him alone."*

Dear friends, do you wonder why God isn't sending revival to His church in America right now? We are joined to our idols and He has left us alone. We have transformed ourselves into the American Church Buffet. We have turned our backs on God and joined ourselves to idols of this world to please the lost with an American Church Buffet that they can choose and declare for themselves. And God says to the church in America, *"Ephraim is joined to idols: let him alone."*

So we have the withdrawn presence of God as a judgment upon us for our replacing God with things of this world to attract new members to our churches. May God have mercy on us! And the sad thing is, most pastors would disagree with this message and call me and it unsound. Well, I may be unsound to them, but I will sound the alarm to awaken the church out of her spiritual lethargy and slumber and remind her of her duty to take the gospel to this generation of hell-bound sinners.

A fellow minister asked me a question last week. He asked, "Aren't you tired of dead churches?" I replied, "I can't use the word tired. The word I would use is nauseated." When I sit in churches and listen to the nonsense that is going on, I get nauseated, sick to my stomach. I just can't take it anymore. I plead with the American Church Buffet today.

AMERICAN CHURCH BUFFET

Listen, brother pastor, don't call yourself a church if you have yoga and Zumba classes. Be more transparent and just call yourself a fitness center. Listen, a pastor is a shepherd over the Lord's sheep. An Eastern shepherd is deeply familiar with the sheep in his care. At night, when the sheep are brought into the sheepfold, the shepherd examines each one carefully to see if their condition needs immediate attention. Some sheep may have had their wool torn off by a thorny branch or the skin may have a sore on it that needs oil poured on it for healing. The shepherd examines each sheep carefully and tends to its particular needs for its ongoing health and restoration.

If you are a pastor and you are not familiar with each member's spiritual condition in your church, you are a poor shepherd indeed. If you're too busy marrying and burying and you don't have the time to visit with each family member of your church and speak with them about their spiritual welfare, why should you complain when they give you trouble and fight you at every turn?

You have no business calling yourself a church if the carpet in your sanctuary isn't wet with the tears of your people, broken over their sins and the sins of the land. Don't call yourself a church if the carpet in your sanctuary isn't soaked with tears of your broken-hearted members as they pray for the lost in your community with anguished heart-cries and pleadings with the Lord for their salvation. How can you call yourself a church if prayer is not the engine that runs your church? Is your church operated by money and man-power and not Holy Ghost power? If that is the case, your lack of prayer is an indictment against you. Jesus said, *"My house shall be called the house of prayer."* Does your church have a regular weekly prayer meeting that truly lays hold of God in desperate agonizing prayer? If your church is not a house of prayer from God's perspective, then why meet at all?

Don't call yourself a church if you don't have an outreach program to the lost in your community. This generation doesn't need to hear the doctrine of election, they need to hear their duty of repentance. We were never meant to have a come-and-hear gospel but a go-and-tell gospel. Whatever happened to knocking on doors and sharing our faith? We're too afraid of making a false convert, so we don't tell anybody about Jesus except our regular church members. Rather, in the gospel of Luke we have this command, *"And the lord said unto the servant, Go out into the highways and hedges, and compel them to come in, that my house may be filled"* (Luke 14:23). Are we doing it?

And we wonder why people are leaving the churches in droves and not coming back. We became the world and people are sick of this world. It doesn't satisfy, so they are sick of the worldly church. It is high time that we get serious with God and go to our knees in repentance and seek His face and forsake our ways. Judgment must begin at the house of God. Instead of our churches being filled with yoga classes and Zumba dancing and worldly entertainment, let us humbly return to the Lord and flood our sanctuaries with the sighs and heart-cries of broken-hearted, repentant people who have turned back to God in holy desperation, pinning all their hope of deliverance upon Him.

We must turn back to the living God of the Bible and preach a pure message of the gospel that isn't politically correct or afraid to offend man. We must have boldness and courage to preach the full counsel of God which speaks of ruin, redemption, repentance, and regeneration. The gospel of the Son of God calls sin "black" and hell "hot." It warns men to flee from the wrath to come through their duty of immediate repentance and faith.

The gospel of the Son of God speaks of a broken law and a curse and an offended God. The gospel declares that man is a sinner by nature and one who stands in need of being reconciled back to a holy God. The gospel speaks of a bloody cross and the Savior who shed His precious blood for sinful man as a substitute for sin and who died and rose again and reigns in glory.

Listen, friends, Christianity differs from other religions. Buddha lived, died, and was buried. Confucius lived, died, and was buried. Mohammed lived, died, and was buried. Jesus lived, died, and was buried, but He rose again. We serve a risen Lord. Christianity was never built on a coffin lid.

Let us forsake the American Church Buffet and let Christianity in America be what it was always meant to be, counter-cultural. Let us have a counter-cultural revolution within the churches of this land and get on our knees and get back to God. God told his rebellious people, *"And I will stretch over Jerusalem the line of Samaria, and the plummet of the house of Ahab: and I will wipe Jerusalem as a man wipeth a dish, wiping it, and turning it upside down"* (2 Kings 21:13).

Oh friends, let us go to our knees as a church and beg God to spare us from being wiped as a dish by His hand of judgment.

Let us pray. *O Great God, forgive us for our wicked ways. Forgive us for turning aside from thee. Forgive us for replacing thee with the idols of this world. Forgive us for our spiritual harlotry and whoredom. Give us the grace, I pray O Lord, give us the grace of repentance to bring us to our knees in mercy rather than bringing us to our knees in judgment like you would wipe a dish and turn it over in disgust. Separate us from our idols, I pray. Purify our hearts. Open our eyes to behold your majesty. For if we could only catch a glimpse of thee, we would see our own rotten hearts for what they are.*

Great God of glory, hear our prayer. Come down and visit this vine once again in a spiritual awakening as you have done in former times in this once great land of ours. Purge thy church of its impurities. Cleanse your people and prepare your bride for the marriage supper of the Lamb. Help us, Lord Jesus, to be candles burning brightly in these dark, sin-soaked days of apostasy. Help us, O Lord, to be on fire for you in a red-hot love relationship with you.

O God, hear this prayer as it ascends to thy throne room and answer it with a mighty outpouring of your grace rather than an outpouring of your wrath upon your disobedient people. Have mercy, I pray.

CHAPTER 23: THE LEGEND OF THE KING'S SWORD

Bible Text: Jeremiah 6:16
Preached On: Thursday, July 18, 2013

Allow me to tell you a story about the Legend of the King's Sword. It is found in my biography on Asahel Nettleton.

> There was a legend about a magical sword used by an old English king. It seems that whenever the king used this particular sword, he experienced success and victory on the battlefield. His enemies learned to fear the king's sword. Eventually, the king grew old and feeble and an adversary of the king began to spread a rumor around the village that the king's sword no longer possessed supernatural powers, that it was now just an average, ordinary sword of little use to its owner. This story began to spread among the peasants until the entire village believed that the king's sword was now impotent.
>
> As the king's heir to the throne matured, he too grew up believing the story about the sword's uselessness and ordered the royal blacksmith to forge him a new sword, a handsome, shiny, engraved sword with jewels, much more beautiful to behold than his father's old sword. This was done. One day, an enemy force attacked the castle village and fell upon the inhabitants, killing and maiming many. The enemy then laid siege to the castle. The young prince grabbed his new bejeweled sword and went forth to defend his kingdom, but to no avail. Rather than defeating his enemy, he was captured. In fact, the entire village of the royal family was now under bondage to this evil enemy.
>
> Time passed and the villagers groaned beneath the oppressive bondage of the evil power. But there was nothing they could do but suffer. Eventually, the old king died and his son, the prince, could not assume the throne because he was still a captive of this evil entity. The entire village groaned and lamented as they served their oppressive and evil new ruler.
>
> During this time, a nephew of the king grew to maturity and one day this lad called on the prince of the castle. The guards allowed

the fair-haired, harmless looking youth entry since he was royalty. The prince was held captive in a chamber with a guard at the door. When the lad was allowed to visit the prince, he asked him where the old sword was that once belonged to the king. The prince pointed to a large cedar chest by the barred window. The chest was opened and there, wrapped in an old blanket, was the leather scabbard which held the king's sword. The lad asked if he could have the sword as a memento of his uncle, the king. The prince nodded yes, telling the lad that it was just an old, worthless sword, of little use today.

The lad left the castle with the sword wrapped in the old blanket. Upon arriving at his part of the village, he stopped by the barber shop to get a haircut. The barber was one of the ancient men of the town. As the old barber cut the lad's locks, he inquired about the bundle by the lad's feet. The lad told the barber about the sword. When the old man heard this, his eyes lit up and his stooped shoulders straightened. He then proceeded to tell the lad about all the powers that the sword formerly possessed. The lad was curious and as he left the barber shop, he visited an old baker. He asked the elderly baker to verify the story of the magical sword. "Oh yes," said the baker, "I was an eye witness to the king's victories with that sword, for I used to be the royal baker until the enemy captured the castle and placed us all in bondage." The baker turned away. His eyes were full of sadness.

The lad left the baker and went home. In his little hovel, he unwrapped the blanket and pulled the old sword from the worn leather scabbard. Though it was large and double-edged, the sword seemed just an ordinary sword. In fact, it was almost too heavy to wield properly. The lad lay down on a mat on the straw floor and fell asleep next to the sword. The lad dreamed of being a king. He dreamed he was king and fighting a battle with the sword. The enemy fled from the lad in fear. Was it the magical sword?

He awoke to sunlight pouring in from a hole in his thatched roof. The lad grabbed the sword. Lifting it up with both hands, he exclaimed, "It must be true." With a new faith, he rushed from his hovel and the first enemy soldier he encountered, he brandished the sword and attacked. The enemy fell down dead. Soon, another enemy was upon the lad, but, brandishing the sword again, he experienced victory. Finally, a troop of enemies fell upon the lad, but the sword saved him once more. There were now eye-witnesses to these events and soon word spread among the villagers that the king's old sword was once again magical.

Word got to the evil ruler at the castle and he personally led his largest band of soldiers to go out and attack the lad. All the lad had to do was to brandish the sword and the enemy fell before him. The lad was a hero. He and the sword set the captives free. The lad was made the new king. The prince was so bewildered and jealous that he killed himself by falling upon his bejeweled sword. From that day on, there was peace in the valley of the king.

Listen, friends, the church has failed with its new swords and methodologies. It is time to seek the old paths once again. In the book of Jeremiah, we read, *"Thus saith the LORD, Stand ye in the ways, and see, and ask for the old paths, where is the good way, and walk therein, and ye shall find rest for your souls"* (6:16). The old paths have weapons that have proven themselves to be mighty weapons against the dark kingdoms of this world. These weapons were used in olden days by men like Jonathan Edwards and George Whitefield, Asahel Nettleton and Charles Spurgeon. What were these weapons so mightily used in revival and spiritual awakenings? They are the sword of the Spirit and the great doctrines of the gospel.

These men were mighty men because they were anointed with the Spirit of God, and they preached doctrinally sound sermons which drove the truth of God into the very heart and conscience of man. Their sword was one of total depravity and utter ruin for mankind; that man was a rebel against a most high God; that man was a guilty sinner who deserved the punishments of an eternal hell and the only way to be reconciled back to a holy God was found at the foot of a bloody cross; that the law of God was severe and strict and all mankind would be judged against the utter strictness and severity of the law of God. All men would fail that test because all of mankind are sinners who need a sin substitute in the person of Jesus Christ. The sword of repentance was greatly used by these men. It cut down its hearers, and then made them tremble before a just and holy God. It declared that it was man's duty to exercise repentance towards God and faith in Jesus Christ, and if he failed to do that, he was justly condemned to a burning hell for all eternity because man, by his very nature, is an enemy of God. God is ready to cut a wicked sinner down with the sword of justice, and man's only hope is in the merit of Christ Jesus.

George Whitefield's great cry was, "Ye must be born again," and he shook two continents for God. The great doctrine of regeneration has fallen into disuse and this particular sword is a mighty one if wielded properly.

Men like Edwards and Whitefield knew how to tread the old paths. They knew full well that a sinner had to be awakened before he could be converted. Their preaching was aimed at the very heart and conscience, to awaken men to their lost and ruined condition, and then show them the remedy for sin through the shed blood of the Son of God, who rose again from the dead and who now reigns in glory.

But sadly, many in our churches today know little about these great doctrines, for they have been seldom preached in our land in for years. And if they've been preached, they have lacked the necessary power attended to them, which is the Spirit of God in an anointed ministry. Few men in the pulpit today understand what is meant by an anointed ministry. Fewer still actually possess it. Most preachers get by with their education and personality, but in the gospel of Luke, John the Baptist declares, *"I indeed baptize you with water; but one mightier than I cometh, the latchet of whose shoes I am not worthy to unloose: he shall baptize you with the Holy Ghost and with fire"* (3:16).

Too many pulpits today lack fire. They lack power which comes from an anointed ministry under the control of the Holy Spirit. But mighty men of past days, like Edwards and Whitefield, Spurgeon and Nettleton, knew they could not preach without this fire. No, they did not speak in tongues, but when they preached, strong men were melted down under the influence of a holy God. When these men preached up the great doctrines of the gospel, men were struck in their conscience as if a sword had just cut them down. They wielded these great doctrines with the strong arm of the Almighty in attendance to the truths they proclaimed. God attended His preached word with such authority that every word had majesty behind it.

These men understood their Bibles and knew they were utterly helpless in proclaiming the doctrines of grace unless the Spirit of God was mighty upon them. And what was the result of their preaching? Spurgeon shook London in his generation. Edwards opened up the realities of hell in such a dramatic fashion that the people of Enfield, Connecticut, felt the heels of their shoes being warmed as he spoke as if hell itself was opening beneath them. Whitefield yielded such great power that 30,000 people would stand out in the open air in the rain to hear him preach, and it was not uncommon for some of his hearers to drop dead while he preached. Nettleton spoke with such power that when it was said he was coming to a town, men feared his preaching because his preaching bowed the hearts of men like a mighty wind would bend trees. These men saw revival because they each were under the discipline of the Holy Spirit and were holy men utterly consumed with God and eternity. They lived so others might live.

But today, when we hear these stories, they seem fanciful to us, as fanciful as the king's magical sword. We just don't believe we can have access to that kind of power today. So many teach instead of preach; many entertain their hearers with funny stories and jokes and make them laugh. We just don't believe that the old paths of the old swords still work, so we have fashioned ourselves new swords, and we are as ineffective as a child operating a nuclear submarine. There just isn't much affect at all. Death is all around us and people are staying away from church and starting house churches because they are sick and tired of the spiritual desolation within the institutional church.

Allow me to read you our passage from Jeremiah once again, for I left out the last sentence earlier. It states, *"Thus saith the LORD, Stand ye in the ways, and see, and ask for the old paths, where is the good way, and walk therein, and ye shall find rest for your souls. But they said, We will not walk therein"* (6:16). And that is the response of the church in America today. It defiantly declares, "We will not walk therein." So what is the result of the new swords in our pulpits? We have the sword of laughter, the sword of entertainment, the sword of conformity, the sword of worldliness, and death is all around us in our pulpits today. And the great tragedy is that, as a nation, we face utter destruction because of the sins of the land, and the pulpits are powerless to do anything about it. Their new bejeweled swords just don't cut the mustard, let alone slay anyone's conscience.

If the priests of the Lord won't lay hold of God, then let the people do so. Let the Average Joe go to his knees in desperate prayer and lay hold of God, that God would be pleased to send a mighty revival to his slumbering bride in the land. Let the women of the church go to their knees in holy desperation and beg God for mercy for the sins of our nation. Let the people of God turn, and forsake their sins, and repent, and seek the face of the Almighty for His manifest presence to break out in revival once again.

The institutional Church of England, in the days of Wesley and Whitefield, was so dead that God had to work outside of it. So he raised up Wesley and Whitefield and others to preach outdoors in the open air and begin a fresh movement of vital Christianity. If the institutional church in America will not rouse herself and throw off her grave clothes, then perhaps God will raise up a Wesley and Whitefield for our day to go and start something outside the institutional church for God and His kingdom.

The institutional church has become like a large ocean liner that is content to stay its course regardless of the warnings all around her. Like the Titanic, it is adrift and sinking and completely unaware of it. Because of the pride of the institutional church in America, and believing itself to be unsinkable, it will surely go down into the deepest recesses of oblivion. And as it does, a New Testament church will emerge, bursting with the remnant on fire for God, and alive with vital Christianity, of whose members it will be said, *"These that have turned the world upside down are come hither also"* (Acts 17:6).

The sword of the old paths lies in a scabbard of disuse. Perhaps a lad will come along and pick it up again and believe the God of the Bible, that He is able to once again do what He has done in former times.

CHAPTER 24: LIFEBOAT OF GRACE IN A SINKING WORLD

Bible Text: 2 Peter 3:3-9
Preached On: Thursday, August 22, 2013

I want you today to picture in your mind the planet earth. Think of the earth and its physical matter and the present world system in which we live. We are born into this world through the pain of labor. It's a struggle to survive. Life itself is full of pain and suffering, disappointments and grief. This earth is little more than a planet filled with sorrow and tears.

Let me describe what this world really is: this world is a wrecked vessel breaking up on the rocks and quickly sinking; all aboard will perish. There is a lifeboat nearby ready to lift the perishing to safety, but they ignore this lifeboat as if it did not exist at all, or they treat it with contempt and indifference, thinking their condition is not as perilous as it appears. But the ship they are on is sinking fast, worse than the Titanic, and soon it will go down, pulling everyone on board down to the lower depths. These passengers will descend to a region they never intended on entering, and that region is hell.

There is a lifeboat of grace in a sinking world but few wish to board it. The lifeboat is the gospel of the Son of God and it gives life to all who enter in. For to be without Christ in this sinking world is to be like someone in the days of Noah without an ark.

My message today is entitled "Lifeboat of Grace in a Sinking World." Our passage is found in 2 Peter 3:3-9. Allow me to read that passage to you as we begin:

> *Knowing this first, that there shall come in the last days scoffers, walking after their own lusts, And saying, Where is the promise of his coming? for since the fathers fell asleep, all things continue as they were from the beginning of the creation. For this they willingly are ignorant of, that by the word of God the heavens were of old, and the earth standing out of the water and in the water: Whereby the world that then was, being overflowed with water, perished: But the heavens and the earth, which are now, by the same word are kept in store, reserved unto fire against the day of judgment and perdition of ungodly men. But, beloved, be not ignorant of this one thing, that one day is with the Lord as a*

thousand years, and a thousand years as one day. The Lord is not slack concerning his promise, as some men count slackness; but is longsuffering to us-ward, not willing that any should perish, but that all should come to repentance.

Now let me say this, dear friends. It's later than you think both for this generation and your life. These, indeed, are the last days where scoffers are all around us, mocking God as in the days of Noah as he built the ark. They laughed at Noah and mocked such an old, foolish man who preached righteousness and warned them to flee from the wrath to come. They ridiculed him and his boat for it was obvious to anyone with any sense that there was no need for it. It had never rained like that before. The old man was just an old fool. Don't pay him any mind. And then we read in Genesis 7:10 the following five striking words, *"And it came to pass."* The text reads, *"And it came to pass after seven days, that the waters of the flood were upon the earth."* In other words, the flood came suddenly and without warning. Destruction to that generation of people came suddenly and without warning. They perished quickly as their homes and buildings began to float and then sink. The perishing scrambled to grab hold of any piece of driftwood that would float and sustain them but the torrents came down in such intensity that they were utterly and finally consumed and drowned.

God judged the former world by flood for its wickedness and sin, for God is a holy God who must punish sin. But many today don't believe in that kind of God. They just don't believe that God is a God who must punish sin. But indeed He is, and indeed He will. To ignore this fact is to be like those spoken of here in this passage of Scripture, *"For this they willingly are ignorant of."* Then it reads, *"Whereby the world that then was, being overflowed with water, perished."* You see, friend, to ignore how God deals with sin and sinful man is to be willingly ignorant, for we have the Scripture record.

The apostle Peter knew Christ personally and intimately. The apostle Peter had heard the voice of God speak audibly and with authority upon the Mount of Transfiguration. The apostle Peter knew his Bible and he knew His God and he says that in the last days, in other words, in the end times right before the second coming of Christ, there shall be scoffers walking about, mocking God, and shaking their fists in His face and declaring, *"Where is the promise of his coming?"*

The very same kind of men scoffed as they impudently passed Calvary. The gospel of Mark describes their talk on that day and the condition of their wicked hearts. Mark 15 reads, *"And they that passed by railed on him, wagging their heads, and saying, Ah, thou that destroyest the temple, and buildest it in three days,*

Save thyself, and come down from the cross" (verses 29-30). Scoffers, mockers as in the days of Noah, as in the days of Christ, are in the world right now. Right now. Men are marrying men and women are marrying women, judges are legislating laws and enforcing them against the very laws of God, shaking their angry fists in the face of God and declaring, *"Where is the promise of his coming?"*

But the apostle Peter solemnly gives a warning that to ignore how God has moved in former days in His dealings with judging sin, is to be willingly ignorant. In other words, willingly ignorant of the very nature of God and the promises of God. Then the apostle Peter issues a very solemn warning with the following words, *"But the heavens and the earth, which are now, by the same word are kept in store, reserved unto fire against the day of judgment and perdition of ungodly men."* Peter states that as the old world was consumed by floods and that generation utterly destroyed, so too the world will once again pass under the judgment of an angry God who will destroy it by fire. He even graphically describes this terrible scene for us in verse 10, *"But the day of the Lord will come as a thief in the night; in the which the heavens shall pass away with a great noise, and the elements shall melt with fervent heat, the earth also and the works that are therein shall be burned up."*

To Peter's hearers in his day, this seemed quite incomprehensible. But not to us today, who live in a nuclear world where any madman can get his hands on a nuclear weapon and start WWIII, setting off a series of nuclear explosions which would quickly and quite suddenly fulfill the promise of the Scripture in which *"the heavens shall pass away with a great noise, and the elements shall melt with fervent heat, and the earth also and the works that are therein shall be burned up."* And, may I add, burned up immediately and finally and utterly. To live in this day and age in a nuclear world and still ignore how the God of the Bible must punish sin is to be willfully ignorant, indeed.

Now, allow me to read the verse which describes the title of my message and is our focus today, verse 9. The title of my message is "Lifeboat of Grace in a Sinking World." Listen to this verse as I read it to you now: *"The Lord is not slack concerning his promise, as some men count slackness; but is longsuffering to us-ward, not willing that any should perish, but that all should come to repentance."*

A lifeboat of grace in a sinking world. The gospel speaks of a Savior who is a lifeboat to the perishing. The gospel speaks of a day of grace and the duty of repentance. The gospel speaks of a longsuffering God who is holy and who must punish sin as He has promised in His written Word. He is not slack concerning that promise, but He is a gracious and merciful, longsuffering God, who loves sinful man so deeply and so greatly that He gave His only begotten Son, to come and suffer and die for sinful man.

Listen, God so loved the world that he built a cross out of the wood of the trees that He made and allowed his Son to hang on that cross and bleed and die for sinful man. God so loved the world that he provided a lifeboat in the days of Noah before the floods came and warned that generation of wicked men to flee to the safety of that lifeboat, which was the ark, but they laughed and scoffed and drowned.

Then a gracious and merciful God sent His only dear Son into this wicked world and allowed Him to be taken by wicked men who scourged Him, and spat on Him, and nailed Him to a bloody tree with cruel mockings, contempt, and ridicule. The very ark of safety was hanging on that bloody tree, but they refused that offer and crucified the Lord of glory.

Now today, the world is perishing and dying and it mocks God as it grows in wickedness. All the while, God offers grace in the person of His dear Son and the invitation of the gospel. The world mocks and holds a longsuffering God in contempt, and it tramples the blood of His dear Son who hung there and died for sinful man. And soon, quite soon, sooner than any of us realize, the God of creation will roll up this world as a fiery garment and destroy it, and all who die apart from a saving faith in Jesus Christ, will die in their sins and be cast into hell and its everlasting burnings.

The Word of God declares, *"The wicked shall be turned into hell, and all the nations that forget God"* (Psalm 9:17). The world will be burned up by fire and all in it shall perish, and then God will declare, *"Let death seize upon them, and let them go down quick into hell: for wickedness is in their dwellings, and among them"* (Psalm 55:15).

Some of you casually listen to this message and act like Felix, who the Scriptures say, *"Felix trembled, and answered, Go thy way for this time; when I have a convenient season, I will call for thee"* (Acts 24:25). You foolishly believe you have all the time in the world, when in reality the Bible declares against you, *"For man also knoweth not his time: as the fishes that are taken in an evil net, and as the birds that are caught in the snare; so are the sons of men snared in an evil time, when it falleth suddenly upon them"* (Ecclesiastes 9:12).

We live in an evil day where you can be gunned down as you stand in line in a public place. You can be murdered and removed from this planet quite suddenly. Sudden death is all around you. You may be killed in an accident or your heart may just suddenly stop, sending you into an eternity that you are quite unprepared for.

Listen, friends, there are no second chances in hell. When you die in your sins and awake in hell, you will no longer be under the longsuffering hand of God who extended a lifeboat of grace in a sinking world, and you not only ignored it, but you held it with complete contempt. God will then hold you in contempt for all eternity as you suffer and burn under His Almighty wrath as it is poured out on you, as a mighty oven does its consuming flames.

You foolishly ignore the storm warnings all around you—that you are living in a ruined and wrecked world that is breaking up upon the rocks, and there is only one place of safety, in the person of Jesus Christ and His blood. A sudden death could suddenly remove you and where would you be? To be reproved and not to bow and submit to the King of Glory is to defy Him. *"He, that being often reproved hardeneth his neck, shall suddenly be destroyed, and that without remedy"* (Proverbs 29:1).

You that are listening to this message may be quite suddenly destroyed and you will die without remedy. The remedy for sin is Jesus Christ. Your duty of repentance is a command from a holy God. Jesus declared, *"Except ye repent, ye shall all likewise perish"* (Luke 13:3, 5). The invitations of the gospel of the Son of God are many. Here, they cry out to you now. Will you heed and submit to the claims of Christ on your life and surrender your all to Him through repentance and faith?

God lovingly declares:

> *Look unto me, and be ye saved, all the ends of the earth: for I am God, and there is none else.* (Isaiah 45:22)

> *Seek ye the LORD while he may be found, call ye upon him while he is near.* (Isaiah 55:6)

> *Let the wicked forsake his way, and the unrighteous man his thoughts: and let him return unto the LORD, and he will have mercy upon him; and to our God, for he will abundantly pardon.* (Isaiah 55:7)

> *Come unto me, all ye that labour and are heavy laden, and I will give you rest. Take my yoke upon you, and learn of me; for I am meek and lowly in heart: and ye shall find rest unto your souls. For my yoke is easy, and my burden is light.* (Matthew 11:28-30)

And the Spirit and the bride say, Come. And let him that heareth say, Come. And let him that is athirst come. And whosoever will, let him take the water of life freely. (Revelation 22:17)

Dear friend, are you hungry for God? He is the bread of life. Are you tired of your sins? Jesus is the remedy for sin. Are you thirsty for Christ? Listen to what Jesus declares, *"If any man thirst, let him come unto me, and drink. He that believeth on me, as the scripture hath said, out of his belly shall flow rivers of living water"* (John 7:37-38). Do you want the living water?

The gospel of the Son of God is for the hungry, the weary, and the thirsty. There is a lifeboat of grace in this sinking world. *"The Lord is not slack concerning his promise, as some men count slackness; but is longsuffering to us-ward, not willing that any should perish, but that all should come to repentance"* (2 Peter 3:9).

I will close this message with this promise to you from God, the living God, the God of the Bible, the God who must punish sin: Jesus declares, *"All that the Father giveth me shall come to me; and him that cometh to me I will in no wise cast out"* (John 6:37).

CHAPTER 25: TEXTUAL DECISIONISTS

Bible Text: Romans 8:9
Preached On: Tuesday, September 10, 2013

There is a cult growing in America and Great Britain today, and it is gaining prominence within major denominations. This cult is more numerous than the Jehovah's Witness and more prevalent than the Mormons. This cult has members positioned in high and influential places. Some occupy seminary chairs, some stand behind a pulpit, but the vast majority of this cult is found occupying the pews within our churches. These cult members seem to enjoy fellowship between themselves, and they are active with an outreach to their communities. They are busy doing good for others. The members of this cult are not confined to any theological grouping, for deists are as plentiful among reform circles as they are among Arminian circles. Nor are the members of this cult limited geographically, for they are prominent both in America and Great Britain. The members of this cult are not confined to a particular denomination, for they flow into each of them quite easily. The members of this cult seem to flourish in times of great spiritual declension, and this cult seems to spread like a plague when vital Christianity is at a low ebb and there is a famine in the land for hearing the Word of God preached with authority and in the power of the Holy Spirit.

The cult to which I refer is called Textual Decisionists. This is what a pastor friend of mine in Glasgow, Scotland calls them: Textual Decisionists. They are people who have entered the church through an intellectual agreement with a certain Scripture, a doctrine, or Christian ideology. At one time in their life, they made a decision to be a Christian by believing a particular Bible verse, such as John 3:16, or they agreed with the concept that Jesus died for sin and rose again. These cult members often join a church because they have believed the fact found in Scripture. They believe in the death of Christ, but their problem is, they have never believed on the Christ who died. They are Textual Decisionists. They base their salvation on a text of Scripture, or a fact found in the Bible, and they have convinced themselves that they are saved because they made a decision to accept Jesus based on that textual foundation. Their hope of heaven rests on a text rather than on a relationship.

These Textual Decisionists have never been awakened, convicted, regenerated, and indwelt by the Holy Spirit. They are best described by Romans 8:9 which declares, *"Now if any man have not the Spirit of Christ, he is none of his."* In other words, they have not the Spirit of Christ dwelling in them because they have never experienced the new birth through regeneration. They have become Christians on their own terms, and by their own means. They seem to flock together in great quantities, and encourage themselves with encouraging words of Scripture. Oh, they love to talk about the rapture of the church and how they just can't wait for Jesus to come and get them. They derive great pleasure from serving in their local church and community in the name of Jesus. They like to pray and have Bible studies, although their Bible studies often focus on a self-help book written by a contemporary Christian author. These cult members are into self-empowerment and having their tents enlarged for the kingdom of God. They are busy, busy, busy, and if you question them on the validity of their conversion, they may fight you and grow very angry with you because if you start killing somebody's gods, they will fight you for it. These cult members have several gods they serve, but they do not serve the living God of the Bible.

These Textual Decisionists claim to be followers of Christ and they rest on their duties and on their good works, but they have never seen the deceitfulness and wickedness of their own heart. They are very self-righteous individuals who like to point out the sins of society and cry against them, but they fail to pursue holiness in their own lives through surrender to the lordship of Jesus Christ. Jesus speaks of these "followers" in the gospel of John 2:23-25: *"Now when he was in Jerusalem at the passover, in the feast day, many believed in his name, when they saw the miracles which he did. But Jesus did not commit himself unto them, because he knew all men, And needed not that any should testify of man: for he knew what was in man."*

Leaders within this cult of Textual Decisionists can occupy a pulpit and compose very interesting intellectual essays to be considered. They can tell amusing stories to keep the audience interested in their message. They can take a Bible truth and wrap it with ideology and expound upon it for weeks upon weeks. The members can take notes and smile and feel they are all doing good in their advancement of the Christian character, but there is something missing among these cult members. There is no spiritual life, no supernatural activity of God among them. You can sit in their congregations and listen to the content of the sermons and these pastors/Textual Decisionists will never call sin "black" and hell "hot." They won't preach on the blood. They won't preach on the cross. They won't warn you to flee from a future judgment for all mankind. They won't warn you of your duty of repentance and the necessity of a work of grace on the heart through regeneration. It is almost impossible to come savingly to Christ under their

TEXTUAL DECISIONISTS

preaching because they do not preach what Jesus preached and the Spirit of God is absent from among them.

If you don't believe me, then go to one of their churches and sit among them and see if you hear what Jesus preached. Jesus preached on the utter necessity of regeneration: *"Marvel not that I said unto thee, Ye must be born again. The wind bloweth where it listeth, and thou hearest the sound thereof, but canst not tell whence it cometh, and whither it goeth: so is every one that is born of the Spirit"* (John 3:7-8).

Jesus preached on man's duty of repentance: *"I tell you, Nay: but, except ye repent, ye shall all likewise perish"* (Luke 13:3, 5).

Jesus preached on the fires of an everlasting hell: *"And if thine eye offend thee, pluck it out, and cast it from thee: it is better for thee to enter into life with one eye, rather than having two eyes to be cast into hell fire"* (Matthew 18:9).

Jesus preached on the cost of discipleship: *"If any man will come after me, let him deny himself, and take up his cross, and follow me. For whosoever will save his life shall lose it: and whosoever will lose his life for my sake shall find it"* (Matthew 16:24-25).

But the doctrine that these Textual Decisionists avoid the most is found in the book of Hebrews: *"Follow peace with all men, and holiness, without which no man shall see the Lord"* (Hebrews 12:14). They will not preach on holiness because the members of their cult would scream bloody murder if they did. They certainly don't want to preach any upsetting doctrine to their fellow cult members, because somebody may get up and leave and go join another cultic church and take their checkbook with them.

I repeat, these individuals have never come savingly to Christ, for they have never been awakened to their lost condition. They've never been convicted of sin by the Spirit of God. They've never been a subject of grace through the work of regeneration upon the heart, and although they claim to be Christ's, they do not possess Christ through an indwelt Holy Spirit. If you challenge them on any of this, they may grow very angry with you and call you a fanatic or a crackpot.

Whenever the church fails to carry out the mandate of the Great Commission and proactively storm the gates of hell, then a vacuum is created. A healthy church advances the true gospel of the Son of God which proclaims what Jesus proclaimed: the necessity of the new birth through regeneration and the duty of sinful man to come to repentance towards God and faith in Jesus Christ. The gospel speaks of a burning and everlasting hell and it warns men not to go there. The true gospel of the Son of God is honest with men and tells them about the cost of discipleship in following a crucified Savior. A healthy church exudes vital Christianity through its born-again believers who strive to live holy lives unto the Lord Jesus Christ. They serve God for the glory of God and not to showcase themselves or their talents.

But when the tide of vital Christianity is running at a low ebb, then their much cultic activity will abound, trying to cover itself with the garments of Christianity, like duties, and ordinances, and activity, in the name of Christ. But they are naked and unaware of their true condition because they are blind and deaf, and have not the Spirit of the living God living in them. They lack the blood-red robe of justification and the white robe of sanctification. Their Jesus is not the bloody Jesus on the cross with all His claims on their lives. No sir, their Jesus is a friendly Jesus who lets you live your life as you please as long as you are in church on Sunday, donate time and money, and rest upon a decision based on a text of Scripture and sit on a foundation that is on sinking sand.

There is a famine in the land today, friends, and it is a famine of hearing the Word of God preached in the power of the Spirit of God. *O Great God, where are the men? Where are the men who preach what You preached? Where are the preachers who call men to repentance? Where are the preachers who are honest with men and preach that man is an enemy against a sovereign King? Who still warn that sinful man must throw down his shotgun of rebellion and surrender all to King Jesus to be reconciled back to an offended God who has every right to consign sinful man to a burning hell? Where are the preachers who warn men about the strictness and severity of God's holy law, that no man is perfect, and all men will one day be held up against the strictness and severity of God's law, and all will fail that test? Where are the preachers that warn man is a sinner and needs a substitute for sin in the person of Jesus Christ, that if man stands on his own merits he will be held up against the utter strictness of that law of God and will be sentenced to an everlasting punishment for breaking that law through sin?*

Man is not a sinner because he sins, rather man sins because he is a big sinner. His heart is wicked and deceitful, and man is a rebel who lives in opposition to a holy God. We need men anointed by the Spirit of God to preach the great doctrines of God and warn men of their danger. We don't need any more intellectual essays to be considered on ideologies wrapped in a biblical truth. The days are too dark, the hour is too late, friends. We need men of action to warn men of their perilous position outside of Christ. Where are the ambassadors who call sin "black" and hell "hot" and preach up the blood and the cross on which the Prince of Glory died?

TEXTUAL DECISIONISTS

Where are the men preaching on the necessity of an act of God upon the heart through regeneration?

The days of Wesley and Whitefield were similar to our day. In the 18th century, the Church of England was apostate and ordaining unconverted men. It ordained John Wesley in 1735 and Wesley came to America as a missionary to the Indians, but the fact remained, he was, at the time, an unconverted minister of the Church of England. It was three years before he came savingly to Christ in 1738.

John Wesley eventually knew about the need for the new birth. Listen to his words that he wrote in his diary:

> In the evening I went very unwillingly to a society in Aldersgate Street, where one was reading Luther's preface to the Epistle to the Romans. About a quarter before nine, while he was describing the change which God works in the heart through faith in Christ, I felt my heart strangely warmed. I felt I did trust in Christ, Christ alone, for salvation and an assurance was given me that He had taken away my sins, even mine, and saved me from the law of sin and death.

John Wesley knew of the change which God works in the heart. Wesley's friend, George Whitefield, experienced the same change when he read a book by Henry Scougal called *The Life of God in the Soul of Man*. And George Whitefield realized that Christianity was not in the amount of works performed for God and the amount of sacrifice suffered for God or the numerous prayers offered up to God. But true Christianity occurred when a sinner was awakened to his ruined condition and through repentance and faith received Christ as Lord with all His claims and demands on a man's life, and that life was a new life because there had been a change wrought on the heart. Now, the life of God was in the soul of man through the new birth, and that was the message preached during the revival of religion of the 18th century, you must be born again.

In our day, friends, when we live in a morally bankrupt society that is growing more hostile towards God and the people of God, when we live in a day of great spiritual declension within the church through a growing cult of Textual Decisionists who know not the Spirit of God in an experiential way through saving faith, then it's time to proclaim the great doctrines that Jesus preached and that comprise the gospel of the Son of God. Surely, the message to this generation must be: *"Repent ye"* (Mark 1:15). *"Ye must be born again"* (John 3:7). Sinners must come under the saving influence of the true gospel and be awakened and convicted and regenerated and converted and indwelt by the Spirit of God.

Let me pray. *O God of glory, raise up a band of preachers to preach like that again. Raise up a band of preachers who call men to repentance and preach your blood on the cross and call sin "black" and hell "hot" and who will preach up the necessity of regeneration once again in the land. These doctrines you've blessed in former days with outpourings of your grace and revival and spiritual awakening. Raise up such an army of preachers who aren't afraid of men but who fear you. Raise up an army of preachers who are so eaten up with eternity and hungry for you, Christ Jesus, and full of the Holy Spirit, that their preaching will be like a hammer that breaks the rock in pieces. Do it, Great God, for Thy name's sake. Amen.*

CHAPTER 26: THAT BLOODY CROSS

Bible Text: Romans 5:9
Preached On: Monday, September 16, 2013

There is an incident that took place during a cruel and bloody war. A commander took an oath in the presence of his troops that he would slaughter the entire population of a certain town. When the soldiers invaded this particular town, they began to slaughter everyone they could lay their hands on. There was a man hiding in a bush, watching in horror as his fellow townspeople were put to death. He watched a number of soldiers as they broke into a house, the inmates of which they put to the sword. On leaving it, one of them dipped a cloth into a pool of blood and slashed it on the door as a token to any who might follow of what had taken place inside. As quick as his feet could carry him, the man in the bush ran away to a large house in the center of town where a number of his friends were concealed and breathlessly he told them what he had just seen. At once, it flashed upon them what to do. A goat was in the yard and immediately it was killed and its blood splashed on the door. Scarcely had they closed the door, when a band of soldiers rushed into their street, but when they came to the blood-marked door, they made no attempt to enter. The sword, so they thought, had already entered therein and performed its work. Even though many innocent people around that town were slain, all within the blood-marked door were saved.

This brings to mind the biblical account of the first Passover as given by Moses in Exodus, chapter 12, where the Lord instructed Moses to speak to the congregation of Israel saying:

> *They shall take to them every man a lamb ... Your lamb shall be without blemish ... and the whole assembly of the congregation of Israel shall kill it in the evening ... And ye shall take a bunch of hyssop, and dip it in the blood that is in the bason, and strike the lintel and the two side posts with the blood.* (verses 3, 5, 6, 22)

The children of Israel were safe in the shelter of the blood. They were in perfect safety for the Lord had said, *"When I see the blood, I will pass over you"* (verse 13).

And when I think of Christianity today and how different it is from what it was intended to be, when I hear the so-called gospel message being proclaimed in our pulpits, there is something missing, and the absence of this item is tragic.

Where, oh where, is the blood? We don't preach up the blood anymore in our land today. We have made the gospel a bloodless gospel because we never preach on sin anymore. Why, that's not politically correct. We may upset somebody if we preach on sin or mention a bloody and gory cross. Why, we may offend someone and we sure wouldn't want to do that.

But the cross on Calvary was an offense. It was a scandal. That cross on Calvary wasn't a cleaned up pristine cross, but we, today, have gotten out our mop buckets and have mopped up all the blood around that cross so it can be more presentable to man. But the fact remains, that cross was a cross of gore. It had the Savior's blood running down all over it. Ephesians tells us, *"But now in Christ Jesus ye who sometimes were far off are made nigh by the blood of Christ"* (2:13). And, again, Ephesians declares, *"In whom we have redemption through his blood"* (1:7).

Listen, friends, when you start preaching the scandal of the cross in America today, you will be an object of hatred because mankind hates that bloody cross. The crowd gathers around it and cries, *"We will not have this man to reign over us"* (Luke 19:14). So we preachers get out our mops and buckets and mop up that cross before we preach it so we won't offend anybody, and the gospel of our present hour is a bloodless gospel that can't save anybody, because when you remove the blood from the gospel, you may as well stick Jesus back in the ground and let Him stay buried in that tomb. There is no need of a resurrected Savior without the blood because the blood of Christ is what washes my sins away.

In the book of Revelation 1:5, it states, *"Unto him that loved us, and washed us from our sins in his own blood."* Did you hear that, friend? But today, a bloody cross is not a politically correct cross. We have removed the blood from our worship in our churches. We used to sing old hymns that spoke of the blood like "There is a Fountain Filled with Blood" and the other old hymn, "There is Power in the Blood." But we just don't believe that anymore, and when we preach, we wash the cross of all that gore and blood because it just isn't presentable to our modern-day crowd. Why, they just couldn't swallow it, so we dilute the gospel and clean up that cross and omit the blood, and that way, we don't have to talk about sin because man's not that bad, anyway. He doesn't need to be regenerated, he just needs to be reformed a little, cleaned up a little, so he can stay in his sins and still go to heaven. That's what we tell folks.

But that bloody cross was a scandal, because divine justice had to be satisfied. The only way to reconcile sinful man back to God was through that bloody cross. Sinful man is under the damning sentence of the law and under the wrath of God.

THAT BLOODY CROSS

The blood of Christ is the only way out. We see this in Romans, *"Much more then, being now justified by his blood, we shall be saved from wrath through him"* (5:9).

The only way to have peace with God is by the shed blood of Jesus Christ. That's what Colossians tells us, *"And, having made peace through the blood of his cross"* (1:20). And in Romans it speaks of that cross, and the Savior's red blood was all over it because of the blackness of sin—because of the blackness of your sin, friends, because of the blackness of my sin. The apostle Peter tells it like this, *"Who his own self bare our sins in his own body on the tree, that we, being dead to sins, should live unto righteousness: by whose stripes ye were healed"* (1 Peter 2:24).

Like those men in that town and like the children of Israel were safe inside that blood-marked door, we're safe behind that blood-marked door. So, you too, friend, you'll be safe from the wrath of God when by faith you come and stand under the shelter of that precious blood. Are you washed in the blood and born from above? Or have you become a Christian some other way? There is no other way but to come and kneel at that bloody cross and lay down your arms. Come to that bloody cross and throw down your shotgun of rebellion and turn from your sins and surrender to a King, the Lord Jesus Christ. Jesus is a risen Lord and that's where you must take Him. He sits on the right hand of God the Father and He got there by way of a bloody cross.

When the apostle Peter speaks of Jesus *"who his own self bare our sins in his own body on the tree,"* that speaks of a sacrifice for sin. Jesus was the Lamb, without blemish and without spot, who was sacrificed for us upon that cross at Calvary. His shed blood stayed the sword of divine judgment for everyone who, by faith, takes shelter in it. When the soldiers came to that blood-marked door, they kept on going and slaughtered the rest of the town, but those inside that blood-marked door were safe. In Exodus we see there was a slaughter going on in Egypt that night, and there was a great cry in Egypt, for there was not a house where there was not one dead. But the children of Israel were safe in that shelter of blood, for the Lord said, *"When I see the blood, I will pass over you."* And when God the Father sees you under the blood of His dear Son, His wrath will pass over you.

The true gospel has blood in it. O Great God, I'm thankful for that bloody cross. O Lord, Jesus, where would I be today without that bloody cross? But today's modern gospel gets out its mop bucket and cleans it all up, mops up all the gore and blood by that cross, and remains silent about the demands that Christ has on a man that comes to Him for salvation. When a man gets saved, something happens: self is dethroned and another is enthroned there, and that other is the Lord Jesus Christ.

And if you don't receive Him as Lord, you haven't received Him. That bloody cross is a scandal. It upsets wicked man because wicked man does not want to throw down his shotgun of rebellion and submit to the lordship of Jesus Christ with all His claims and rights on that man. You start preaching the lordship of Christ and repentance and a bloody cross and they will surely throw bricks at you today in America. You preach up the lordship of Jesus Christ and call sin "black" and hell "hot" and call sinful man "a rebel" and "an enemy against a holy God," and you'll have the deacons mad at you. They will be standing on the steps of the platform when you get through preaching. They'll be waiting for you and they will grab you by your ear, and escort you out the door, because American Christianity doesn't want to hear about a bloody cross because of sin. American Christianity doesn't want to hear about the demands of the lordship of Jesus Christ. No sir, they will reject you and your message.

But if you get out your mop bucket and clean up the gospel a little, and omit some offensive things, then more people can swallow it and fill our churches and pay our bills. Our churches are filled with individuals who know nothing of surrender to the lordship of Jesus Christ. They rest on a foundation of self-righteousness, and sit on the throne of their heart, and rule there, and drink iniquity like water, because they are like that verse found in the book of Proverbs which declares, *"There is a generation that are pure in their own eyes, and yet is not washed from their filthiness"* (Proverbs 30:12). They are church members in good standing but they've never been washed in the blood.

In our verse today, the apostle Peter declares that a Christian is one who is dead to sin and who lives in righteousness, but I fear many today that fill our pews and name the name of Christ, are not dead *to* sin, but dead *in* sin. They are not washed in the blood because they were fed a bloodless gospel that never warned them to flee from the wrath to come, that never warned them that they who die in their sins will go to a terrible place called hell, that unless you repent, you will all likewise perish, that you must be born again. But, today, we've gotten out our mop buckets and mopped up the duty of repentance and the necessity of regeneration. Why, there is no need when there is no blood.

Let me tell you what happened on that bloody cross. The Prince of Glory died there for sinful man. Redemption took place there. Peter tells us *"ye were not redeemed with ... silver and gold"* and a mopped up gospel of our day, *"But with*

THAT BLOODY CROSS

the precious blood of Christ, as of a lamb without blemish and without spot" (1 Peter 1:18-19).

You see, when the early church preached the gospel, they were honest with men. They warned men about hell. They preached a living Lord who reigns on a throne. They preached a scandalous cross that was an offense, that had blood all over it because of sin. They didn't clean up the gospel to make it more presentable to sinful man. They told men the truth. They warned men to flee from the wrath to come. Their God was the God of the Bible, a God who must punish sin.

The apostle Paul preached up that blood. In Colossians we read, *"In whom we have redemption through his blood, even the forgiveness of sins"* (1:14). Paul knew how to be honest with men and warn them. *"Knowing therefore the terror of the Lord, we persuade men"* (2 Corinthians 5:11). But today we have, with our modern gospel, removed the teeth from it. We've taken the terror out of it and the scandal of the cross out of it. We've mopped up around Calvary to such a degree that you could sit there and have your lunch, it's so pristine and pleasant. Just come to Jesus. Walk an aisle with a silly grin on your face and agree to a few facts about the death of Christ and you can join the church, stay in your sins, and go to heaven some day because you were told about a sparkling clean cross that has no demands and no cost of discipleship.

But there is only one way to heaven, and that is by way of a bloody cross on which the Savior died, and unless you come to God by way of that cross, and get under that blood, and throw down your shotgun of rebellion, and submit to the claims of the Lord Jesus Christ on your life, and obey His commands, you will die in your sins and fall into the regions of hell for all eternity. That bloody cross is where Jesus gave Himself for me, and it's a scandal to man, an offense, because where there is a cross, there is always a crucifixion, and to be a believer means to live a crucified life. *"I am crucified with Christ: nevertheless I live; yet not I, but Christ liveth in me: and the life which I now live in the flesh I live by the faith of the Son of God, who loved me, and gave himself for me"* (Galatians 2:20). Thank you, Jesus, for that bloody cross. I'd be lost without it.

It is time in this great land of ours, that has fallen to such low levels, to preach that message once again. It's time to put the blood back into the gospel, even if they hang us for it. There is power in that blood.

CHAPTER 27: WHAT PAUL PREACHED

Bible Text: Romans 1:16
Preached On: Thursday, September 19, 2013

When I read my Bible and examine what the apostle Paul preached, and compare that to what is preached in the majority of our churches in America today, I see little similarity. If Paul were to show up today and enter a pulpit and preach the message that he preached in his day, he would be quickly escorted out of the church by the good deacons. I submit to you that the apostle Paul would not be allowed to preach in the majority of the churches in America today and, not only that, he would be persecuted by the church for preaching the message that he preached in his day. Some of you may be saying to yourself, "How can you come to that conclusion, Preacher? That's a pretty bold statement." It's true, friends, if Paul came back today to the church in America, they would persecute him and reject his message. "Well," you might ask, "what in the world did Paul preach that would make him an enemy of the church today?" I will tell you, he preached the unvarnished gospel of the Son of God, and if you start preaching that gospel to this generation, to the churches in America today, they will surely hate you for it. You will be considered a trouble-maker, a church-divider, and a heretic.

Well, what did Paul preach? The best place to look is in our Bible. Let us first turn to 2 Corinthians 4:5, *"For we preach not ourselves, but Christ Jesus the Lord."* Let's start there because that is where Paul began. The apostles preached a risen Lord, Christ Jesus the Lord, Christ on a throne sitting at the right hand of the Father, and He earned that right by way of a bloody cross. Jesus is Lord. If you want to come to Him savingly, you have to come to Him there, to where He is, on a throne. He reigns there, and if you want to be savingly converted, you'd better listen to Paul and receive Christ as Lord.

You see, the church in America parted with the gospel about fifty years ago when they separated Jesus from Lord. They made two things out of one. The church in your day and mine declares you can have Christ as a Savior and go to heaven, but you don't have to submit to His claims on your life as Lord. You can accept Jesus as your personal Savior and go on in your sins and reign on the throne of your heart and go to heaven just fine. That's the gospel of our day.

But not in Paul's day, no sir. Paul preached Jesus the Lord and if you wanted Him, you had to approach Him there and bow to Him in utter surrender. If you don't bow to Him now, He will put His foot on your neck at a future day and make you bow then, when He makes His enemies as a footstool. Any person, any church member or non-church member who has not submitted to the lordship of Christ, is lost.

Now, you start preaching that and the good deacons will wring your neck. They'll take their shoes off and throw them at you because the church in America has told people, "You can have Jesus as a Savior, but you don't need Him as a Lord." And thousands upon thousands and millions upon millions have walked an aisle with a grin on their faces and accepted Jesus as their personal Savior, and they never saw themselves as lost, in a ruined estate, and an enemy of God. They never threw down their shotgun of rebellion and surrendered to the King of Kings who is Lord. They were never convicted of their sins, nor were they converted because they never repented from their sins. They were never filled with the Holy Spirit and they call themselves Christians. They run our churches and seminaries and denominations.

If Paul came back today and addressed a national convention for a major denomination, and if he dared preach the message that he preached while he was here in the flesh, he would not last long at the podium, because the heads of that denomination would be shouting for his head. The apostle Paul preached the lordship of Jesus Christ, a risen Lord, who sits on a throne, and if you want Him savingly, you have to do business with Him there. Is that too hard for you? Can't swallow that? Well, take it up with old Paul and the old Book.

The next thing Paul preached is found in Ephesians 2:1-4, and this will really make you mad.

> *And you hath he quickened, who were dead in trespasses and sins; Wherein in time past ye walked according to the course of this world, according to the prince of the power of the air, the spirit that now worketh in the children of disobedience: Among whom also we all had our conversation in times past in the lusts of our flesh, fulfilling the desires of the flesh and of the mind; and were by nature the children of wrath, even as others.*

Now, Paul mentions several things here that are foreign to many in our churches today. They've not heard this message because it's not preached much. Many sermons grab their texts from inoffensive passages of Scripture and men preach those up because they won't offend anybody. After all, you can't upset your congregation. If you do, you won't have a congregation. We live in a day of the positive encouraging word and a positive encouraging God. We have positive encouraging Christian radio, positive encouraging pastors, and so-called Christian bookstores that sell positive encouraging books. That's the day we live in, friends, a positive encouraging day when society is falling apart all around us and people drop into hell by the minute, and we preach nice, little, positive encouraging sermons to soothe their little minds and calm their little hearts.

And if Paul came back today he would preach that all mankind is dead in trespasses and sins, that they serve the devil because he is the prince of the power of the air, that because they are lost and ruined they live in a kingdom of darkness. He would preach they are the children of disobedience who live to fulfill the lusts and desires of their flesh and drink iniquity like water, because they have a nature that is ruined. They are the children of wrath. They are objects of God's wrath. Now, do you want to go preach that message, brother preacher? If you want to be like Paul, you can, but be willing to have his scars, because he was mobbed and stoned and beaten and whipped and run out of town for the message he preached, which was Christ and Him crucified.

Well, let's look at the next thing Paul preached. Turn in your Bibles to Acts 17:30. Paul was addressing the pagans in Athens, and if Paul came back to pagan America today and addressed it, he would preach the same message to it that he preached to those pagan Greeks. This is what he preached to them, *"And the times of this ignorance God winked at; but now commandeth all men every where to repent."*

Paul preached man's duty of repentance, that God commands all men, Greek and American and Chinese and Russian and African and Indonesian, and all men everywhere, to repent. You start preaching man's duty of repentance today and you will have a mob at your door. They horse-whipped Mordecai Ham for preaching repentance; they pistol-whipped him in Texas for preaching repentance. But Mordecai Ham, although he had some scars on his body, he was like Paul. Old Ham saw over 200,000 people come to Christ during his ministry and one of them was Billy Graham.

But we soft-soak the gospel today, and the problem is, people join our churches and sit Sunday after Sunday and listen to our encouraging words for the day, and we are not honest with men and women and honest with boys and girls. We just don't warn them of the fact that Jesus declared, *"Except ye repent, ye shall all likewise perish"* (Luke 13:3, 5). That means that if you came into a church any other way than through repentance towards God and faith in Jesus Christ, you are a hell-bound sinner who needs to repent, even if you are the chairman of the deacons. But if you preach on repentance, then you have to mention sin, and then you have to mention a place called "hell," and then you have to talk about a holy God who hates sin. "Why, that's just not politically correct."

So, the gospel of our day and the gospel of Paul's day are two different gospels, friend, and here is the difference—we don't see many true conversions today with our peanut God-shrunk gospel. But Paul had his because the gospel he preached is found in Acts 20:27 which states, *"For I have not shunned to declare unto you all the counsel of God."*

Paul preached the gospel in its purity and proper order. He preached the full counsel of God. He didn't leave anything out to make it more palatable to sinful man. He was not ashamed of it like we are today, and we are so ashamed of it, we don't want to preach all of it. But the gospel Paul preached had something that today's modern gospel lacks: P-O-W-E-R. In Romans, Paul declares, *"For I am not ashamed of the gospel of Christ: for it is the power of God unto salvation to every one that believeth; to the Jew first, and also to the Greek"* (Romans 1:16).

Our gospel of today lacks power because we have diluted it of all its threatenings and terrors and warnings to sinful man. We don't want to warn sinners to flee from the wrath to come today. We just want to give them some encouraging word and smile and play church and sit back, while society crumbles all around us and this nation turns its back on God. The churches are too afraid to preach the full counsel of God and be honest with men and tell them what they are: ruined, lost rebels, enemies of God.

We paint God all wrong, too, and say He's just a God of love when, in reality, He is also a God of wrath, and who declares, *"God is angry with the wicked every day. If he turn not, he will whet his sword; he hath bent his bow, and made it ready"* (Psalm 7:11-12). We don't tell men that God is ready to cut them down any moment because of sin. The only prayer God ever hears of an unsaved person is this: "God, be merciful to me a sinner." No, the God of today is only a God of the encouraging word. Why, the God of today just wouldn't punish sin. He wouldn't send anybody to hell. But Paul knew better. He warned men. He called a spade a spade. He didn't soft-soap the gospel and shrink God down to man's level like many of us have done today.

Well, what else did Paul preach? If you're not mad yet, you will be after you hear what he preached next. Turn to Ephesians 1:4-5, *"According as he hath chosen us in him before the foundation of the world, that we should be holy and without blame before him in love: Having predestinated us unto the adoption of children by Jesus Christ to himself, according to the good pleasure of his will."*

WHAT PAUL PREACHED

This speaks of election, that God is the God of salvation, not man, *"For by grace are ye saved through faith; and that not of yourselves: it is the gift of God: Not of works, lest any man should boast"* (Ephesians 2:8-9).

Paul would surely be thrown out of many of our churches today for preaching that message, and if he capped it off by saying that we were saved to be holy, why, that would drain the blood out of the good deacons' faces. You start saying that without holiness no one shall see the Lord and they will scream, "We will not have this man rule over us." And if you really want to make some church-folks mad, tell them that the Christian life is a crucified life where self is dethroned and another is enthroned there.

Paul preached on the crucified life: *"I am crucified with Christ: nevertheless I live; yet not I, but Christ liveth in me: and the life which I now live in the flesh I live by the faith of the Son of God, who loved me, and gave himself for me"* (Galatians 2:20).

Paul preached that when we come to Christ we have a new Master; our life is not our own for we are bought with a price. Our body is not our own, our time is not our own, our money is not our own. Jesus is Lord and as Christians, we live crucified lives as we follow a crucified Savior. Paul said in Colossians 2:6, *"As ye have therefore received Christ Jesus the Lord, so walk ye in him."*

Paul would be in bad shape if he came back today and tried to evangelize the American church. Vance Havner used to say, "I could've led a few more people to the Lord had they not already joined the church." Yes sir, you start preaching up election and holiness and repentance and start calling man a rebel, why, you just might as well wear a football helmet when you preach, for the rocks will surely come. But Paul knew that, because in his day, man was as wicked as he is in our day, and in Paul's day, he had his share of rocks thrown at him.

When I sit in big congregations and listen to big dogs preach, I often hear a big round of applause when they are done with their message. Boy, the crowd just loves them. Do you want to hear the kind of applause Paul received? I will close with Paul's laundry list for preaching the gospel of the Son of God as it is found in 2 Corinthians 11:23-28:

> *In labours more abundant, in stripes above measure, in prisons more frequent, in deaths oft. Of the Jews five times received I forty stripes save one. Thrice was I beaten with rods, once was I stoned, thrice I suffered shipwreck, a night and a day I have been in the deep; In journeyings often, in perils of waters, in perils of robbers,*

in perils by mine own countrymen, in perils by the heathen, in perils in the city, in perils in the wilderness, in perils in the sea, in perils among false brethren; In weariness and painfulness, in watchings often, in hunger and thirst, in fastings often, in cold and nakedness. Beside those things that are without, that which cometh upon me daily, the care of all the churches.

And you know what care that is, brother pastor. It's a mighty care indeed.

Paul didn't have a 401k and health insurance and a standing ovation when he left the pulpit and finished his ministry because he preached a different gospel than is preached in many of our churches today. I remember Leonard Ravenhill saying this, "When we get to heaven, Jesus won't be looking for medals pinned on us, but scars." It is my prayer that a sovereign Almighty will raise up a new generation of preachers who are willing to be scarred for preaching the gospel of the Son of God in its purity and proper order, and they won't be men who fear men, but that they will be men who walk humbly in the fear of the Lord.

CHAPTER 28: LOST GENERATION WITH ONE FOOT IN HELL

Bible Text: Book of Judges
Preached On: Tuesday, October 1, 2013

Last week I preached during chapel at a local Christian school. My audience was a group of teenagers and I fear I failed miserably in my task to reach them or move them. On my drive home, I was grieved at how greatly this generation of teenagers has been cheated. How this generation has never seen a true move of God in their midst or felt his power and presence in true revival. How this generation of teenagers has been abused by the culture in which they live, which is a godless culture and a pagan nation. How this generation of teenagers has been exposed to graphic sex as no other generation preceding them. How this generation of teenagers has been the target of Satan through the rise of suicides and self-harm. How this generation of teenagers has been neglected by the true gospel. And how this generation of teenagers has not heard the law thundered in their ears, awakening them to their lost condition and ruined estate. How they have not heard a Spirit-anointed message on the blood and the cross and sin and hell and the need for repentance and the necessity of regeneration. How this generation of teenagers is comprised of more atheists, more bisexuals, more drug users than any generation preceding them.

And as I thought of this time in chapel with this group of church teenagers that I couldn't move with a bull-dozer, a verse of Scripture came to my mind. It is found in Judges 2, beginning in verse 10. Let me read it to you now: *"And also all that generation were gathered unto their fathers: and there arose another generation after them, which knew not the LORD, nor yet the works which he had done for Israel. And the children of Israel did evil in the sight of the LORD, and served Baalim."*

I submit to you today, that this generation of church members who are teenagers has grown up in the church, but many, I fear, have not met the Head of the church, Jesus Christ. They are the most gospel-hardened generation of lost youth this earth has ever known.

The title of my message tonight is "Lost Generation with One Foot in Hell." There are five main reasons why this generation is the lost generation.

1. The church in America is to blame by trying to reach the youth with the world rather than the Word of God. Youth groups have been one of the worst things to happen to the church in America. If you want to lose your kid, place him in the youth group at your local church. That's how bad it's gotten.

2. Preachers are to blame for not preaching the true gospel of the Son of God. We live in a time of the no-gospel preacher. Pastors teach and inform rather than preach and transform.

3. The third reason why this generation is a lost generation is divine judgment in the form of the withdrawn presence of God in the land.

4. The death of the weekly prayer meeting which is the engine of the church.

5. A poor example of parents who have not lived like they should have as believers. There is no godly example in the home, no family altar, compromise everywhere, and a "do as I say" mentality rather than a "do as I do."

Listen, friends, this is the lost generation with one foot in hell. They don't care about your Jesus or your God. They just don't see any need for Him or doubt even if He exists at all. And brother preacher, you can offer them Jesus until you're blue in the face and they might take Him like they would an antibiotic, reluctantly.

I'm going to go over these five reasons to blame for this lost generation tonight. Let me address the first reason and that is this: the White House isn't to blame, the courthouse isn't to blame, the church house is to blame. We've dropped the ball as a church with this generation of young people. The culture we live in is a culture of the spoiled kid, and the church has spoiled the kids by giving them what they want instead of giving them what they need. They wanted more of the world in the worship time and we handed it to them. They wanted more entertainments in the church and we provided it for them. They wanted this and they wanted that and we handed it to them on a silver platter, and they are still disinterested in spiritual things, and discontent with their lives, and disconnected socially. Oh, they have 300 or 500 friends they text, but they don't know how to handle a real-live relationship. They are disenchanted, disengaged, depressed, and although they've grown up in the church and accepted Jesus into their hearts when they were four or five, they know not the living God of the Bible, nor have they ever seen a revelation of the Son of God in their lives. They are lost. They are lost. They are lost.

And much of their lost spiritual condition is our fault as poor shepherds. The church in America created a program for the youth instead of giving them the living Word of God. There is no church discipline from the pulpit on down in the church today. The church in America is spinning out of control. The church in America is like a spoiled and pampered child crying for more candy, more amusements, more attention, and more gratification. It has become self-focused, self-absorbed, and self-destructing. And we wonder why our kids hate going to church. We invited the world into our congregations and pushed God right out the back door. If I were a teenager today, I wouldn't go near the average church in America. Why would I want to?

The second blame for this lost generation is the no-gospel preacher. The no-gospel preacher is a minister who does not preach the gospel of Jesus Christ. He is a nice man who likes to keep everybody in his congregation happy. He will teach Bible truths enwrapped with morals, and do a great deal of fill-in-the-blank teaching, where you write the next obvious word in your church bulletin where the blank is. This keeps the congregation occupied during the service and teaches them some spiritual truths, and they leave the service with a little more information than when they came in. But they also leave the same way they came in. There is no transformation. There is no spiritual activity. Teaching informs, preaching transforms, and the no-gospel preacher will say anything he can to keep your attention and not upset you. But you will not hear about your duty to repent from your sins. You will not hear about a bloody cross, nor a crucified Lord. You will not hear about a terrible place called "hell," nor will you hear about the necessity for regeneration, which is an act only God can perform. The no-gospel preacher will never preach the terrors of the law to awaken you to your sins. Rather, he will be a soothing, encouraging fellow who likes to talk about heaven, but is quite unable to get you savingly there. This generation of young people has been victimized by the easy-believe gospel of our day. They have accepted a Jesus they've never seen. They made a decision to be a Christian without ever being awakened, convicted, and converted by the Holy Spirit of God. The no-gospel preacher has ruined this generation of young people and has gospel-hardened them to the reality of what true, saving faith really is.

The next blame for why this is a lost generation of hell-bound sinners with their young is the fact that we are living in a day of divine judgment in the land. The church in America is experiencing the withdrawn presence of God. There was a time not too long ago in the early 1950s and even in the early 1970s when God was afoot in the land—God was moving in seasons of revival. If you were a young person back then and you were in a meeting at church, you felt the presence and power of the Almighty in your midst. You could not wait to get into a prayer meeting. You could not wait to get back to church because God was there. Now it's death all around us, deadness everywhere. Teenagers today have never felt the power of God in a meeting. They just don't know what it's like to be bowed under His presence in a service.

The blame lies at the door of the church. We have cheapened the gospel message. We've removed the duty of repentance. We've omitted the blood and we've pushed God out of the back door of the church and replaced Him with worldly entertainment, and God has left us to our own devices. He has withdrawn His presence from among us. Why should a teenager want to attend church today? Our preaching is void of the Holy Spirit. Our sanctuaries are absent of the presence of God. Why should the teenagers even listen to any of us any longer? Somewhere the church in America forsook the great God of the Bible and the passage in Judges applies to us today. *"And they forsook the LORD God of their fathers, which brought them out of the land of Egypt, and followed other gods, of the gods of the people that were round about them, and bowed themselves unto them, and provoked the LORD to anger"* (Judges 2:12).

The fourth reason we have a lost generation on our hands today is the very fact that we, as a church, have killed the weekly prayer meeting and buried it in obscurity. We replaced it with classes on social reform and exercise. You won't have any trouble finding a divorce recovery class in your church, or a yoga class, but you'll be hard pressed to stumble into a room with people lying on their faces, broken over their sins and crying out to God. Where are the church members weeping over the lost in our churches today? The weekly prayer meeting is the engine of the church, and this is why so many churches are out of gas and stalled out. What a difference it would make in the life of our teenagers if they could witness the reality of prevailing prayer by brokenhearted believers crying out to God, interceding for the sins of this nation, humbling themselves before the Almighty, crying out for mercy through nights of desperation and travailing prayer. No, we give the kids movie night. We give them football night. We give them pizza night. But we don't give them the opportunity to learn about corporate prayer in the life of the church. Perhaps the greatest failure of the church in America over the last forty years has been the death of the weekly prayer meeting.

Listen, friends, when I was a boy many years ago, it impacted me to see grown men and women on their faces crying out to God and moaning and groaning over their sins, begging God for mercy, begging God for a fresh move of his presence. Where is that in our churches today? I know there are a few faithful churches still in the land, and they still have a weekly prayer meeting, but the majority of churches in America have killed the weekly prayer meeting and cut off the only access to the living God that they had. When the church in America became a self-reliant church, that's when it replaced the prayer meeting. Who needs God when money and man-power can get the job done a lot quicker?

The last point, the fifth blame for this generation of lost teenagers, is the actual parents themselves, the parent who says, "Do as I say and not as I do." And the kid sees a double standard and Pharisees in the home, an adult who is a Christian at church but a hypocrite when back at the house.

I witnessed revival in a church years ago whereby I was merely an observer at what God was doing in a local body of believers in the South. I heard about a church where a true move of grace was occurring, and it was worth the drive out of town to get there and get in on what God was doing. When I arrived there at that church, it was well into the service on a Saturday night, and there was silence in the sanctuary as I took my seat. I was mystified by the non-activity: no pastor was in the pulpit and the choir sat silent and weeping, handing the Kleenex box back and forth between them. Suddenly, I felt like crying. I felt an overpowering presence of the Almighty. It was as if God had sat down on that congregation with His awful presence and all one could do was to be still and soak up that majesty.

I later learned the cause of that move of God in that local church. You see, the men of the church had attended a retreat some weeks earlier and God had moved in on them, in their midst. While these men were holed up with God, God began to change their hearts. They began to live for the Lord, and when they went back home from this retreat, they started being the spiritual leader of the home as they were intended to be. The wives were so taken aback by their husbands' new demeanor, gentleness toward them, and godliness, that the wives gave themselves to God in a fresh way. Their lives were also transformed, and they began to live in the home as godly women should do.

Well, when the teenagers in these families saw what it was like to have genuine Christian parents, the teenagers went forward in a church service and gave their lives to Christ in surrender, and that was the night I had arrived at that church. I missed the first part of the service where the teenagers had come forward in submission to the Lord. God had sat down on that group of people and transformed them one by one. As each one surrendered to the lordship of Jesus Christ in their lives, the teenagers in that church could not wait to get back to church and they stayed there all odd hours of the night crying out to God in the sanctuary.

Listen, friends, when the people of God get right with God and humble themselves and confess their sins and turn from their wickedness and seek the Lord of glory, great things are done. God promises us, *"Return unto me, and I will return unto you"* (Malachi 3:7). Revival hangs in the balance in regard to our duty to follow the requirements set out in 2 Chronicles 7:14 which declares, *"If my people, which are called by my name, shall humble themselves, and pray, and seek my face, and turn from their wicked ways; then will I hear from heaven, and will forgive their sin, and will heal their land."*

Let me ask you, friends, does our land need healing? Do our teenagers need saving? Are their souls worth you stopping all you're doing right now, getting on your face before a holy God, and crying out to Him to forgive you for not living for Him as you should? Are the souls of our teenagers today, the young girls who are harming themselves, the young boys who are drugging themselves, and all the young people who are perverting themselves, are not their souls precious in the eyes of the Lord? Are we willing to cease the nonsense in our churches and forsake our man-made programs and turn out of our churches everything that is an abomination to the Lord? Are you willing, brother pastor, to reinstate the weekly prayer meeting even if it upsets your deacons? Are you willing to start preaching up the blood and the cross and call sin "black" and hell "hot" for the sake of our teenagers and their precious souls? Will you call them to their duty of repentance and warn them to flee from the wrath to come? Are we willing as a church to forsake our ways, get back to the old paths once again, and seek the Lord of glory and beg Him and invite Him to once again be pleased to dwell in our midst?

Let me pray. *Great God, forgive us for ruining this generation of teenagers. Forgive us for not living for you as we should. It lies in surrender and holiness. Forgive us, Great God, for replacing you with things of this world and bowing down to these idols rather than humbling ourselves before your face and seeking mercy and forgiveness from you, O Lord. Give us the grace, I pray, the grace of repentance. Wake us up, O Lord, to our great responsibility for the souls of this generation that does not know you.*

O Lord of glory, look down, come down, flow down, by your Spirit upon this vine once again. Breathe fresh fire into your churches by your Holy Spirit. Cleanse us, O Lord, of our great wickedness and, O Lord, may you say to your church in America today as you spoke to King Solomon whereby you declared, "I have heard thy prayer and have chosen this place to myself for a house of sacrifice." O Great God, O Ancient of Days, be pleased to visit your church in America once again with your presence. Come in revival, O Lord. Come rain righteousness upon this dry and forsaken land. Do what you've done in former times for your great glory and great name's sake, I pray. Amen.

CHAPTER 29: ONE FOOT IN THE AISLE AND THE OTHER IN HELL

Bible Text: Matthew 7:13-27
Preached On: Saturday, October 12, 2013

I have been to the stone marker in Exeter, New Hampshire, which marks the spot where George Whitfield preached his last sermon. He preached in the fields of Exeter on September 29, 1770, to a crowd of 4,000 in the open air. His chest was heaving from asthma and he stood bolt upright for two hours proclaiming the glories of Christ Jesus his Savior. His text was taken from 2 Corinthians 13:5 which states, *"Examine yourselves, whether ye be in the faith; prove your own selves. Know ye not your own selves, how that Jesus Christ is in you, except ye be reprobates?"*

As the great Whitfield preached, his voice pierced the autumn air as he cried out, "Works, works. Can a man get to heaven by works? I would as soon think of climbing to the moon on a rope of sand." Whitfield finished his sermon and died the next morning. To the day he died, he preached the necessity of one being born again. He shook America with that message during the Great Awakening. Whitfield preached for true conversions in his day and his message was "Ye must be born again."

If George Whitfield were alive today he would be greatly alarmed at what passes for the gospel in our land. He would be shocked by the irreverent behavior of most ministers in the pulpit, and he would be saddened by the great many who sit in our churches and have their names on the church membership roll, but their names are not written in the Lamb's Book of Life.

We live in a day in America, where the majority of church members are in an unconverted state. We live in the day of the unconverted church whereby a good too many have walked an aisle, repeated a prayer, believed a verse and a fact about the death of Christ, and made a decision to become a Christian in the same careless manner they would make a decision to join a health spa. They occupy our pews and serve on our committees and are very vocal about their profession of faith, but they've never been awakened to their lost and ruined condition. They have never been convicted by the Holy Spirit of their sins and they've never come savingly to Christ through a true work of grace upon the heart in regeneration. They sit proudly as chairman of the deacons. They teach a Sunday school class. They sing in the choir. Some even stand behind the pulpit. They have one thing in common with the foolish virgins who had no oil of testimony in their lamps, and that is this very fact: they strongly believe themselves to be true believers, but they are lost, lost, lost and they are on their way to a terrible place called "hell." Hell fills up every day with unconverted church members who sit in church with one foot in the aisle and the other in hell.

And that's the title of my message today, "One Foot in the Aisle and the Other in Hell." My text is found in the gospel of Matthew chapter 7, beginning in verse 13. You can turn in your Bibles there now. I want you to know that Jesus didn't make it easy to be His follower. He turned away the rich young ruler and many who believed on Him because of His many miracles. He did not commit Himself to them because He knew what was in their hearts. Listen to me, you may be able to deceive yourself, you may be able to fool your family and friends with your profession of faith, but Jesus knows your heart and He knows if you are sitting upon a false foundation of self-righteousness and good works. If you are deluded, if you have been cheated by the gospel of this day—a gospel that is no gospel because it is so diluted it does not point you to a bloody cross and to a risen Lord who reigns on a throne, a risen Lord who demands repentance, submission, and surrender—you may have swallowed hook, line and sinker a feeble counterfeit that could not save a flea. The Jesus you have been told about is so impotent and shrunk down to man's size that he just couldn't save anybody.

Listen, friend, if you have never seen the rottenness of your vile and wicked heart, if you have never been lost and realized your need of a Savior, if you have never seen a revealed Christ, if you have never had a work of conviction of sin upon your heart and conscience, if you've never turned from your wicked sins in true gospel repentance, and if you have never had your heart of stone turned into a heart of flesh through a work of God exercised upon you in regeneration, you have never been truly united to a living Lord in saving faith. For years, you have served your church faithfully. For years, you have verbally testified of being a Christian. And for years, you have remained unchanged and unconverted, and unless you exercise repentance toward God and faith in Jesus Christ in a saving way, you will die in your sins and drop into hell.

My passage today is from the very lips of the Lord Jesus Christ. There are few who are saved and those who are, are saved with great difficulty. For too many years I have sat and listened to very sincere men in the pulpit proclaim a gospel that made it too easy to become a Christian. They made it far too easy to walk an aisle and come to Christ. I've seen people walk an aisle in response to an invitation of, "Come to Jesus. Come to Jesus. Jesus said if you are sincere, you will come to

Him. Accept Him now. A public testimony is necessary to show how you are so sincere. So, if you come to Him publicly, he will not turn you away." And thousands have walked that aisle with a silly grin on their face, repeated the Sinner's Prayer, and were able to give the right answer to a couple of questions in an adjoining room. Then they were patted on the back and their hands were shaken and they were told they were saved. They joined the church, served on its boards and committees, taught Sunday school, and sang in the choir, and when they died, a great many of them dropped into hell as unconverted church members.

They were victims of an easy-belief gospel, misled by a sincere minister who was ignorant of the ways of saving faith, and they accepted a Jesus they knew nothing about and one whom they never truly met. They took the name of "Christian" but their hearts remained unchanged. A true Christian is a person who has experienced change, and there are many today who have been that way for a long time. They put on a good front at church and in front of their friends, but when they are alone and the devil crooks his finger at them with a temptation, they follow him like a zombie and lie in their sins like a pig wallows in the mire. They drink iniquity like it's water because they have never been wrought upon by the Holy Spirit in conviction and conversion. They are unconverted church members who give the church of Jesus Christ a bad name because of their hypocritical lifestyle. They are hypocrites in the home, hypocrites at the office, and hypocrites when they are alone.

They rest upon a false foundation of self-righteousness and good works and are very vocal about their Christianity. Oh, they just can't wait for Jesus to rapture them out of this present evil age. They love the doctrine of the rapture of the church because it assures them they won't have to be found out when Antichrist comes and places a mark upon them to buy and sell, for they would surely take that mark and forsake their Christ to save their skins. So, they love to speak of the rapture and talk about it all the time in a selfish way, not caring that the very delay of Christ's return is because he's a long-suffering God, not willing that any should perish, but that all should come to repentance and faith.

Here now is the passage from the gospel of Matthew. Listen carefully to the words of the Lord Jesus Christ for they may be an indictment against your brand of Christianity and they may be a means, by the mercy of God, to bring you off your false foundation of security, show you your ruined and lost condition, and reveal to you the Son of God in all His glory and power in a saving way. Listen, friends, to my solemn warning to you today: there are few who are saved and those with great difficulty.

Enter ye in at the strait gate: for wide is the gate, and broad is the way, that leadeth to destruction, and many there be which go in thereat: Because strait is the gate, and narrow is the way, which leadeth unto life, and few there be that find it. Beware of false prophets, which come to you in sheep's clothing, but inwardly they are ravening wolves. Ye shall know them by their fruits. Do men gather grapes of thorns, or figs of thistles? Even so every good tree bringeth forth good fruit; but a corrupt tree bringeth forth evil fruit. A good tree cannot bring forth evil fruit, neither can a corrupt tree bring forth good fruit. Every tree that bringeth not forth good fruit is hewn down, and cast into the fire. Wherefore by their fruits ye shall know them. Not every one that saith unto me, Lord, Lord, shall enter into the kingdom of heaven; but he that doeth the will of my Father which is in heaven. Many will say to me in that day, Lord, Lord, have we not prophesied in thy name? and in thy name have cast out devils? and in thy name done many wonderful works? And then will I profess unto them, I never knew you: depart from me, ye that work iniquity. Therefore whosoever heareth these sayings of mine, and doeth them, I will liken him unto a wise man, which built his house upon a rock: And the rain descended, and the floods came, and the winds blew, and beat upon that house; and it fell not: for it was founded upon a rock. And every one that heareth these sayings of mine, and doeth them not, shall be likened unto a foolish man, which built his house upon the sand: And the rain descended, and the floods came, and the winds blew, and beat upon that house; and it fell: and great was the fall of it. (7:13-27)

Notice that Jesus states the road to hell is broad and there are many on it. The majority of the people on this earth at this hour will live their lives unto themselves and one day get sick and die or be caught out of this world quite unexpectedly and die in their sins and drop into hell.

Let's look at this majority, the many who are marching on their way to hell. Let's look first at the many religions in the world who serve a different god than the God of the Bible. Jesus declared that if any man try to go up any other way than Jesus, he is a thief and a robber. Jesus declared, *"Verily, verily, I say unto you, He that entereth not by the door into the sheepfold, but climbeth up some other way, the same is a thief and a robber"* (John 10:1). That describes all the world religions today. Jesus is the door; He is the only way. Listen, Buddha lived, died, and was buried. Confucius lived, died, and was buried. Mohammed lived, died, and was buried. Jesus lived, died, and was buried, but he rose again. We serve a risen Lord. Christianity was never built on a coffin lid. So, we have the many on the broad way of world religions who try to reach heaven some other way other than through Jesus Christ.

Then add to them others who claim to serve the God of the Bible and they gather around the foot of the cross, yet they are the ones spoken of in this passage from Matthew who say, "Lord, Lord, have we not prophesied in thy name and done many wonderful works?" But these, too, are on their way to hell because, although they gather around the foot of the cross, they refuse to get up on the cross in submission to the Lord of glory. So, there are few true believers in the world today in comparison with the world population. And it's been that way in every generation since the days of Noah when the flood came upon the earth and destroyed all mankind, except for eight persons who were placed in the ark of safety.

There are few today who take refuge in the ark of safety in the person of Jesus Christ, who are washed in the blood and born from above. Jesus makes a great distinction between the many and the few. The few are the ones who do the will of the Father. That means those who repent of sin, believe in Christ, live a holy life and who love one another, for if we fail to comply with the will of God and disobey His commands, we mock Christ by calling Him Lord, when He was never truly Lord of our lives. And that is the great issue which is separating us today. It's the separating line between true believers and false professors. When a person comes savingly to Christ, self is dethroned and another is enthroned there—the Lord Jesus Christ.

But many today who are willing to take Christ as their Savior, reject Him as their Lord and cry out, *"We will not have this man to reign over us"* (Luke 19:14). But the fact remains, a false professor will not submit his neck to His yoke and be under the lordship of Jesus Christ. You see, today we have made two things out of one: we preachers mislead people by telling them they can have Jesus as Savior now and later on take Him as Lord if they want to go deeper with Him. In other words, you can still go to heaven and still sit on the throne of your life and rule there in self-gratification.

But Jesus spoke about taking up a cross when you follow Him, and denying yourself daily. In your day and mine, the vast majority of the pulpits in the land are silent on the issues of the cost of discipleship in becoming a Christian. There is a cost and it must be counted, for what costs counts and what counts costs. It cost Christ His very blood. Listen, Christ is a Savior to those only to whom He is a Prince and who are willing to obey Him. Christ is a risen Lord who sits on a throne and reigns there, and if you want Him, you must meet Him there. He is a sovereign King who will have no rebels in His kingdom. You come to Him one way, and that's by way of a cross, where you kneel in surrender and submission to all His claims and rights upon you, because you are bought with a price, and that price is His blood. He must be a complete Master. Your life is no longer your own.

The greatest failure of the church in America over the last fifty years has been cheapening the gospel and omitting the duty of repentance and submission to the lordship of Jesus Christ. That is where people drive a stake into the ground and scream, *"We will not have this man to reign over us."* The two things Satan hates more than anything else in a gospel presentation is repentance and the lordship of Jesus Christ. I look at the ministry of a man like Mordecai Ham, who preached those two doctrines, and he was horse-whipped, pistol-whipped, dragged by a mob to be tarred and feathered, and run out of town because of what he preached. Mordecai Ham preached that man is under a curse because of sin, and if you die under that curse, you will surely go to hell, and the only way of escape from that curse is to repent of your sins and by faith submit to the lordship of Jesus Christ. That's what that man, Ham, preached. Hence, he saw 200,000 people come to Christ under his preaching, and one of them was Billy Graham.

But the great danger of a false profession is this: you remain unconverted while you sit upon a false and shaky foundation of sand, and when trials come, and they surely will, when a severe time of testing blows into your life, your Christian profession will break apart on the rocks of adversity. The great dividing line in our passage today is that word "Lord." Jesus is not recognizing those professors who claim they know Him and call, "Lord, Lord," when He was never Lord of their life and living in their hearts through the new birth. And at the judgment of all mankind, "Many will say to me in that day, Lord, Lord, I've taught Sunday school for twenty years. Lord, Lord, I handed out tracts on a regular basis. Lord, Lord, I was a deacon in my church for ten years. Lord, Lord, I was pastor of the church." But Jesus will say unto them, *"I never knew you: depart from me, ye that work iniquity"* (Matthew 7:23).

The church in America is quite unprepared for the coming persecution to it. We will soon be in a day where it is either Caesar is lord or Jesus is Lord. When it comes down to renouncing Christ to stay out of jail or to keep your job or your home, then you will find that the church membership in America will thin out immensely. There won't be enough people to pay the bills to continue to operate these big church campuses, and many churches will have to close their doors. It will be a phenomenon in America that is kind of like that in Great Britain today, where there are empty churches that sit as house cafes and libraries and night clubs.

Let me ask you, is Jesus your Lord? Can you honestly say when you get up in the morning, that throughout your day He is Lord of your life? Ruling there? Reigning there? Directing you under the discipline of his Holy Spirit? Or are you still sitting on the throne of your life? A true believer has laid down his shotgun of rebellion at the feet of a sovereign King and submits to His yoke upon his neck from that point forward. The typical American Christian is a self-ruling person who sits on the throne of his life like the rich young ruler. They've never counted the cost of following a crucified Savior. They've never surrendered to the lordship of Christ in their lives with all His claims and rights on them. Like the rich young ruler, they are quite willing to call Jesus "good Master" but quite unwilling to be mastered by Him. Yet, if they are not brought off from their false security of self-righteousness, they will soon die and be buried and drop into hell. I repeat: this is the day where a church member sits in the church sanctuary with one foot in the aisle and the other in hell. He claims to know Christ but is not known *by* Christ.

People often ask me about the subject of revival. It was not long ago in our once great land that the fires of revival were burning here and there. Even in the early 1970s, you could still come across an older pastor who was a teenager back then, and his face will light up as he speaks about the power of God in meetings. You see, there was a stir in the land, for God was afoot. They'll talk about how the presence of God was so strong in prayer meetings to where the teenagers could not wait to get back to church and get into that manifest presence of God.

Would you like to know what the two main doctrines were that were being preached in those days of revival fires? Repentance and the lordship of Christ. Go research it yourself if you don't believe me. God was honoring the preaching of the great doctrines of repentance and the lordship of Jesus Christ. But today, we see no revival fires burning across our land because we preach nice little sermons that don't upset anybody. We've diluted the very gospel that once had power to save, and we've insulted the God of the Bible by replacing Him with the things of this world in our sanctuaries. And we, today, experience the withdrawn presence of God rather than the manifest presence of God. God have mercy on us!

It is my prayer that the Lord of glory will raise up a new generation of preachers who do not fear man but fear God, who will preach up the great doctrines of the Bible with clarity and power, who will preach man's duty of repentance and surrender to the lordship of Jesus Christ and proclaim once again, *"Ye must be born again"* (John 3:7), who will preach that regeneration is a work of God upon the heart that only a sovereign God can perform. Man does not come to Christ on his terms but on God's terms. And I say to you, friend, if you've been sitting in your church with one foot in the aisle and the other in hell, if you know that when you are alone you are quite unchanged because you drink iniquity like it's water, that you rest upon a false foundation, I say to you now: repent and turn from your sins. Beg God for mercy. Ask Him by His Holy Spirit to break up your false foundation before it's too late.

Submit, friend, submit to the claims of Christ on your life and His lordship and come to Him in surrender of all you have and all you are. Become a seeker of Him and ask Him for the grace to believe savingly on Him. I beg you, *"Examine yourselves, whether ye be in the faith; prove your own selves. Know ye not your own selves, how that Jesus Christ is in you, except you be reprobates?"* (2 Corinthians 13:5).

I repeat: there are few saved today and that with great difficulty, *"Because strait is the gate, and narrow is the way, which leadeth unto life, and few there be that find it"* (Matthew 7:14).

CHAPTER 30: REVIVAL: AN ABUNDANCE OF RAIN

Bible Text: 1 Kings 18:30-40
Preached On: Sunday, October 13, 2013

There is a generation among us dying off who knows what true revival is; they have spent their lives in the study of it. I spent decades praying for it and preaching on it. Some have even seen the power of God in a meeting of real revival. I fear we live in a day where the vast majority of Christians do not know what a true revival of religion is. We live in a day where many pastors in the pulpits know very little of the subject of revival because they've not pursued an interest in it nor prayed desperately to see it. And it grieves my heart that if God came in revival in the land at this hour, that many in the church would fight that revival and try to put an end to it, because of their great ignorance of the movements of God in past time in the history of spiritual awakening and revival.

I've been fortunate to know men of revival, men like Stephen Olford and Ted Randall, Ian Murray and Richard Owen Roberts, men who have immersed themselves in the study of revival. They have written wisely upon it and preached on it and prayed for it in their lifetimes. I, myself, have spent decades studying the subject of revival and I've written many books on revival. My Ph.D. dissertation was on the revival of religion in Great Britain in the mid-18th century under Wesley and Whitfield. I've immersed myself in the study of revival for years. But many young preachers need to know what true revival is. They need to be aware of the vast distinction between evangelism, which is what we can do for God, and revival, which is what only God can do. Revival is not a series of meetings with loud music, loud preaching, and loud shouting, but revival is a true work of grace when God takes the field and everyone present is bowed down by the awful presence of the Almighty. Revival is when God breathes new life into His bride to energize her for the task at hand, to equip her to reach this generation of perishing souls with the gospel of the Son of God.

Our study today is a look at revival and its principles as found in the first book of Kings, in chapter 18, beginning in verse 30. You can turn there now in your Bibles. There is a pattern to follow to prepare our hearts for a visitation from on high. Listen, we cannot produce revival, it is a sovereign work of God. However, we can set our sails and align ourselves rightly to God to catch those winds of revival when they do blow. My message today is entitled "Revival: An Abundance of Rain" and we will look at the life of the prophet Elijah and how he was used of

God to turn a people back to Himself, to where the drought ended, and there was an abundance of rain, because that's what revival is, an outpouring of divine effusions of grace upon the people of God like showers from glory. It is heaven come down to earth and God dwelling among man. All our human props are kicked out from beneath us when God takes the field and saturates a church or community with His manifest presence. And that's what we need so desperately today, the power of God in a meeting, bowing hearts in repentance and surrender, and where the preaching of God's Word is, once again, like a hammer that breaks the rocks in pieces. Oh, for those days again. Oh, for the great God of the Bible to come down in His glory once again.

Let us look at this passage found in 1 Kings and I will lay out for you today the five great aspects of this passage in the relation to the reality of revival. That was the title of my first book on revival, *Realities of Revival*. Stephen Olford took my manuscript with him on his last vacation and he added to that book very carefully before it even went to print. Dr. Olford taught me much on the subject of revival and I want to share with you today some vital aspects on how to prepare ourselves for revival. Like I said, there are five aspects seen in our passage today. We see:

1. A repaired altar
2. A prepared sacrifice
3. An accepted offering
4. A revived people
5. A healed land

Let me read you our passage today as found in 1 Kings 18, beginning in verse 30:

> *And Elijah said unto all the people, Come near unto me. And all the people came near unto him. And he repaired the altar of the LORD that was broken down. And Elijah took twelve stones, according to the number of the tribes of the sons of Jacob, unto whom the word of the LORD came, saying, Israel shall be thy name: And with the stones he built an altar in the name of the LORD: and he made a trench about the altar, as great as would contain two measures of seed. And he put the wood in order, and cut the bullock in pieces, and laid him on the wood, and said, Fill four barrels with water, and pour it on the burnt sacrifice, and on the wood. And he said, Do it the second time. And they did it the second time. And he said, Do it the third time. And they did it the*

> *third time. And the water ran round about the altar; and he filled the trench also with water. And it came to pass at the time of the offering of the evening sacrifice, that Elijah the prophet came near, and said, LORD God of Abraham, Isaac, and of Israel, let it be known this day that thou art God in Israel, and that I am thy servant, and that I have done all these things at thy word. Hear me, O LORD, hear me, that this people may know that thou art the LORD God, and that thou hast turned their heart back again. Then the fire of the LORD fell, and consumed the burnt sacrifice, and the wood, and the stones, and the dust, and licked up the water that was in the trench. And when all the people saw it, they fell on their faces: and they said, The LORD, he is the God; the LORD, he is the God. And Elijah said unto them, Take the prophets of Baal; let not one of them escape. And they took them: and Elijah brought them down to the brook Kishon, and slew them there.*

This is the Word of the Lord. May God attend it with His holy blessings.

The first aspect of revival as seen in this striking passage of Scripture is this: we notice a repaired altar. In verse 30 we see that Elijah repaired the altar of the Lord that was broken down. Is there an area in your life, in your walk with God, that has become broken down? Has a sin separated you from the sweet fellowship of Jesus Christ? Have you been neglecting the daily quiet time with your God? Is your Bible a closed book and are your eyes dry when you pray? Perhaps the altar in your own life is broken down and it needs to be repaired. That's the first step to revival: re-entering a right relationship with God. Repair your altar and get your wood in order.

Listen to this poem written by Evan Roberts of the Welsh Revival. In Wales in 1904, God showed up under the ministry of a young layman called Evan Roberts, and it spread through other preachers. Revival spread all over Wales until it was said that from that revival, over 100,000 people came to Christ. Listen to this very last poem of Evan Roberts which speaks of repairing our altar before God.

> Here I have built my altar,
> The wood I've placed in order;
> The sacrifice is ready now,
> Send Thou, O Lord, the fire.

Is that what you need, my friend? Do you need to place the wood which represents the things in your life that are wood, hay and stubble; place them on the altar of sacrifice and offer them up to God in repentance? Do you need to be the sacrifice where you get up on that altar, where you can say, "Send Thou, O Lord, the fire?" So, we have this first aspect of revival of a repaired altar.

The second aspect is this: a prepared sacrifice. Look at verse 33 from our passage today, *"And he put the wood in order, and cut the bullock in pieces, and laid him on the wood."* Our hearts, friends, must be prepared to seek God in revival. We must realize the sacrifice involved in seeing revival, that in God's economy there is always a cost involved. Our very redemption had a cost and that cost was Christ's blood. What counts costs and what costs counts.

Too many pastors give up on praying for revival; they lose their passion for it. Their burden of prayer grows cold. I used to meet with a group of local pastors each week on Thursday mornings to pray for revival. These men faithfully came for about three months. Then they stopped coming. There must be importunity in desperate prayer for revival. There is a great sacrifice of prayer in seeing revival. It's a sacrifice of time and a sacrifice of self. Self must get up on the altar if we desire to see revival. So, we have this aspect of a prepared sacrifice.

The third aspect of revival is an accepted offering. We see this in verse 38, *"Then the fire of the LORD fell, and consumed the burnt sacrifice, and the wood, and the stones, and the dust, and licked up the water that was in the trench."* It is as if God was so pleased with the faith of Elijah that He consumes his offering as if at a great banquet, licking His lips in delight. We see that it's only after the altar is repaired, and the wood placed in order, and a sacrifice offered up, that God then sends the fire. When the people of God get right with God and return to Him in repentance and humility, and seek His face in desperate prayer, and turn from their wicked ways, then God accepts that offering. It is an accepted offering.

How about you, friend? Have you offered yourself to God lately? Or are you just a taker? Are your prayers just self-centered and it's all about you? Or are you willing to be laid up on the altar of sacrifice for others and have those flesh hooks pin you down so you can't crawl off there? Can you say of your life right now, before God, that it is an accepted offering? If not, then get your wood in order.

Now notice the fourth aspect of revival as found in our passage today. Look at verse 39, *"And when all the people saw it, they fell on their faces: and they said, The LORD, he is the God; the LORD, he is the God."* We see a people revived. That's what true revival is, friends; it's when God comes and revives His people and takes a sluggish church, a downcast remnant, and breathes fresh life into them to where they have an apostolic faith and an apostolic walk. True revival is like the book of Acts all over again, where it was said of the believers that they turned the world upside down.

Once revival comes and the people of God are rejuvenated by His Spirit, then it's all action, action, action. Evangelism is ignited. Missionary enterprises are activated. Family altars are reinstated in the homes. The very spiritual life of the church and community is altered because of what God has done. Christians become firebrands, drawing others to Christ as a revived people of God.

Now let us see this last aspect of revival and that is a healed land. We see in 1 Kings how a mighty drought has plagued the land, cattle have been dying off. It has been a blight upon the people of God, but when God comes with His presence and accepts the offering of the prophet, then the drought ends. Look at verse 41 from our passage, *"And Elijah said unto Ahab, Get thee up, eat and drink; for there is a sound of abundance of rain."* And that's what true revival is, friends, an abundance of rain. God promises in His Word that he will pour water upon him that is thirsty, and floods upon the dry ground. The thirsty heart is flooded by the presence of the Holy Spirit. The text says in verse 45 that *"there was a great rain."* When revival comes, the lost are swept into the kingdom of God through a spiritual awakening. More is accomplished in seasons of revival than in years of steady evangelism.

So, we see this aspect of a land healed. What does it say in God's Word for a land to be healed? Look at 2 Chronicles 7:14. I will read it to you. *"If my people, which are called by my name, shall humble themselves, and pray, and seek my face, and turn from their wicked ways; then will I hear from heaven, and will forgive their sin, and will heal their land."*

That's the pattern, and its mirror is laid for us in 1 Kings 18. Let us remember that if we truly have a desire to see God come in His manifest presence in the midst of revival and heal our land with an abundance of rain, with showers of blessings, then we must each come to that place before Him personally, where we are willing to have a repaired altar, a prepared sacrifice, an accepted offering which results in a revived people who then dwell in a healed land.

Let the people of God turn back to the God of the Bible in these last days and cry out to Him to forgive our sins, notice our sacrifice, and accept our offerings of ourselves before it's too late, and rather than His blessings received in revival and spiritual awakening, it is drought and judgment and ultimate destruction. Let us realign ourselves back to God right now. Right now. And turn our hearts towards Him in repentance. Turn our eyes on the Lord Jesus Christ and tune our ears to expectantly hear the sound of abundance of rain.

It is my prayer to see revival in your day and mine. I will close this message with a poem I wrote on this very subject entitled "A Repaired Altar."

> Give me a fire, O Lord,
> Give me a fire for thee.
> Give me your fire, O Lord,
> Let it burn brightly in me.
>
> Give me a fire, O Lord,
> The wood of my life I give to thee.
> Consume my ashes, O Lord,
> And let a revival begin with me.
>
> Give me a fire, O Lord,
> Give me a glimpse of hell and eternity.
> Make me a fire, O Lord,
> So my life may be burned out for thee.
>
> Give me a fire, O Lord,
> Increase my desire for thee.
> Make me a flame, O Lord,
> That draws others to you through me.

INDEX OF WORDS AND PHRASES

1910, 9
400 million souls, 28, 130
450 prophets of Baal, 15
5,000 an hour, 28
66 books, 41
800,000 a week, 28
Aaron, 67, 68
Abraham, 24, 25, 47, 105, 183, 241
absence, 37, 61, 67, 68, 69, 70, 71, 137, 213
absences, 67, 71
acrostic, 184, 186, 187, 188
Adrian Rogers, 70, 104
adulterers, 28
African, 77, 221
agora, 108
Alan Redpath, 36, 37
ambassador, 76, 131
America, 11, 13, 14, 16, 17, 19, 20, 21, 29, 35, 36, 37, 38, 39, 47, 56, 59, 60, 61, 62, 63, 64, 67, 69, 70, 71, 81, 86, 87, 106, 107, 112, 123, 124, 125, 126, 127, 137, 138, 139, 153, 169, 180, 190, 192, 199, 200, 207, 211, 214, 216, 219, 220, 221, 226, 227, 228, 230, 231, 236
Amos, 5, 13, 14, 15, 105, 142
Ancient of Days, 91, 139, 168, 172, 230
Andrew Murray, 9
antediluvian, 112
apostate, 59, 60, 61, 62, 65, 211
Arminian, 153, 207
Asahel Nettleton, 89, 92, 97, 137, 167, 195, 197, 253

atheists, 28, 225
author of salvation, 55
axe, 103, 183, 185
Baal, 15, 241
backslide, 67, 68
backsliders, 141
Baxter, 110, 112, 113
beggar, 24, 75
Bell Inn, 35
bema seat, 18, 132
Benjamin Franklin, 123
Beyond Death's Door, 27
bitter, 87, 115
black stallion, 114, 115
blind beggar, 75
blood, 13, 19, 25, 32, 33, 41, 42, 43, 45, 53, 56, 61, 63, 64, 92, 94, 97, 106, 107, 108, 116, 117, 118, 124, 127, 129, 134, 143, 144, 146, 147, 152, 157, 158, 159, 166, 192, 198, 204, 205, 208, 210, 212, 213, 214, 215, 216, 217, 223, 225, 228, 230, 235, 236, 242
bloody cross, 26, 41, 42, 53, 57, 61, 86, 99, 134, 192, 197, 214, 215, 216, 217, 219, 227, 232
bottomless pit, 33, 167
British Parliament, 126
Calcutta, 41
Calvinist, 153
Campbell, 86, 176
Canada, 64
Cappuccino, 59, 60, 61, 62, 63, 65
cardiologist, 23, 27
Carly, 3

245

Charles Spurgeon, 24, 143, 163, 197
Chicago, 23, 132, 135, 180
children of wrath, 52, 220, 221
Christian bookstores, 117, 221
Christianity, 9, 14, 60, 89, 120, 126, 192, 199, 200, 207, 210, 211, 213, 216, 233, 235
Christless, 26, 50, 75, 130
clean hands, 82, 83
coal mine, 23
Coal Mine, 23
Colin N. Peckham, 2, 10
colony, 106
complete harmony, 83
compromised gospel, 47
compunction, 92
convict, 54, 100
conviction of sin, 32, 54, 55, 56, 93, 94, 163, 166, 232
courthouse, 64, 90, 123, 226
crucified lives, 83, 133, 223
cult, 207, 208, 209, 211
cultural revolution, 192
Daily Bread, 116
Damocles, 127
danger, 9, 29, 31, 50, 51, 53, 77, 97, 185, 210, 236
David Wilkerson, 71, 113
dead wooden Jesus, 134
death, 16, 23, 24, 26, 27, 29, 30, 35, 41, 42, 44, 50, 52, 53, 54, 60, 74, 75, 77, 95, 98, 100, 107, 108, 115, 132, 138, 151, 152, 153, 154, 155, 156, 158, 159, 160, 184, 199, 204, 205, 207, 211, 213, 217, 226, 227, 228, 231
debauchery, 35, 68
deeper walk, 99, 114
demon, 27

demons, 24, 26, 27, 28, 30, 53, 112
denomination, 207, 220
discipleship, 90, 99, 100, 106, 130, 209, 210, 217, 235
disinterest in spiritual things, 81
disobedience, 28, 62, 81, 125, 181, 220, 221
disposition, 56, 96, 109, 157, 187
doctor, 26, 115, 156, 180
doctrines, 11, 89, 90, 92, 100, 101, 197, 198, 210, 211, 212, 236, 237
dog, 42, 75, 178
Donald Trump, 114, 151
drunkards, 28
Duncan Campbell, 86, 176
E. A. Johnston, 2, 9, 11
E. M. Bounds, 112, 164, 166
Earthquakes, 16
easy believism, 62
Edinburgh, 2, 9, 10, 52, 153, 165
Edwards, 98, 181, 198
Elijah, 15, 103, 112, 239, 240, 241, 242, 243
Elisha, 103, 104, 109, 110
embarrassed, 13, 36, 60
enduring hardship like a soldier, 100
Englishman, 41
Enoch, 83, 112, 179
eternal suffering, 24, 29
eternal worth, 17, 18, 19
Evangelism, 83, 90, 243
everlasting burnings, 23, 31, 204
Every day 120,000 people fall into hell, 28
evidence, 9, 25, 56, 59, 81, 89, 109, 125
exagorazo, 108
Faith Bible College, 2, 10
false converts, 90, 93, 95

INDEX OF WORDS AND PHRASES

famine, 15, 126, 207, 210
farmer, 42, 100, 148
Felix, 204
fields of Exeter, 163, 231
fiery prophet, 14
financial collapse, 16
financial crisis, 185
fire is not quenched, 31
firebrands, 11, 243
first aspect, 83, 241, 242
first message of that bloody cross, 25
flee from the wrath, 50, 58, 61, 63, 97, 133, 183, 192, 202, 216, 217, 222, 230
Florida, 31
followers, 63, 105, 106, 108, 117, 125, 130, 134, 208
funeral, 70, 151, 152, 156
furnace, 31, 47, 48, 91
Gehazi, 103
Genesis, 6, 25, 47, 48, 49, 83, 105, 111, 112, 119, 202
George Whitefield, 11, 35, 56, 59, 75, 92, 94, 111, 123, 163, 197, 198, 211, 253
Georgia, 106
Gilbert Tennent, 11
Gill, 154
gin-house, 35
global depression, 16
goats, 64
golden thread, 84
Gomorrah, 25, 28, 47, 48, 57
grace, 11, 31, 45, 52, 53, 55, 57, 75, 76, 78, 79, 84, 87, 88, 89, 95, 121, 123, 131, 134, 141, 149, 155, 157, 159, 160, 172, 181, 192, 193, 198, 201, 203, 204, 205, 206, 208, 209, 212, 223, 229, 230, 231, 238, 239, 240
Great Awakening, 56, 59, 89, 123, 137, 167, 231, 253
Great Awakenings, 89
grocery store, 31, 48
guilty, 29, 52, 55, 57, 84, 94, 98, 134, 159, 197
hands of God, 37, 90, 92, 130, 148
hands of men, 90, 92
Harrold, 24
Hartford Seminary, 167
haunted, 26, 136
heartbroken, 82
heaven, 14, 19, 20, 23, 24, 25, 47, 48, 50, 58, 62, 73, 77, 78, 86, 91, 93, 104, 108, 111, 112, 114, 115, 118, 124, 132, 137, 140, 141, 154, 155, 157, 158, 159, 164, 166, 167, 170, 172, 181, 186, 207, 214, 217, 219, 224, 227, 230, 231, 234, 235, 240, 243
Hebrides, 86
hell, 11, 13, 15, 21, 23, 24, 25, 26, 27, 28, 29, 30, 31, 32, 33, 43, 44, 50, 51, 52, 53, 54, 55, 57, 58, 59, 61, 63, 65, 89, 90, 91, 93, 95, 97, 98, 99, 100, 108, 109, 112, 116, 117, 125, 130, 136, 137, 138, 145, 152, 153, 155, 156, 157, 158, 160, 169, 170, 171, 172, 181, 186, 190, 192, 197, 198, 201, 204, 205, 208, 209, 210, 212, 216, 217, 221, 222, 225, 226, 227, 230, 232, 233, 234, 235, 236, 237, 238, 244
helmet of salvation, 144, 147
Henry, 211
Hezekiah, 20, 21
historical periods of revival, 82

Hollywood, 13, 36, 37, 38
Hollywood video, 36
horizontal relationship, 83, 84, 85
humiliation, 17, 32, 126
hymn, 120, 176, 177, 214
idols, 21, 37, 68, 71, 137, 169, 172, 189, 190, 192, 230
Ignatius, 44
inquirer, 97
intellectual agreement, 207
intercession, 10, 118
Iza, 112
J. Sidlow Baxter, 71, 110, 112
Jaazaniah, 138
Jabbok, 118
Jay Leno, 60
Jericho, 103
Jesus is Lord, 219, 223, 236
Jewish, 16
John Gill, 153, 154
John Owen, 137
John Sung, 108, 145
John the Baptist, 117, 163, 183, 185, 198
John Wesley, 54, 94, 106, 107, 111, 153, 154, 172, 211
Jonah, 57, 127
Jonathan Edwards, 11, 60, 89, 92, 97, 123, 197
Jonathan Parsons, 11
Jones, 35
Joseph Harrold, 24
Josephus, 137
Judgment, 15, 64, 76, 192
King Hezekiah, 20, 21
King of glory, 82, 86, 87
King of Terror, 32
King Solomon, 151, 152, 153, 158, 230

Knox, 181
Krushchev, 67
Laban, 119
Lamb, 42, 54, 76, 78, 93, 120, 121, 134, 157, 193, 215, 231
lamentation, 123
law, 9, 43, 54, 55, 57, 63, 90, 92, 94, 96, 98, 100, 106, 107, 138, 154, 158, 192, 197, 210, 211, 214, 225, 227
law before grace, 94
Lazarus, 24
Lee, 133, 134, 159
Leonard Ravenhill, 17, 71, 118, 170, 224
leprosy, 103
Lewis Awakening in Scotland, 86
lifeboat, 201, 203, 204, 205, 206
living Lord, 54, 79, 96, 99, 159, 217, 232
lizards, 129
London, 35, 41, 107, 125, 126, 143, 165, 180, 198
loneliness, 30
lonely place, 30
lost, 19, 24, 30, 42, 45, 50, 51, 52, 53, 55, 56, 59, 60, 61, 77, 81, 87, 89, 90, 92, 93, 95, 96, 97, 100, 103, 109, 116, 118, 130, 131, 132, 134, 135, 136, 137, 142, 148, 157, 166, 167, 172, 177, 179, 181, 187, 190, 191, 198, 209, 217, 220, 221, 222, 225, 226, 227, 228, 229, 231, 232, 233, 243
Lot, 47, 48
Louis Klopsch, 43
lukewarm church, 89
Luther, 85, 107, 154, 181, 211
Martin Lloyd Jones, 35

INDEX OF WORDS AND PHRASES

Martin Luther, 61, 85
martyr, 44
Matthew Henry, 73
Maurice Rawlings, 23
McCheyne, 110
memoirs, 110
Memphis, 104, 133, 134, 159
Methodist church, 69
methodologies, 61, 163, 197
Microsoft, 13
Moabites, 103, 104
Moody, 36, 43, 97, 132, 135, 136, 163, 165, 180, 181
Moody Church in Chicago, 36
moral compass, 13
Mormons, 207
Moses, 45, 67, 68, 78, 91, 107, 141, 160, 213
Mount of Transfiguration, 202
Mount Sinai, 91, 94, 95, 141
murderers, 28, 155
Murray, 239
museum, 23
national calamity, 16, 38, 39
native servant, 77
negative effect, 84
nether regions underground, 23
Nettleton, 98, 167, 198, 253
new creation, 96, 107
Nikita Krushchev, 67, 70
Nineveh, 57, 127
Noah, 28, 49, 50, 57, 201, 202, 203, 204, 235
obey, 53, 124, 217, 236
Old Hans, 114, 115
old paths, 90, 197, 198, 199, 200, 230
Old time preachers, 89
Olford, 70, 77, 104, 118, 166, 180, 239, 240, 253

omits the necessity of repentance, 93
one stop prison, 33
Only Believe Gospel, 93, 98
out of step, 81, 83
Owen, 239, 253
Payday Someday, 133, 159
pearl of great price, 56, 78, 79, 96, 100, 131
pearls before swine, 95
pen ministry, 133
people of Noah's day, 49
perverts, 28
pestilence, 16
Pharaoh, 107
physical pain, 30
Pittsfield, 167
place of weeping and gnashing of teeth, 30
politically correct gospel, 47, 57
prayer life, 18, 81, 84, 118, 147, 148, 169, 171, 172
preaching, 9, 11, 21, 24, 47, 49, 56, 57, 63, 81, 89, 90, 94, 96, 98, 100, 101, 111, 114, 117, 118, 123, 125, 127, 132, 133, 143, 145, 159, 163, 164, 165, 166, 167, 168, 171, 172, 180, 183, 198, 209, 211, 212, 214, 216, 219, 220, 221, 223, 224, 226, 227, 228, 230, 236, 237, 239, 240
Precious Remedies Against Satan's Devices, 144
President of the United States, 17
pride, 64, 84, 86, 87, 141, 179, 200
prince with God, 119, 170
prodigal son, 76
prophet, 71, 91, 103, 125, 127, 239, 241, 243
pruning knife, 117

pulpits, 47, 50, 59, 60, 61, 64, 81, 90, 91, 96, 101, 105, 124, 137, 164, 167, 169, 172, 179, 198, 199, 213, 235, 239
punishes, 25, 94, 125
punishes sin, 25, 94, 125
punishment, 23, 24, 25, 26, 43, 94, 210
pure heart, 82, 83
Puritan fathers, 92
Puritans, 112
purpose of the law, 55
R. A. Torrey, 180
R. G. Lee, 133, 159
racquetball, 84
rapists, 28
Ravenhill, 17
Rawlings, 24, 27
rebellion, 26, 29, 32, 44, 51, 56, 93, 157, 158, 186
recollection of sin, 54
Redeemer, 75, 106, 112, 143, 188
redemption, 57, 61, 63, 90, 92, 100, 108, 134, 184, 192, 214, 217, 242
regeneration, 11, 53, 57, 63, 81, 90, 92, 96, 100, 107, 134, 152, 153, 154, 161, 192, 198, 208, 209, 211, 212, 216, 225, 227, 231, 232, 237
repent, 10, 16, 17, 20, 29, 33, 45, 48, 57, 58, 59, 64, 69, 71, 74, 79, 93, 98, 127, 131, 139, 141, 175, 176, 178, 199, 205, 209, 216, 221, 227, 235, 236, 238
repent of your sins, 20, 45, 236
repentance, 10, 11, 17, 20, 21, 32, 38, 42, 45, 50, 53, 55, 57, 61, 63, 71, 75, 76, 79, 88, 90, 92, 93, 96, 97, 98, 100, 117, 127, 130, 131, 133, 134, 139, 141, 142, 159, 163, 181, 183, 184, 191, 192, 197, 202, 203, 205, 206, 208, 209, 210, 211, 212, 216, 221, 223, 225, 228, 230, 232, 233, 236, 237, 240, 242, 243
repercussions, 62
reprobates, 32, 56, 231, 238
revealed Christ, 54, 78, 99, 232
revival, 9, 11, 14, 15, 16, 19, 20, 21, 39, 56, 64, 67, 81, 82, 83, 84, 86, 87, 89, 92, 101, 117, 123, 134, 137, 139, 142, 159, 167, 169, 171, 173, 190, 197, 199, 211, 212, 225, 227, 229, 230, 237, 239, 240, 241, 242, 243, 244, 253
Robert Murray McCheyne, 110, 145
Roberts, 239, 241, 253
Rogers, 70, 104
Rolfe Barnard, 253
Roman emperors, 28
root of bitterness, 185
ruin, 9, 14, 19, 21, 57, 63, 67, 90, 92, 100, 134, 139, 145, 186, 187, 192, 197
Samson, 36, 179
Samuel Chadwick, 36
sanctified themselves, 21
sanctuaries, 21, 39, 71, 127, 139, 173, 192, 228, 237
Satan, 15, 108, 143, 144, 145, 146, 147, 183, 186, 225, 236
saving faith, 55, 92, 95, 99, 204, 211, 227, 232, 233
Savior, 32, 42, 51, 54, 61, 62, 90, 94, 99, 106, 132, 149, 192, 203, 210, 214, 215, 217, 219, 220, 223, 231, 232, 235, 236, 237
Scottish pastor, 110, 145
seeker, 52, 55, 58, 95, 238
seeker of God, 55

INDEX OF WORDS AND PHRASES

Self, 53, 61, 133, 242
serial killers, 28
Sermons on Revival, 9
serpent, 29, 45, 78, 160
shallow preaching, 89
Shaphan, 138
sheep, 51, 55, 64, 78, 85, 186, 191, 234
Shekinah glory, 36
shepherd, 60, 191
shield of faith, 143, 144, 147
shotgun of rebellion, 32, 56, 75, 93, 99, 133, 158, 210, 215, 216, 217, 220, 237
shower, 52, 153
shrunk, 141, 222, 232
Shunemite, 103, 109
sinkholes, 31
slippery place, 32, 53, 153
Sodom, 25, 28, 47, 48, 49, 51, 57, 137
Sodomites, 47, 48
Solemn Assembly, 138, 139, 140, 141, 142
Soviet Premier, 67
spirit of antichrist, 19, 35, 169
Spurgeon, 9, 24, 143, 165, 166, 181, 198
stamp collecting, 18
standing, 35, 51, 54, 70, 82, 83, 85, 86, 92, 94, 95, 104, 157, 169, 201, 216, 224
statue, 129
Steven F. Olford, 19
substitute, 26, 37, 41, 43, 54, 55, 57, 63, 76, 94, 106, 108, 133, 158, 181, 192, 197, 210
Sudden death, 29, 153, 204
Sung, 108, 145

supplanter, 119, 170
sword, 16, 38, 51, 98, 127, 143, 144, 147, 195, 196, 197, 198, 199, 200, 213, 215, 222
Teen Challenge, 113
teen gang members, 113
The Christian in Complete Armor, 144
The State of the Church, 9
thieves, 28, 189
Thomas Brooks, 126, 138, 144
three great absences, 67
torment, 30, 31, 51, 98
Torrey, 180
tortillas, 129
tragic spiritual declension of the church in America, 59
traveling preacher, 18
TV commercial, 69
unction, 10, 100, 163, 164, 165, 166, 167
unforgiveness, 84
United Nations, 67
UT School of Medicine, 23
Vance Havner, 71, 223
vertical relationship, 83, 85
W. Graham Scroggie, 36
Walking with God, 120
war, 15, 16, 184, 213
warned, 13, 23, 31, 50, 51, 57, 58, 61, 97, 98, 110, 183, 202, 204, 216, 217, 222
Wesley, 35, 106, 107, 111, 153, 154, 172, 181, 199, 211, 239
Western church, 9
White House, 17, 64, 90, 123, 226
Whitefield, 35, 56, 59, 95, 111, 123, 163, 181, 198, 199, 211
wicked dead, 24, 28

Wilkerson, 113, 114
William Gurnall, 144
William Halper, 120
wind blows, 83
World Missionary Convention, 9
worldly lives, 18
worm dieth not, 23, 31, 97
worst fear, 30

wrath, 26, 31, 39, 41, 48, 50, 52, 57, 69, 76, 86, 94, 98, 124, 125, 127, 161, 188, 193, 205, 214, 215, 221, 222
wrestle with God, 118
Yellowstone National Park, 111
Zoar, 47

ABOUT THE AUTHOR

E.A. Johnston, Ph.D., D.B.S. is a fellow of the Stephen Olford Center for Biblical Preaching and an evangelist and conference speaker with Ambassadors For Christ Intl.-USA.

Dr. Johnston has been a student of revival for several decades and his ministry passion is toward revival in the Church and spiritual awakening in the world.

Dr. Johnston is the author of seventeen books. The last three books of Dr. Johnston, published by Revival Literature, are *George Whitefield: a Definitive Biography* in two volumes, clothbound with dust jacket, containing 1172 pages and 48 photos. The foreword and preface were written by Dr. J.I. Packer and Richard Owen Roberts; *God's "Hitchhike" Evangelist: The Biography of Rolfe Barnard* with a new look at one of the nation's unique evangelists in the 20th Century that will prove to be captivating reading for those interested in revival; and *Asahel Nettleton: Revival Preacher*, a clothbound book of 519 pages, also commended by Dr. J.I. Packer who says: "The momentous ministry of the Edwardsean evangelist Asahel Nettleton, a key figure in the Second Great Awakening, has been effectively forgotten during the past century and a half of less-than-Reformed revivalism. Dr. Johnston's masterful and thorough biography is a long-overdue tribute to this outstanding servant of God, and is priority reading for all who care about evangelism today."

www.ingramcontent.com/pod-product-compliance
Lightning Source LLC
Chambersburg PA
CBHW060504090426
42735CB00011B/2101